Getting Started

Developing Critical Learning Skills for Children on the Autism Spectrum

A STEP-BY-STEP GUIDE TO FURTHER THE DEVELOPMENT OF CHILDREN WITH MINIMAL LANGUAGE SKILLS

James W. Partington, Ph.D., BCBA-D

Behavior Analysts, Inc.
311 Lennon Lane, Suite A
Walnut Creek, CA 94598
PartingtonBehaviorAnalysts.com

Getting Started: Developing Critical Learning Skills for Children on the Autism Spectrum

Teach Your Children Well® Series

April, 2014
Version 1.0

Partington, James W.

The Teach Your Children Well® Series is designed to provide research-based practical information in a non-technical manner to parents, educators, and other professionals who interact with or attempt to teach skills to individuals with an autism spectrum disorder or other developmental delay. However, the presentation of this information does not make recommendations for any specific child. The selection of educational and behavior change goals and interventions are tasks that should be undertaken with input from competent professionals. Furthermore, it should not be viewed that the use of this information with a child with a developmental disability would result in "normal development or functioning." It is not within the scope of this book to determine the appropriateness of any educational goals and objectives, nor the priority of a child's needs. It is recommended that parents confer with trained and experienced professionals to evaluate an individual's need and to determine appropriate educational priorities and programming decisions.

ISBN: 978-0-9882493-2-5

Publisher: **Behavior Analysts, Inc.**
311 Lennon Lane, Suite A
Walnut Creek, CA 94598
www.behavioranalysts.com
(925) 210-9378
FAX (925) 210-0436

Dedication

To Terry Partington, my loving wife and steadfast companion who shares my desire to make the world a better place for individuals with special needs.

JWP

Acknowledgements

This work would not have been possible without the help of many individuals. Some people assisted by providing a conceptual analysis for understanding behavioral teaching methodology, while others provided me opportunities to work with their children to refine the implementation of the teaching methods necessary for the development of critical language and learning skills. Finally, others devoted a considerable amount of time to help with the editing of this work to ensure that the reader was able to clearly understand the information being presented.

Most of the conceptual analysis of behavioral teaching methodology has been acquired from the work of my mentors Dr. Jon S. Bailey, Dr. Richard Malott, and Dr. Jack Michael. Dr. Jon S. Bailey and Dr. Richard M. Foxx also provided me with the inspiration to translate all of my works into non-technical language so that it could be useful to those not well versed in the technical language of a behavior analyst.

The day-to-day efforts by the staff at Behavior Analysts, Inc. to provide high-quality services to the children and families have also been an inspiration to me. My consultant staff: Jessica Curell, Michael Edmondson, Holli Henningsen-Jerdes, Kathy Kilby, Carmen Martin, and Marian Woodside, work hard everyday so that all the children we serve have the best possible chance to develop to their fullest potential. The author is also appreciative of the administrative support provided by Alex Arnold, Autumn Bailey, Tammy Pease, Cathy Santopadre and Laurie Winkler who helped find time to get the work done. I am also grateful to Brian Beasley, and Sue and Rick Ranft for their support in helping me be able to devote time to this and other major projects.

I wish to thank the individuals who provided editorial comments to help improve the readability of this work. The editorial review by Autumn Bailey, Jessica Curell, Kathy Kilby, Dion Ma, Scott Partington, Terry Partington, Rita Shreffer, and Lisa Squadere-Watson has been invaluable. I also wish to thank Dawn Nozaka for her very valuable guidance and support with graphic design of the book and for her artistic work in the design of the cover. I would also like to thank Blake Knight for his assistance with typesetting the book.

Most importantly, I would like to acknowledge my family for enduring our endless hours of work on this project. I owe a great deal to my wife, Terry Partington, and my children, Scott and Sonja Partington, for their patience and support. Scott provided significant input to help clarify the descriptions of several key teaching procedures. Terry spent countless hours transcribing, reviewing, and editing the document; without her help the book wouldn't have been possible.

Of course, this work would be meaningless if it were not for the parents and children served by devoted professionals and their staff. Thanks especially to all the children who have taught me so much.

JWP

Preface

This book is a "must have" for every parent or educator of a child who has no—or very limited—language skills. It is written in non-technical terms and provides critical information on what and how to teach initial skills to such children. It provides the rationale for teaching six critical learning skills and the procedures necessary to develop them. Step-by-step instructions allow a parent or teacher to implement training and track the child's acquisition of these important skills. In addition, it provides the reader with strategies to motivate the child to participate in those learning activities.

Week after week, parents bring their children to my clinic for evaluations of their son's or daughter's skills so that my staff and I can make programming recommendations that will help the child reach his or her fullest potential. These parents have found themselves in a situation that they never anticipated; they need to find the best possible actions with the best possible outcomes that can help their children minimize or overcome delays in their development. It is difficult enough to raise a typically developing child, but children with delays in language and social skills bring even more challenges into the mix. Parents must then seek help from experts who have experience in such situations. Parents are willing to do whatever they can to help their child, "leaving no stone unturned"—often unaware of what options are available, and which specific actions on their part may be critical in helping their child.

There is an abundance of information available to parents of children with developmental delays through a variety of sources. The Internet, pediatricians, state sponsored agencies, and local school systems all have information that might assist these children and their families. The Internet provides access to a wide range of resources, some of which provide accurate data and are worthy of the time spent in checking them out. However, there is also an abundance of information that can be misleading, or lacks conclusive empirical support to confirm the effectiveness of the proposed interventions. Furthermore, even if the information is credible, it is often extremely difficult to sort and use to develop into a meaningful plan of action that will increase the rate at which a child learns new skills.

There are also private agencies that specialize in providing intervention services based upon the principles of Applied Behavior Analysis (ABA). This type of intervention service has been demonstrated to be effective in helping many children develop skills that are needed for participation in a wide variety of school, family and community activities (Howard, Sparkman, Cohen, Green & Stanislaw, 2005; & Lovaas, 1987; National Research Council, 2002; Sallows & Graupner, 2005; Thompson, 2007 & 2011). The input from physicians and professionals from the various community agencies (including the school system) has been of some assistance to families and children with special needs. However, the professionals from these various systems often do not have knowledge and skills to develop and implement a comprehensive and effective intervention plan for the child.

I believe that parents need to become the child's best teacher. Regardless of the resources available to a family, it is critical that parents learn how to teach skills to their own child. Although well-trained professionals can help in teaching skills, parents spend the greatest amount of time caring for their child. It is important that they know how to develop the child's skills while they interact with him during his daily activities. Parents have the most to gain from their child learning to interact with others and care for himself. Every waking moment provides opportunities for the child to learn new skills. When a parent has learned how to teach and implement those teaching techniques, both the child and the parents will be able to reap the benefits.

The main focus of this book is to help parents, teachers and caregivers identify the critical elements of an effective intervention program. The aim is to help in identifying the specific needs of a particular child, so that parents and educators can develop specific individualized program recommendations. Finally, the book will assist in identifying appropriate teaching strategies to develop those skills that are being targeted for intervention.

The book is not written primarily for academicians (although it can be used in college classes to teach students how to develop effective programs), but rather for parents and teachers and other individuals who want to see the child succeed. Written in layman's terms, the book is designed for individuals who care about a child, but do not need to learn a technical vocabulary to be effective in teaching new skills.

Because individuals with a diagnosis of autism vary greatly in their skill levels, it is not possible to write a single book that can cover all the learners with that diagnosis. Therefore, this book is geared toward those children who are currently nonverbal or have a vocabulary of less than 20 words. The focus is on developing programs that will teach the child beginning basic language and social interaction skills, along with other critical skills that allow the child to learn from his everyday interactions with others.

GETTING STARTED: DEVELOPING CRITICAL LEARNING SKILLS FOR CHILDREN ON THE AUTISM SPECTRUM is one in a series of books. The skills that are presented herein provide the foundation upon which to build a wide variety of other important skills. A child must develop an extensive vocabulary, and he needs to be able to talk about items and events. Additionally, he must learn to put words together in the correct order and in combination. Separate books in this *Teach Your Children Well®* series provide additional information regarding how to teach skills such as understanding and using adjectives, pronouns, prepositions, and to develop conversational skills. However, these advanced skills are dependent upon the child learning the basic skills addressed in this book.

My aim is to provide a useful tool to help a child's team of parents and educators make informed decisions about intervention strategies for optimal advances in development. It is important to remember that every child is unique and all decisions regarding teaching-based interventions must consider all aspects of the child's life. Therefore, the information from this book should be used in conjunction with input from other professionals who know the child and are knowledgeable in providing services to children with autism or similar developmental delays.

JWP

Table of Contents

1 Establishing Initial Skills

A child who doesn't understand what is being said to him and who cannot communicate needs to begin receiving services to help him learn those skills. One of the first steps in developing an educational program to teach a child to understand and use language to communicate with others is identifying what skills to teach first. There are many skills that a child needs to acquire, but the selection of the initial skills to be taught will have a significant impact on the outcome of the child's development. This chapter identifies six critical skills that should be included in a program for children who are either nonverbal or use only a few words to communicate with others.

The Goal: Learning to Learn

The parent or teacher of a child with language delays is often easily able to identify language deficits by comparing the child to typical children of the same age. For example, a typical five-year-old child is able to readily ask for a variety of items and activities, can name and receptively identify thousands of items and activities, knows colors, numbers, letters, and is able to learn a variety of new concepts with relatively little effort. Thus, for a child of that age who has no communication skills or only a limited vocabulary, there are clearly many skills that he could develop to reduce the discrepancy in skill levels from his typically developing peers.

Unfortunately, merely identifying deficits does not often result in the identification of skills that should be taught first. A skill that may appear at first glance to be a relatively simple task (e.g., follow instructions to pick up a pencil, or point to colors when asked) may prove to be difficult for a child, and may result in frustration for him as well as for his parents and teachers.

For the child with autism or other developmental disabilities, it is often critical that those who attempt to teach him (1) are well trained in behavioral teaching methodologies and (2) have a well-sequenced curriculum that can be individualized to meet the specific needs of a child. The combination of effective teaching practices and an appropriate curriculum can help to maintain a child's motivation during the instructional activities.

Although one could attempt to identify and teach all the specific skills that a child needs to learn, this approach may not be practical. A more efficient strategy may be to focus on the basics that will allow him to learn additional skills to promote developmental growth without the need for highly specialized instruction. Therefore, a curriculum should emphasize teaching a child a set of "basic learner skills" in a manner that sets the stage so that children can "learn to learn" (Partington, 2010).

The Assessment of Basic Language and Learning Skills-Revised (The ABLLS-R®) provides such a curriculum. The ABLLS-R® is a criterion-referenced assessment that measures a child's ability to perform 544 skills. The assessment provides a comprehensive review of 25 types of skills from four major areas of development. The major groupings of skills are the Basic Learner Skills (which includes many language skills and the skills included in this book), Academic Skills, Self-Help Skills, and Motor Skills. The assessment lists skills in order from those that are easier to more difficult to learn. Thus, it helps a parent or educator identify what skills a child already has, and the next ones that should be taught (Partington, 2010).

The Basic Learner Skills

The Basic Learner Skills section of *The ABLLS-R® Protocol* (the book where the assessment is conducted) provides a basis for a curriculum that emphasizes skills that are important for being able to "learn to learn." This section is comprised of 15 skill areas that are critical to being able to learn from everyday experiences. These skill areas include the child's cooperation with learning activities, specific receptive and expressive language skills (vocal imitation, requesting, labeling, and talking about items and experiences), motor imitation, social interaction, appropriate play, participation in group instruction, following classroom routines, and generalization of acquired skills to new people, places, and materials.

The skills contained in the Basic Learner Skills section are ones that typically developing children acquire before entering kindergarten (Partington, Bailey, Pritchard, Nosick & Doerr, 2010). Thus these skills represent a reasonable, age-based target for young children who are in early intervention programs, while also continuing to provide important educational goals for older learners. It is important to consider that if an older learner has not yet acquired some of these basic skills, the development of these skills would still help the individual gain access to a wider range of options for involvement in community activities.

Because these basic learner skills provide a foundation for the development of a wide variety of social, academic, and functional living skills, the majority of instructional time should be devoted to fostering their development (Payne, Radicchi, Rossellini, Deutchman & Darch, 1983). While other skills (e.g., self-help and motor skills), may also be taught concurrently (Partington & Mueller, 2012), it is often beneficial to postpone certain tasks (e.g., traditional academic skills) until progress has been made on the basic learner skills (An exception would be if the child shows a high degree of interest in learning in those areas).

However, in order to teach these critical learner skills to a child, it is important to:

- Identify developmentally appropriate skills to teach
- Establish a sequence of interactions to teach those skills
- Get the child to actively participate in the learning activities

The active participation of the learner in the developmental activities is a critical factor in the acquisition of the skills. If the child does not actively respond, his behavior will not have the opportunity to be strengthened by coming in contact with either naturally occurring or other reinforcers being used during the teaching sessions.

Developing a Child's Cooperation

When attempting to teach a new skill either in a formal teaching session or in the context of performing an activity of daily living, it is important that the child cooperates with the parent or teacher. However, many children have learned that if they engage in disruptive behaviors, take too long to respond, or just fail to respond to the parent's or teacher's instructions, they will no longer be asked to participate in those instructional activities; the adults will simply do what is necessary for the child. The adults find it is easier just to save time and disruption by doing the tasks for the child. In essence, the child has learned how to avoid following the instructions of others. Thus, one of the priorities of the teaching process should be to ensure that the child is consistently following directions and otherwise cooperating with the adults who are attempting to teach him. The development of the foundational skills identified in this book can help to develop a learner's cooperation and can be used to establish instructional control while facilitating the development of both a child's ability and his willingness to follow instructions (**A Section**)*.

Multiple Payoffs for Teaching a Skill

When teaching a specific task to a student, it is important to remember that the teaching activity can facilitate the development of several other important skill areas. For example, when teaching a child to request an item (e.g., raisin), the instructor has an opportunity to reinforce the child's looking at the adult and

* Note that references to both ABLLS-R® skill areas and specific skills will be provided (e.g., **A Section**, **B 1**, **C 14**, etc.).

attending to her instructions. Reinforcement will also follow cooperation with the instructor's prompts and instructions, thus increasing the likelihood of future cooperation. Additionally, the instruction will result in the further development of the child's imitative skills (if using sign language) or vocal imitation skills (if speaking). Finally, the instruction may result in the child attending to praise, the changes in the instructor's facial expression, and the tone of voice that precedes the delivery of the reinforcer. The careful pairing of the instructor's praise with the delivery of other reinforcers often results in the child being willing to work for more naturally occurring social reinforcement (e.g., praise, smiles).

> **Technical Note:** Although people often refer to reinforcing a child for exhibiting a certain behavior, it is actually the behavior that is being reinforced.

The completion of a simple puzzle provides another example of how multiple benefits can occur when teaching a specific skill. For example, when teaching a child to put puzzle pieces into an inset puzzle board, the instructor can be developing the student's attention to the materials, independent completion of the task, coordination of fine motor movements, and looking for instructor feedback. Thus, it is possible for a well-trained instructor to teach the child how to listen, attend for longer periods of time, scan his environment, and attend to more complex instructions.

The Six Critical Skills

There are six critical skill areas that need to be developed for a nonverbal child or a child with minimal language. It is important to teach him that good things happen when he interacts with others. He must learn that attending to what others are doing and saying helps him gain access to his reinforcers. He must also learn that language works for his benefit when he requests items or actions that are of value to him.

Critical Skills to Teach a Nonverbal Child or One with Minimal Language Skills

1. Social Interaction
2. Receptive Language
3. Motor Imitation
4. Vocal Imitation (Echoic)
5. Requesting (Manding)
6. Visual Performance Tasks

The first six skill areas include: approaching and interacting with others, listening to and understanding what others are saying, watching and imitating actions, listening to and repeating sounds and words, requesting desired items and activities, and paying attention while manipulating objects. These skills have been identified by professionals as being important for the development of additional advanced skills (Sallows & Graupner, 2005; Weiss, 1999). The skills involved in each of these areas—and their importance—will be reviewed below. Following this chapter, an individual chapter is devoted to providing an in-depth description of how to develop each of these skills.

Parents Teaching Critical Skills During Daily Activities

It is important to note that all of these skills can and should be worked on throughout the day. (The only exception is a situation in which a child can't control his vocal musculature and may need to develop his motor imitation skill prior to an attempt to teach imitation of specific vocalizations.) Many parents report that due to busy schedules involving careers and/or taking care of their other children, they find it difficult to arrange times to work on the development of these critical skills. Although it is important for the child to have specific "teaching sessions," **these skills can also be developed anytime**

a parent is helping the child to engage in the typical daily routines of eating, dressing, and bathing. Even those parents who leave for work before the child wakes up can still find "teachable moments" to work on the development of these skills in the evening while bathing the child and helping him get ready for bed.

Skill Area 1: Social Interaction

One of the major deficit areas for individuals with an autism spectrum disorder (ASD) is related to the ability to socially interact with others. Therefore, it is critical that a child learn to pay attention and interact with others they encounter. There are many subtle skills that are needed by individuals to be able to interact with and learn from their peers. A child must learn to greet others, pay attention to the reactions of others, and generally interact with others according to his cultural expectations. Looking at people when they are talking, excusing himself when necessary, helping others, and waiting to take a turn during activities are just a few additional examples of social skills that increase the likelihood that others will want to include the child in their activities, hence, enriching his life.

The Social Interaction chapter of this book (Chapter 2) covers the development of initial approach and interaction behaviors. This chapter describes the motivation behind why we interact, and how to encourage a child to initiate an interaction. It also covers topics such as how to develop eye contact, initiate and return greetings, and interact with others while engaged in fun activities (**L Section of ABLLS-R®**).

Skill Area 2: Receptive Language

Another critical learner skill is to be able to attend to and understand the words of others (Bloom, 1974; Wynn & Smith, 2003). This ability is necessary for tasks such as following simple directions. Many children with ASD have never learned the benefits of paying attention to the words and instructions spoken by others. The receptive language skills of these children are often a major area of weakness. When the spoken words of others doesn't help children gain access to things that are important to them, they often begin to "tune-out" the verbalizations of others. Therefore, it is important to establish the ability to pay attention, understand, and be able to respond to the words of others.

The Receptive Language chapter of this book (Chapter 3) covers the child's first few responses to specific instructions. This chapter explains how to motivate and teach a child to respond to his own name, and come to an adult when called. It also describes how to teach a child to follow instructions in the context of ongoing daily activities, and explains how to teach him to listen to instructions and then perform specific actions (e.g., wave, clap), and how to select common objects on request. Methods for selecting the first words to teach a child and for tracking the development of receptive language skills are also presented (**C Section of ABLLS-R®**).

Skill Area 3: Motor Imitation

The importance of being able to imitate or copy another person's motor movements has been recognized by parents and professionals as critical to the development of a wide variety of language, self-help, motor, academic and social skills (Rogers & Vismara, 2008; Schreibman, 2005). Many skills are acquired by watching and then imitating the actions of others. When people are unsure of how to respond in a certain situation, one of the most effective courses of action is to look at what others are doing and to respond in a similar fashion. Unfortunately, many children with autism don't pay attention, let alone close enough attention, to the actions of others. Without the ability to watch and replicate the actions of others, a child will not be able to learn many critical skills. Thus, it is important to ensure that every child is able to pay attention to the actions of others and be able to replicate those actions in a very precise manner. Furthermore, the child must be able to attend for a sufficient amount of time to learn sequences of responses being modeled by others, perform sequences of actions that require him to switch between actions at the same time as others, and to be able to recall and replicate those actions following demonstrated sequences of actions.

The Motor Imitation chapter of this book (Chapter 4) describes how to develop a child's initial imitative skills. Methods are described regarding how to teach a child to watch a person perform an action using objects and then imitate the manipulating of those objects. Additionally, methods to teach the imitation of gross motor movements involving arms, hands, and feet are provided. Specific procedures are presented that detail how to teach the imitation of fine motor actions involving fingers, and how to teach imitation actions that are presented by standing in front of a mirror. Finally, a description as to how motor imitation is related to the development of vocal imitation skills is presented **(D Section of ABLLS-R®)**.

Skill Area 4: Vocal Imitation (Echoic)

If a child is going to be able to communicate with others using speech as the medium of communication, it is important that he is able to vocally imitate what others are saying. He must be able to produce patterns of sounds that imitate not only individual sounds, but also combinations of sounds that result in accurately spoken words, phrases and sentences. If a child has delays in this skill area, programming must be implemented to overcome deficits in this repertoire **(E Section of ABLLS-R®)**.

The Vocal Imitation chapter of this book (Chapter 5) describes how to develop initial vocal imitation skills. Methods are presented on teaching a child to attend to specific sounds and then replicate sounds made by objects. Because vocal imitation involves making a variety of sounds, procedures to increase the number of sounds and amounts of specific sounds made by a child are described. Specific procedures to identify which sounds may be most easily taught to imitate are described along with a system for tracking the child's development of specific sounds. Finally, teaching strategies are provided to develop the ability to repeat a variety of sounds on request, make sound combinations, form words, and produce variations in volume and tone of the words.

Skill Area 5: Requesting (Manding)

There are many types of receptive (Kent, 1974; Spradlin, 1974) and expressive language skills (Partington & Bailey, 1993; Skinner, 1953; Spradlin, 1963; Wynn & Smith 2003) that a child must develop in order to effectively interact with others. Professionals from the field of behavior analysis (Hart & Risley, 1975; Lerman, Parten, Addison, Vorndran, Volkert, & Kodak, 2005; Sloane & MacAuley, 1968) and from speech and language pathology (Van Riper, 1978) have developed a variety of techniques to help individuals learn these necessary skills. The cumulative effect of the development of many of those language skills results in gradual improvements in interactions with others over time.

However, there is one expressive language skill that results in immediate and powerful benefits to the child—the ability to ask for a desired item or activity (i.e., manding).

Every child must be able to use his language skills to ask for things that he needs or desires. (Note that the ability to request can be either by speaking, using sign language, writing, or typing.) Whether the item is within view or out of sight, the child should be able to get access to those items or activities. He also must learn how to request that others stop undesired activities or to be removed from unpleasant situations. Furthermore, when the child needs information about the location of people who are momentarily important to him, or about activities that may occur in the future, he should be able to gain access to information about those individuals or activities. He also needs to be able ask for items and activities by stating and describing the specifics about where an item is located, when an activity should occur, and delineate the specifics of the items and actions he would like to access or engage using a variety of adjectives, adverbs, pronouns and prepositions **(F Section of ABLLS-R®)**.

The Requesting chapter of this book (Chapter 6) describes exactly how to teach a child to request items and activities. Because he can be taught to ask for items even if he isn't able to speak, a description as to how to select the initial method of requesting is presented. However, as most people talk to each other when interacting, speech would always be the preferred method of communication. For children who have difficulty controlling their vocal musculature enough to be able to reliably produce sounds and words (the reason vocal imitation is one of the critical skills included in this book), it is still helpful to teach them to learn to ask for items even before they can use their voice to ask for them. This chapter describes not only what to teach a child to request, but also what not to teach. The information in this chapter identifies how to avoid common mistakes made when attempting to teach a child this invaluable skill.

Skill Area 6: Visual Performance

It is very important for a child to pay close attention to the items that he can see during his everyday life. For example, he needs to be able to identify his jacket and backpack among those that belong to others. He also needs to be able to pay close attention to the difference between a dog and a cat to be able to learn to name the two different types of animals. If a child is to learn common daily activities such as matching socks or putting away silverware, he must be able to "match" or sort identical items.

The Visual Performance chapter of this book (Chapter 7) describes the development of the child's ability to attend to items and his own actions as he manipulates those items. This chapter covers how to teach a child to complete tasks such as placing single puzzle pieces into the correct space in an inset puzzle board, and how to select various shaped pieces, visually locate an identically shaped space, and then insert into the appropriate holes in a form box. Additionally, a detailed description is presented on how to teach a child to look at a display of items, locate an item identical to the one he's been given, and then place his item beside the matching item (often referred to as a matching-to-sample procedure). Finally, a similar procedure is described in which the child must scan and then select an item that matches the one shown to him by his instructor (a reverse matching-to-sample procedure) **(B Section of ABLLS-R®)**.

Daniel's Story

Daniel was a nonverbal three-year-old boy who had a very busy schedule. He had six hours a day of therapy sessions at my clinic with competent instructors and two weekly appointments with a speech and language pathologist. His father worked long hours so his mother was in charge of Daniel's care. She reported that scheduling and driving him to each of his appointments and caring for her older son left her exhausted and without time to conduct therapy sessions with her son.

I scheduled an early evening appointment to visit Daniel and his mother in his home. I quickly identified numerous interactions that could easily be turned into teaching opportunities. When Daniel wanted something to eat, he approached his mother in the kitchen and pulled her toward the refrigerator. I suggested that rather than just immediately giving him some food, she could use the opportunity to teach him to use American Sign Language (ASL) signs to request (mand) for her to "open" the refrigerator, and to request something to "eat."

When talking with the mother about Daniel's nighttime routine, she indicated that she usually undressed her son, got him into the tub and washed him and then supervised him while he enjoyed sitting in the tub and playing with his toys. Afterwards, she would put on his pajamas and then put him in bed.

As it approached the time for Daniel to take his bath, I suggested that he could be taught some additional skills during this evening routine. Rather than merely removing his clothes, I prompted his mom to use physical and verbal prompts to help him learn how to take off each article of clothing. Although he couldn't remove some of the items without assistance, he could be taught how to engage in some actions to help with their removal. Also, once the clothes were off, I prompted his mother to have him follow the instruction to "put your clothes in the hamper." Once again, it was necessary for Daniel to be physically and verbally prompted to put each piece of clothing in the hamper. After putting away his dirty clothes, he was able to get into the tub.

Daniel seemed very happy when he got into the tub. His mother quickly washed him and then allowed him to play with his toys. He clearly enjoyed splashing in the water, and he spontaneously made a variety of speech-related sounds as he played. I then pointed out that while the mother had to sit and watch him, she could also work on teaching him a few skills. Because he needed to work on improving both his motor and vocal imitation skills, I suggested a way to capitalize on his enjoyment of seeing and hearing water splashing.

I demonstrated how she could start by scooping some water in a container and then get his attention as she poured it quickly back (i.e., splashing) into the tub in a very animated manner. After she did this action a few times, he started to watch her in anticipation of the next "splash" (a powerful reinforcer at that moment). She then scooped the next container of water but then asked him to "give me five" (i.e., tap his hand on hers). Since he already was able to follow this request, he immediately tapped her hand, and she then poured the water into the tub. After a few more successful "trials," Daniel was still very excited about seeing his mother pour the water in a fun way. I then had her give him an instruction to imitate clapping his hands. I knew that he had already learned to imitate this action. He readily imitated the actions and mom then poured the water into the tub.

I instructed her that it was now time to attempt to teach him to imitate other actions such as tapping the top edge of the bathtub. She then asked him to watch her and to "Do this" as she tapped the top edge of the tub. On the first trial, she needed to physically prompt him to tap the tub before she poured the water. By the third trial, he was independently imitating the action.

We both noticed that when Daniel watched the water pouring into the tub, he would make several speech-related sounds. I asked the mom to playfully repeat his sounds and pour a little more water while doing so. Very quickly, he started increasing the frequency of making a certain sound. I asked the mom to get the container full of water and then make that sound for him. Daniel then made (i.e., imitated) that sound immediately after she gave that vocal model, so she then excitedly poured the water into the tub. She repeated this vocal imitation task a few more times before she stopped to let him just play for a few minutes on his own before getting out of the tub.

After Daniel was in his pajamas, the mother told me that she was excited to see that she could work on so many skills while just doing the usual nighttime routines. Teaching him to follow directions, and imitate her actions and vocalizations was actually fun for both her and Daniel. She remarked that there were so many "teachable moments" and it didn't really require any extra time for her to teach him those skills. The best part for her was that Daniel enjoyed having fun with her.

The Need to Develop Each of These Critical Skills

It is important to remember that each of these six critical skills is involved in the development of more complex skills. In essence, they are skills that lay the foundation for the child's development. Therefore, it is crucial that the development of these skills is made a priority, and that everyone who works with the child knows how to teach them. There must be a plan as to what specific tasks are presented, and there must be consistency in how everyone attempts to teach these skills. Most importantly, all of these skills must be worked on throughout the day in a variety of locations and situations. Everybody who interacts with the child should be well aware of the skills he needs to learn and how to teach them. Simply stated, the more opportunities the child has to work on these skills, the more quickly he will learn them (Payne et al., 1983).

Bob's Story

Bob is the father of two boys. As with many fathers, he works a full-time job that sometimes requires travel. He and his wife, Lisa, learned that their youngest son's delays were consistent with the diagnosis of autism. Lisa, who did her homework and began an early intervention program for their son, became a very competent teacher. Their intervention approach was based on verbal behavior teaching strategies and included a team of therapists and a variety of professionals. They were using the *Assessment of Basic Language and Learning Skills* (The ABLLS-R®) to identify his learning objectives.

Lisa asked me to review their son's program and to help provide guidance and training to his intervention team. When I went to their home to observe their son's intervention program, I was able to provide the feedback and guidance that she requested.

During my visit, Bob approached me and said, "Dr. Partington, I want you to spend time alone with me. I know you're here to work with the team but I'm his father and I want to know how to work with my son. Leave some time at the end of your visit to show me what to do to get him to interact with me, and how to teach him." I promised him that I would meet with him when I was done with his team of therapists.

That day, Bob and I spent about an hour discussing intervention strategies and how he could get more involved in the process. I had him practice working with his son using the strategies and procedures described in this book. I coached him so that he would experience success in teaching skills to his son. Although his mother Lisa is still the main manager of their son's program, and his most effective teacher, Bob has continued to implement the strategies we discussed and has remained an active participant in his son's intervention. I must say that I was so happy to hear a father's request to learn what to do to help his child. There may be others who are better trained in effective teaching methods, but as I've always said, it is crucial that parents learn how to teach skills to their own child—the parents should become the child's best teachers.

Good work, Bob!

Summary

There are six critical skill areas that need to be developed by a child who is either nonverbal or who has minimal verbal skills. It is important to teach him that good things happen when he interacts with others. He must learn that attending to what others are doing and saying helps him gain access to his reinforcers. He must also learn that language works for his benefit when he requests items or actions that are valued by him. It is important that he learn to attend to and imitate the actions of others. In order to be able to communicate by talking, he must learn to control his vocal musculature so that he can vocally imitate sounds, words and phrases (Van Riper, 1978). It is also crucial that he learn to carefully attend to his own actions while manipulating objects. Finally, he must be able to scan displays of items and be able to match identical items. These important skills are foundational for the development of a wide variety of other critical life skills (Partington & Mueller, 2012). They increase the opportunity to maximize his potential and overall development. Parents and educators need to learn the procedures that can help the child learn these skills, and must be able to identify those teachable moments when they can further the child's development. These skills should be worked on throughout the day under a wide variety of circumstances (e.g., while dressing, eating, and bathing), and everyone who interacts with the child needs to know his best level of responding and should require him to use those skills.

2 Developing Initial Social Interaction Skills

The responsiveness of a six-month-old child to an adult who interacts with him is an enjoyable moment for both the child and the adult. Even though the child is unable to talk, the attentiveness to the adult's actions and the excitement that is shown through the child's facial expression and body movements provides a great source of reinforcement for the adult's interactions. In addition, the child also enjoys these interactions and learns to attract further attention by looking at the adult and moving or making vocalizations. When the child engages in such actions, adults will often notice him and interact with him, reinforcing the child's initiation behaviors. The result of these interactions is an "emotional connection" between the two of them. There is enjoyment that is derived solely from the interaction itself. As the child learns to walk and talk, he soon learns more sophisticated ways of socially interacting by not only hearing what is said to him, but also attending to the tone of voice and posture of others as they are speaking with him.

One of the major defining characteristics of an Autism Spectrum Disorder is the failure of a child to develop those types of social interaction skills (American Psychiatric Association's Diagnostic and Statistical Manual [DSM-V], 2013). Parents of such children often report being saddened by the "lack of connection" between them and their child. However, every child is a unique individual, and there is a wide range of differences in social interaction skills among those who have been given this diagnosis (Siegel, 2003; Wing, 2003). Many children may lack or avoid making eye contact and may even avoid interacting with others unless that person has something that is currently desired by the child. Some children do show interest in the actions of others but lack the language skills or awareness of the more subtle nuances of interactions that will allow them to successfully interact with others. Other children may have sufficient language skills, but lack an interest in interacting with others. In any of these situations, both the parent and the child miss out on the reinforcers associated with simply "socially connecting" with each other.

Because there is such a wide range of skills involved in becoming competent in socially interacting with a variety of individuals, this chapter will limit the focus on this topic to the establishment of the earliest forms of social interaction by individuals with little to no verbal skills. Specifically, we will consider the issues of approaching and responding to initiations from others to engage in interactions. Once these basic social interactions are established, it is possible to have the child learn additional social interaction skills that are necessarily reliant on the development of language skills.

Why We Interact with Others

Regardless of a child's language skills, it is important for parents and educators to consider the motivation behind social interactions (Partington, 2008). Parents often report being saddened by the fact that their child doesn't take an interest in attending to the actions of others. When left alone, some children seem to prefer to entertain themselves primarily by engaging in isolated activities. These activities are often very limited and frequently they are ones that cause concern for the parents.

One of the types of concerns can be due to the danger involved in the activity. For example, some children like to climb which may result in injury. Other children like to explore different locations that may lead them to dangerous items (e.g., sharp objects) or harmful substances (e.g., cleaning supplies, poisons, etc.) found in cabinets, or even leave the house when not under constant surveillance (i.e., wandering/elopement). Other types of concern involve damaging of objects (e.g., tearing books, breaking objects) and engaging in repetitive behavior (often referred to as "self-stimulation;" e.g., arm-flapping).

Parents are often perplexed as to why the child seems so interested in doing these isolated activities instead of engaging in socially interactive activities. However, the fact that the child does continue these actions indicates that he is getting something out of the activity. Simply put, if he was not receiving some reinforcement for the behavior, he wouldn't be doing it. (Note that in order to help reduce or eliminate these undesired behaviors, it is necessary to teach him alternative appropriate ones that result in his receiving reinforcers that are more highly valued than the ones that automatically result from the undesired behavior.)

When a child engages in a certain behavior, the reinforcement often comes directly as a result of his own actions. Professionals often refer to this phenomenon as "automatic reinforcement" (Laraway, Snycerski, Michael, & Poling, 2003; Michael, 1993). For example, he may enjoy watching paper rip, hearing the sound of the tearing, and the feel of the paper as it is being ripped. Furthermore, he can get this type of stimulation without needing the help of others. Playing with electronic tablets or computers that allow him to watch movies or changes on the display provide direct reinforcement for his actions. He doesn't need to ask for help or follow anyone's instructions; the paper-ripper can get access to those reinforcers by simply engaging in the behavior whenever paper is available. The reinforcement is available without needing to respond to anyone else.

The reinforcement derived from social interactions often requires following directions or going along with requirements from others. Additionally, the "reinforcement" for engaging in the social interactions may not actually be a reinforcer (i.e., it doesn't strengthen the behavior). Although a child may enjoy some of the outcomes, the value of the supposed reinforcer may not be sufficient for the amount of behavior being required. If the benefit derived from interacting with others is greater than the enjoyment of engaging in isolated activities, the child will want to engage in those interactive activities. If, on the other hand, he chooses to engage in isolated activities, this fact would suggest that the effort to engage in activities with others just isn't worth the effort compared to what he can get on his own for free (i.e., from his own activities).

The critical point is that parents and educators need to help the child obtain stronger forms of reinforcement for engaging in behaviors involving interaction with others. Thus, when attempting to increase the child's interactions with others, it is critical to ensure that his participation with them is actually reinforcing. Initially, it is important that the responses being required of the child are not too complicated and don't require too much effort. The responses should be easy for the child, and the reinforcement for engaging in those responses should be highly desired by him at that moment.

Reasons Children May Avoid Others

> "We want the children to run to us, not from us." ~ JWP

While adults want children to be eager to interact with them, the child may not be as interested. Each adult who interacts with a child needs to establish a good working relationship with him. The child must learn that good things are likely to happen when he sees the adult approaching. However, adults often approach a child to get him to do activities that he may not necessarily enjoy.

Children must be prompted to perform daily living tasks and taught a variety of skills. Because a child on the spectrum is delayed in understanding and using language skills, he may not understand why he is being made to do certain daily living tasks. The same situation may occur when adults attempt to teach a child a new skill. If the teaching sessions are not carefully designed, the child may find many of the learning tasks to be difficult and not enjoyable.

If the adult's interactions are mostly ones that stop the child from engaging in preferred activities (or require him to engage in non-preferred activities), the child will not be very interested in interacting with that adult. If, however, the interactions have been more positive than negative overall, the child will be more likely to approach and interact with that adult. It is most important that the relationship with the adult results in the child wanting to "Run to us, not from us."

Reinforcement of Approach Behavior

In order to develop social interaction skills, it is necessary for two individuals to interact. However, some children with developmental delays rarely approach others unless they want something from the other person. The majority of interactions are a result of others approaching the child to start the interaction. Obviously, if a child lacks interest in approaching others to initiate an interaction, this outcome is related to a motivational factor due to his past experiences with others. Simply put, the child is receiving greater amounts of reinforcement for his behaviors that do not involve interacting than he is for those that do. Much of his existing reinforcement may be from the direct changes in stimulation resulting from of his own actions (i.e. automatic reinforcement). For these children, it is not only important to reinforce the child's participation when it has been prompted by an adult, but it is especially important to reinforce the spontaneous approaches from the child.

When a child does approach another person (child or adult), it is important to remember that **the child is initiating an interaction**, and that his initiation behavior needs to be reinforced. It is critical that the child seeks out and enjoys the interaction. The more attempts a child makes to interact with another person, the greater the opportunity to teach him a wide variety of social interaction skills. Thus, the main result of his approach behavior is that he enjoys the outcome of the interaction.

When a child approaches, he may be doing so because the adult either clearly has something he wants, or will be able to get something for him. These situations are wonderful opportunities to encourage the following of simple directions, imitating, or requesting (i.e., manding) specific items. However, **one of the most important reasons for a child to interact with another person is not just to get specific items from others, but rather to get the person to do something with him**. Therefore, it is important for adults (and other children) to develop playful or other interactions that involve doing things with the child that he enjoys but isn't able to do without the other person.

For example, if a child likes a particular doll, he may enjoy being able to hold and manipulate the toy. However, the child may also enjoy the interaction that occurs when someone else makes the doll pretend to say certain phrases in a funny voice as it is bouncing around and is then tickled into the child's chest. Because the child enjoys this particular type of play with the doll, and he can only participate in this activity with another's involvement, the reinforcing activity can only come through social interaction. Similarly, if a child enjoys jumping on a trampoline, but prefers being able to jump higher when an adult holds his hand, the activity is better with the adult's participation. Thus, the value of the reinforcer is increased because it involves the actions others (Partington, 2008).

Another example involves the child who likes to be squeezed or rubbed in a certain manner. If an adult makes fun sounds or says "Squeeze!" or "Rub, rub, rub!" in a fun voice while squeezing or rubbing the child, the child may enjoy that activity enough to approach her again for that activity. Even if the child isn't able to specifically request the squeezing or rubbing, his actions (e.g., backing up to the adult and moving her arm around his chest) will be sufficient for her to know what the child would like her to do. The value of interacting with the adult is increased because she can provide him with something he can't get without her.

It is important for adults and other children to establish similar reinforcing interactions. Although it is great that the child spontaneously approaches when another person can get him something, it is much better when he will also approach because of the forthcoming interaction with that person.

One method of encouraging a child to approach involves an adult making certain words, sounds, and/or actions that have previously been paired with a fun (i.e., reinforcing) activity. For example, if a child enjoys being tickled, an adult may playfully say, "Tickle, tickle, tickle!" starting with a slow and low voice progressing to higher-pitched words, while making exaggerated finger movements (i.e., tickling motions) as she leans closer to the child. Finally, as the child is watching her approach, she will then rapidly say, "Tickle" multiple times as she tickles the child. Thus, the child comes to associate the adult making the tickling motions and saying "Tickle" with that reinforcing activity. When the child notices (i.e., hears and turns toward the adult) the adult saying "Tickle, tickle...," and looks at her hands making the tickling motion, the child may then move toward the adult to be tickled.

Although the interaction is initiated by the actions of the adult, this type of activity has several beneficial outcomes. It provides reinforcement both for the child's attending to the changes in the adult's actions, and for the child approaching the adult. Although a child may attend to and approach an adult who has a specific reinforcing item (e.g., a food item, an electronic pad) in this type of interaction, the reinforcer is the specific interaction with another person.

Desired Outcomes

The child will:

- Approach to interact with others
- Engage in interactions
- Have praise, smiles and recognition become actual reinforcers

Approaching the Child in a Fun Way

A child can often tell by the way the adult is approaching whether the interaction is likely to be fun. The child may not understand what an adult is saying, but he may be able to identify what is likely to happen based upon what he can observe. For example, after dinner a parent may go into the bathroom and turn on the water to fill the tub. If the child enjoys taking a bath, he may be excited to see his mother approaching him with his pajamas in her hand; he knows he will be able to get in the bathtub and play in the water. Similarly, children can often identify when an adult is approaching that a task is not likely to be fun. When a parent or teacher approaches with a serious looking face and tone of voice, the child may be able to identify that she is not happy about doing the activity.

When approaching the child, it is usually beneficial for the adult to approach with an attitude and corresponding actions indicating that the activity will be fun for the child. With the right approach, even typical daily activities can be made into pleasant interactions. If the child is able to identify that the approaching adult is likely to engage him in a fun activity, he is more likely to want to interact with her.

Keeping the Child Engaged

One of the most important aspects of developing initial social interaction skills is to make sure that the child is actively engaged with others throughout the day (Grandin, 2012). As indicated above, those interactions should overall be positive in nature so that the adults become conditioned reinforcers (i.e., the child likes the adult and the adult's praise and attention increases positive behavior). If the child is not actively engaged in activities with adults or children, he may start to entertain himself by engaging in undesired activities (e.g., repetitive or "stimming" behaviors). As stated above, he is most likely to go along with interactions that are enjoyable. However, even if the child resists some of the interactions, it is important to adjust the activities to keep them enjoyable for him so that he will not want to "escape" from the interactions.

Interactions During Play

Although it is desirable for a child to engage in appropriate independent play for short periods of time, adults can also take the opportunity to play with the child after he has begun a certain activity. The main idea is to make the play activity **more fun** for the child when the adult is present. For example, some children enjoy dropping balls into a ball maze and watching it travel along the track. If the child has initiated playing with the toy, an adult may simply join the activity and comment or make fun comments (e.g., "There it goes, down, down, down" in a funny voice). If one of the balls rolls away from the child, the adult can retrieve it and simply hand it to the child (i.e., without requiring any response from the child). If the child enjoys the actions of the adult, he will often start to glance at her to see what she is going to do. At that moment, the adult can engage in a playful manner to reinforce the child for looking at her.

Fun activity with eye contact.

Remember that the goal is to establish a positive working relationship with the child so that he will want to remain near the adult. Although it will be necessary to gradually present instructions, it is often helpful to simply narrate or add to the child's self-initiated play activities. Initially, it is better to let him lead the activities, and have the adult's actions make the activities "more fun" for the child.

Establishing Facial Change as a Reinforcer

As was described earlier, it is important that the adult's facial changes become associated with the delivery of reinforcers (i.e., a conditioned reinforcer). Whenever an adult is about to do something the child likes (e.g., give a reinforcer, engage in a preferred activity), it is desirable to have him see the changes in the adult's face and hear the change in his voice that go along with being excited. When the child sees the change in expression just prior to having something good happen, he will associate that change with the delivery of the reinforcing item or activity. Prior to giving the child a reinforcer, the instructor can hold the reinforcing item near her face as she is smiling and praising the child. When the child looks at the reinforcer, he is more likely to also see the instructor's smile. Thus, the smile and praise will get paired with the delivery of the reinforcer. After this pairing has occurred multiple times, the child will often start to look to the adult's face on other occasions to see if good things are about to happen (e.g., fun activity, delivery of a reinforcer).

Require Eye Contact

It is expected that people look at each other when interacting with one another (**L 17**). Although there are varying cultural expectations as to how much eye contact is considered to be appropriate, a certain level is always expected. Many individuals diagnosed with autism spectrum disorder have noticeably low rates of making eye contact when interacting with others (Jones & Klin, 2013).

There are two types of interactions that are especially important for the development of eye contact. These situations are when the child is requesting (i.e., manding) an item or activity and when greeting others.

When an instructor has control over an item or activity that the child wants, she can control what the child must do in order to get it. In Chapter 6, the process of teaching a child to request a reinforcer by prompting and then gradually fading the prompts is described. In each of the steps, the child is systematically required to do more before he is given the item or activity he is requesting. As he is learning to request (i.e., mand) an item, he can be required to look **at the person** when he is asking for it. In essence, the child needs to ask the person who will be giving him what he is requesting. The person can hold the item beside her face, or merely prompt the child to look by saying, "Ask me," or "Look at me," and then wait for the child to make the request while simultaneously looking at the person. Using the power of the child's motivation to get something is a great way to get him to make eye contact (**F 7**).

Establishing Eye Contact When the Child Can't Mand

Children who are unable to speak or imitate ASL signs will often let adults know when they want something. They may lead a parent to the refrigerator when they are hungry, bring them a cup when thirsty, or lead the parent to the TV when they want to see a movie. Although the child isn't able to verbally ask for specific items or activities, he is showing what is referred to as "communicative intent" **(F 1)**. For these children, teaching them to imitate sounds and actions so that they can learn to request those items should be a major part of the child's intervention program.

However, because the child is indicating that he wants something from the adult, the adult is able to require additional responses (e.g., eye contact) prior to giving the child the desired item. For example, when a child wants a push on a swing, the adult can stand in front of him and only give him a push when he looks at the adult. For a child who enjoys going down a slide multiple times, the adult can block him from sliding when he gets to the top of the slide and require him to look at her prior to allowing him to go down the slide. In these examples, the adult would need to use and fade prompts to teach the child to make eye contact, and would praise the child for looking (e.g., "Thank you for looking at me!") as well as giving him a push or letting him go down the slide (See Shaping Johnny's Eye Contact on page 33).

Importance of Teaching Requesting Skills (Manding)

One of the most powerful reasons for a child to approach others is that he needs something that the other person can supply. It is for this reason that early language training should focus on teaching the child requesting skills (See Chapter 6) **(F Section)**. As a child learns that he can go to a person and ask for a specific item (e.g., mand for getting something to eat, listening to music, getting tickles, watching a movie, etc.), the person who delivers such items becomes more highly valued by the child. The child often becomes excited when he sees the person who helps him get reinforcers. If there are two other people in a room and the child sees the one who has delivered reinforcers when requested, he is most likely to approach the person who has provided the requested items. Thus, when teaching a child to request items (i.e., mand) it is important that he be taught to request items and activities from a variety of individuals.

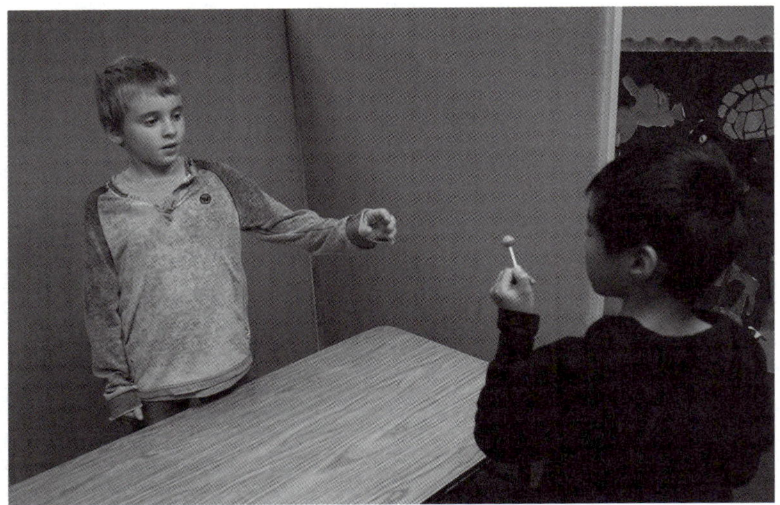

Boy asking his peer for a lollipop.

The child also needs to learn that in addition to adults, other children can help him gain access to his reinforcers (**L 18**). If the requests are reinforced only when he mands to an adult, he is not likely to attempt to use these skills with other children. Therefore, once the child has learned to request items from several adults, it would be beneficial to enlist the support of a cooperative peer. When the child is motivated to receive an item, the other child can be given the desired item, and the adult can direct the child to ask the peer for it (be sure to reinforce the peer for giving the requested item to the child!). Once the peer has provided the child with requested reinforcers, the child will now have learned that he can also ask his peers for items. Thus, he will be more likely to begin to use his new manding skills with peers.

Eye Contact When Returning Greetings

Child greeting/waving with eye contact.

Another important time to develop a child's eye contact is when greeting or when leaving a person. Upon seeing a known person for the first time each day, it is expected that the person will be greeted. That greeting will usually include a statement such as "Hi," "Good morning," or "How are you?" It is expected that the other person will then return a similar greeting (L 10).

However, many children with language delays not only fail to initiate a greeting (L 21), but also don't return greetings (L 10). When adults or peers attempt to greet a child and he consistently doesn't respond to those greetings, those individuals will often stop attempting to interact with him in that manner (i.e., their greeting behavior is "on extinction"). The result is that the adults and peers are more likely to avoid initiating other interactions with him. However, when the child does return greetings, his behavior reinforces the initiation of social interactions from others, thereby increasing the probability of additional interactions. Thus, to increase the social interactions with others, it is necessary to teach the child to at least return greetings.

Responding to Visitors

When friends and extended family members come to visit, it is customary for them to greet all the family members when they arrive. However, if the child doesn't respond to their greetings, the natural effect is that they often stop attempting to greet the child. It is crucial that the child reinforce the visitor's initiations by returning the greeting.

There are two potential factors that may explain why the child isn't returning the greetings. The first is that he may not have learned how to respond to those greetings. The second is that there is inadequate motivation to respond. With a language-delayed child, the failure to respond is often a combination of those variables. Therefore, it is often effective to address both issues at once.

The usual approach is to have someone greet the child by standing directly in front of him, getting him to look, and then both waving and saying "Hi." The greeting should be as easy as possible at first. The child would then be prompted to make eye contact with the person, wave, and if able to speak, say "Hi." For a child who is unable to control his vocal musculature enough to say "Hi," he would merely be required to make eye contact and wave. The child should be prompted as much as necessary to get him to return the greeting. Vocal prompts (i.e., "Hi"), imitative prompts (i.e., waving), and physical prompts (e.g., physical assistance to wave) may be necessary during the initial stages of this training. Those prompts will need to be eliminated as he learns to return the greeting without requiring such assistance (Charlop & Trasowech, 1991). Praise and additional reinforcers (e.g., tickles, hugs, raisins, etc.) should be delivered following the returned greeting.

It is important to note that the reinforcement for returning greetings should be positive in nature (i.e., praise and other reinforcers). However, for many children, praise is not actually a reinforcer (i.e., it doesn't increase positive behavior).

Therefore, other actual reinforcers may need to be presented following the child's response.

Additionally, it is sometimes necessary to require only that the child respond. In essence, a child must learn that he will be required to respond to greetings, even if the person doesn't have something he wants at the moment. In such situations, just the fact that the other person is "getting out of his face" or escaping the demand serves as the reinforcer. Although this approach is generally not as desirable, it is sometimes necessary to get a response. However, children are required to do many tasks that they may not want to do, and this is another one of those tasks. If this type of escape motivation is necessary (i.e., he only returns the greetings to get the adult to stop requesting him to do something) it is very important to continue to use strong forms of positive reinforcement so that the child may eventually respond for the positive outcomes, rather than just responding to eliminate the demand.

Shaping Johnny's Eye Contact

Johnny rarely made eye contact with anyone. However, during one of his intervention sessions, the therapist decided to directly reinforce him for making eye contact. Since Johnny liked to be pushed on a swing, his therapist decided to reinforce his looking at her with pushes.

When they arrived at the park, the therapist put Johnny into a child's seat that would prevent him from falling off the swing. She then stood in front of him and began to give him as few pushes as possible to get the swinging started. Johnny liked the feel of the swing moving quickly. Since Johnny couldn't "pump" his legs to keep the swing in motion, he needed to have occasional pushes from his therapist to keep the swing going quickly.

The therapist began to use a "shaping procedure" that involved delivering a reinforcer for those responses that were closer to the desired behavior, and withholding reinforcers for lesser responses. As the swing began to move more slowly after the initial pushes, the therapist crouched down so that her face would be directly in front of Johnny at the top of his forward swinging motion. She looked at him and when he began to move his head in her direction, she said, "Good looking at me," as she gave him a push.

She continued to crouch in front of him and look for him to turn his head in her direction. After several pushes that followed him turning his head towards her face, she began to only give a push when she saw that he was looking directly at her face. He soon began to look at her face and occasionally he made brief eye contact with the therapist. She then decided to only give a push and praise when he made direct eye contact. Because only minimal effort was required at each step in the process and the value of receiving a push was strong, Johnny continued to turn his head and make eye contact with the therapist to get a push to keep the swing in motion.

The next time they went to the park, the therapist again put him in the swing, but began the swinging in a different manner. She began by pulling Johnny forward and released the swing (to start it in motion) after he had first turned his head toward her (i.e., reinforcing turning his head toward her). She again began to give him a push (and praise) only when he looked at her face. After a few pushes, she only gave pushes when he made eye contact with her. Since then, every time they go to the park, the therapist only gives him pushes when he makes eye contact with her. She had taught him that when he makes eye contact with her, he can get what he wants.

Additional Methods to Teach the Child to Attend to Others

Children walking with their grandfather.

Walking with others is another way of teaching the skill of attending to the actions of others. When a child walks with an adult or a peer, he can either be physically prompted to start and stop or turn in a certain direction, or he can be taught to pay attention to when the others make those same movements. The critical distinction is that the child needs to be reinforced for attending to the actions of others rather than being physically guided. He needs to learn to watch what others are doing and adjust his actions based on the changes in the actions of others **(C 7 & L 25)**.

For example, when an adult starts to walk quickly or walks in a certain direction, the child should notice the alteration in pace or direction and adjust his pace or direction to stay alongside the adult. Similarly, if walking in a line with other children, he should be prompted and reinforced for starting to walk when the others walk, stop when they stop, and maintain an appropriate distance from the person in front of him. The main issue is that his actions are in response to the changes in the other children's actions.

Assisting Others in Moving Items

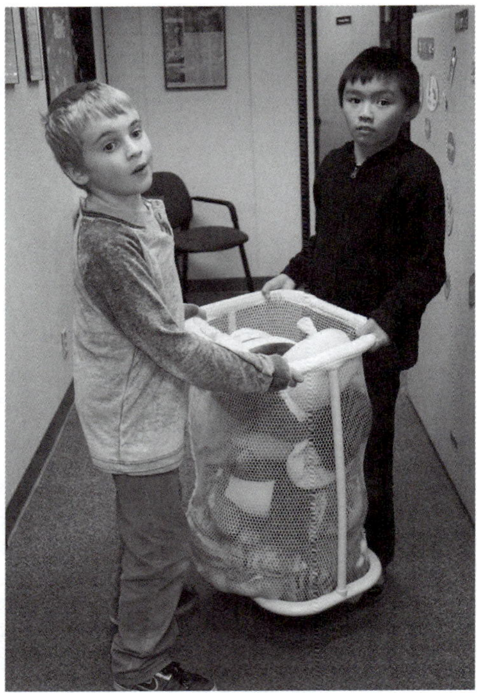

Boys working together to move a basket.

Another approach in teaching a child to attend to the actions of others involves the joint manipulation of objects. For example, a child could learn to help carry a large object with another person. He could be prompted and reinforced for helping another child pick up, carry and place a plastic container with a few objects on a table. This type of activity requires the child to attend to when the other child is lifting the container, when he is starting to move, where he is walking, and when he begins to lift the container onto the table. Similar activities such as lifting arms to make a parachute move up and down and swinging a jump rope provide opportunities to have the child notice and adjust his behavior in relation to the actions of others **(K 13)**.

Imitation

Teaching a child to imitate the actions of others requires that he first attend to those actions, a necessary skill in the development of social interaction skills (Nadel & Peze, 1993; Slaughter & McConnell, 2001; Tomasello, 2001; Wolfberg, 2003). At first, an instructor will teach the child to attend to and imitate her actions. As the child learns to imitate the actions of the instructor, she can also teach the child to attend to and imitate the actions of others. The main difference is that instead of the child imitating the instructor and then receiving reinforcement from her, he now must focus on another adult or peer to receive the reinforcement from the instructor. (See Chapter 4 for additional information.)

Singing With Others

Imitating together during "Head, Shoulders, Knees, and Toes" song.

Many children enjoy hearing people sing songs, and teaching them to sing along with peers or adults is another important way to teach them to attend to others. Many children's songs are often accompanied with certain movements. For example, "The Wheels On the Bus" song has specific motor actions that are done with specific verses. Even if the child is not able to imitate sounds or words, when he participates with others who are singing the song and making the actions, instructors can teach him to imitate the actions along with the group. The use of prompts, fading of the prompts and reinforcement used to develop other behaviors would also be used to develop the child's participation in this type of activity. The benefits of this activity are that it is often an enjoyable activity for the child and provides the opportunity for instructors to teach him to not only look at - but also focus on - the actions and changes in those actions by others. As the child participates in this activity, he can also be developing his motor and vocal imitation skills. If his vocal imitation skills begin to develop, he may even begin to be able to start filling in words during songs (i.e., develop some early intraverbal skills) (H 1).

Playground Possibilities

A child's attention to others can often be developed while on a playground with other children. A skilled instructor will not just let a child play on the equipment, but will also use that opportunity to get him to notice what others are doing. For example, if other children are playing on a slide, the instructor might say, "Look at the children sliding," get the child to look at the children on the slide, and then say, "Let's go slide!" The instructor gets him to focus on others and then leads him to an enjoyable activity. He is also learning to watch and imitate the actions of others required to engage in the activity. This same approach can be used to get him to watch others and then do other enjoyable playground activities (e.g., jumping on a suspended bridge).

During these interactions, the instructor will have the opportunity to teach the child to attend to others so that he can identify when it is his turn to do an activity, and when he needs to wait for others to finish their turns. For a child who has developed some speech, he may also be taught to use his requesting skills to get a push on a swing or to have a turn going down a slide (F 8).

Teaching a child to attend while rolling a ball.

Another great activity in teaching the skill of attending to others involves having him participate in simple ball games (**K 12**). Activities such as sitting on the floor and rolling a ball to another person can help him attend to when the other person is ready to roll the ball back to him, and when the other person is looking so that he can roll the ball to that individual. Additional variations can be included if the child is able to throw and catch a ball or bounce a ball to another person. Rather than just taking the child to the playground to "get his energy out," a skillful adult will be able to use that opportunity to develop a wide range of activities that involve attending to and interacting with others.

Nick Likes People Now

A four-year-old boy was brought to the STARS Clinic for an assessment and to receive help with the development of his language skills. However, when Nick first walked through the door, I noticed that he didn't even look at any of the people in the room. When he wanted something to drink, he just said "juice" without even initiating an interaction with either his parents or any other adult.

I commented to his parents that when he requests items, he should be directly asking someone for the things that he wants. We immediately began to teach him that in order to get a desired item, he would need to look at the person who had the item. When he wanted some juice, he was required to look at me and request "juice." Each time he asked, I would only give him a small amount of juice in a cup. In this manner, I was able to have him practice multiple times in a row to look at me when making his request.

Nick and his parents received daily intervention services over a 10 week period. They moved a long distance to be near our site, while his siblings remained at home. Our staff worked directly with Nick each day on learning new skills while his parents were learning our teaching methods.

Everyday when Nick would enter the clinic, he was required to look at, wave, and say "Hi" to each of the staff. As he left at the end of the day, he was also required to make eye contact with everyone, wave and say "Bye." The first few days, getting him to engage in these behaviors required many prompts. However, after the first week, he would greet and say "Bye" whenever he was approached by an adult as he entered or exited the clinic with the need for only an occasional prompt. After several weeks, he would easily make eye contact when entering the clinic and on some occasions even initiate saying "Hi."

After approximately nine weeks of services, his brother and sister were flown to our area to stay with the family for the last week of Nick's stay at the clinic. One evening, the parents talked with Nick's older brother and sister about the changes that they saw in Nick. His older brother replied, "He likes people now." When his father asked his son what he meant by that comment, he replied, "He looks at us."

When I later heard this story from Nick's father, I was overwhelmed. The impact of teaching a child the simple skills of looking at people when he wants something, and looking at others when being greeted, had such a profound effect on how this boy was viewed by his brother. Teaching him to look at people had made an important emotional connection between Nick and his brother.

Summary

One of the major defining characteristics of an Autism Spectrum Disorder is the failure of a child to develop those types of social interaction skills. It is important to ensure that the child finds that approaching, paying attention to, and interacting with others results in him enjoying the interactions. Adults often must approach children when they need to be made to participate in routine daily activities. Those interactions may result in the child needing to stop engaging in enjoyable activities to engage in lesser or non-preferred activities. Therefore, it is extremely important that adults approach the child at other times in a manner that suggests the activity will be fun and that it actually results in an enjoyable outcome. Instead of stopping his activities, the adult may simply join the child and help make his current activity even more enjoyable. In essence, the interactions should result in desirable events for the child.

It is important to have the child attend to the actions of others throughout the day. Singing songs with actions, playing on playground equipment, imitating others, and assisting others to manipulate items provide numerous opportunities to encourage him to notice what others are doing. A child should be required to make eye contact while return greetings from others. One of the most effective times to teach a child to make eye contact is when he approaches to request (i.e., mand) desired items. Because an adult has something he desires, the adult can require him to look at her before he is able to get the reinforcer.

Potential Learning Objectives Related to the Development of Social Interaction Skills

The following objectives are provided to assist a parent or teacher in targeting specific skills that may be appropriate for a child's intervention plan. Please see the ABLLS-R® to assess the child's skills and to identify additional objectives for further skill development.

Each child is a unique individual and requires input from a variety of people who know him and are familiar with effective programming strategies. Therefore, these learning objectives are not being prescribed for any particular child, but rather are being provided as examples of objectives that are consistent with the skills described in this chapter.

A 7 (Child's name) will be able to demonstrate and use skills learned when working with three or more instructors and with novel instructors at about the same rate and quality of responding demonstrated with familiar instructors.

C 1 (Child's name) will look at or come to a person when called by his name at least 80% of the time.

C 7 (Child's name) will follow instructions to walk nicely beside adults, adjusting to changes in speed and direction of travel, and when stopping and starting to walk.

F 7 (Child's name) will make eye contact when asking a person for items or actions at least 80% of the times that he makes requests.

K 12 (Child's name) will play a simple game involving sitting with legs spread apart, attending to partner, and rolling a ball at least three feet to a peer or an adult for at least five exchanges.

L 6 (Child's name) will approach and attempt to physically engage others in interactions even when the other person does not have a reinforcing item at least 20 times per day.

L 10 (Child's name) will return greetings from adults and peers at least 80% of the time without prompts.

3 Teaching Beginning Receptive Language

The main goal in the development of receptive skills is to teach the child to correctly respond to the language of others. While a few children may not understand any spoken words, most children (including nonverbal children) can successfully follow some instructions (e.g., "Look at me," "Sit down"). These skills are important because the child must be able to both attend to and respond to the language of others. He must also eventually learn to follow a wide variety of instructions, some of which require multiple and complex discriminations. Some of the earliest instructions require the child to engage in a single specified action (e.g., "Stand-up," "Come here," "Jump"), while others require the child to attend to others (e.g., "Go with Bill."), or to discriminate between a selection of items or pictures (e.g., "Give me the red ball.").

When a child is able to follow a few simple directions, it is important to determine the extent of his ability to understand the words spoken by others. There are a variety of ways in which one must be able to respond when others talk to him. It is necessary to determine if the child can follow directions in routine situations **(C 7)**, follow instructions to demonstrate specified actions **(C 9)**, and select objects and pictures upon request **(C 11-14 & 16-17)**. We also need to know exactly what items, actions, and concepts a child understands when accessing his receptive language capabilities.

Teaching Initial Receptive Skills

When a child is not able to follow any directions, including those that are given in the context of regular daily activities, it is necessary to directly teach him to listen and respond to words spoken by others. As with other basic learning skills, we need to review the motivational factors involved in getting the child to listen to our words, and to identify specific teaching procedures to develop the various types of receptive language skills (Grow, Carr, Kodak, Jostad, & Kisamore, 2011).

Why Children Might Not Attend to Words Spoken by Others

Many children with ASD have never learned to benefit from paying attention to the words and instructions spoken by others. When children have found that the spoken words of others don't help them gain access to desired things, they often begin to "tune-out" the verbalizations of others. Additionally, some children actually have a negative history with respect to hearing others speak. Some have learned that when an adult who is talking approaches, they will soon be made to stop the current enjoyable activity and be made to engage in a non-preferred activity. Thus, hearing words is "not a good thing" because it signals that an undesired event is about to occur. Furthermore, when the child frequently hears his name being called prior to such changes, the sound of his name may also be associated with unpleasant transitions. Therefore, it is important to establish a new and positive history of the child paying attention to the words of others and responding appropriately.

The first step in developing a child's receptive language skills is to get reinforcement associated with listening and responding to spoken words. The child needs to learn that when he hears certain words, and then performs a certain action related to those words, good things will happen (i.e., reinforcement). It is important that the initial attempts to develop these skills involve responses that are relatively easy for the child, and correct responses should be immediately reinforced.

For example, when a child is sitting at a table and is about to place a ball in a ball maze, the adult could give the instruction, "Put it in." When the child drops the ball into the track, the adult can praise the child for complying with the instruction. Another example would be when a parent is leading a hungry child to sit in his seat at the dinner table. She could say, "Sit down," as the child is about to sit in his chair. The child would be praised for sitting in his chair and would then be given something to eat. The desired outcome is that the child will start paying closer attention to the words of others, and that some of those words (i.e., praise) will start to become actual reinforcers.

Motivation to Follow Instructions

The fact that a child may "understand" what is said to him does not mean that he will respond as instructed. The ability to follow instructions also involves the child's motivation to follow the instructions. For example, a child may follow a direction to get his shoes when he wants to go outside to play, but if he is engaged in a highly enjoyable activity and his parents want to go to the store, he may not follow the direction to get his shoes on and get in the car because he would rather not leave his current activity. It is critical that he learns that following directions results in reinforcement; he must learn that good things happen when he follows instructions. Therefore, when starting to teach a child to follow instructions, it is best to start by having him do simple responses that are requested of him when he is not actively engaged in a highly reinforcing activity, and when it is apparent that the adult will provide a powerful reinforcer (e.g., item or activity that he would currently like).

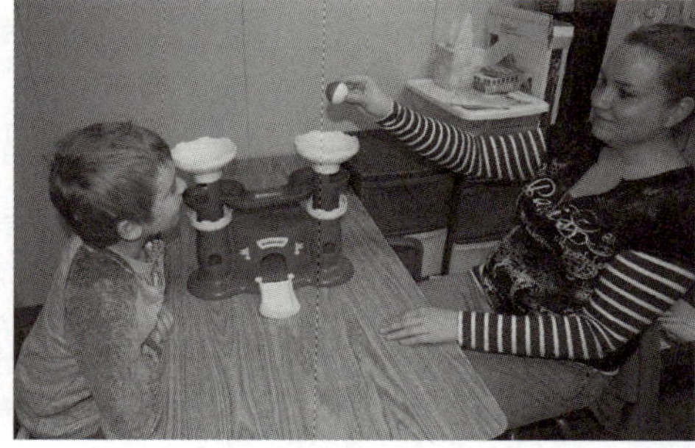

Boy imitating dropping a ball into a ball maze.

Following Instructions in Context

Many of the first receptive responses naturally acquired by typical children involve those that occur in the context of ongoing reinforcing events in their daily lives. For example, when the parents are clearly getting ready to leave the house to drive to a store (e.g., putting on their coats, holding their car keys, and walking towards the front door of the house), and as they are leading their child towards the front door, they say, "Get your shoes." The child will get his shoes and sit on a step so that the parents can help him put them on his feet. These types of interactions are likely to occur at least once or twice a day. In addition, there are other interactions in which the child is given instructions requiring him to get other items. Praise is frequently provided, reinforcing the following of instructions. Through the combination of these interactions, typically-developing child learn to follow directions to get named items.

However, children with significant language delays may not learn to follow those instructions without the contextual cues. Parents and teachers often believe that a child is able to follow an instruction (i.e., "understands" the instruction) when they see him respond correctly in specific contexts, but are then surprised to learn that he is unable to respond correctly when the contextual cues are not present. For instance, he may be able to get his shoes when it is obvious that the parents are about to leave the house, but when it is not apparent and the parent tells him to, "Get your shoes," he doesn't follow the instruction. Therefore, he isn't able to "understand" the instruction without the contextual cues of the activity of leaving the house. In essence, most of the indicators (i.e., stimuli) associated with the activity that require the child to get his shoes are not present, and thus he no longer follows the same direction.

A child has the opportunity to learn many skills when a parent or instructor plans a little extra time to devote to teaching them while engaging in routine daily activities. The responses that do occur in specific contexts can be used to teach the child to follow those same instructions outside of those situations. The main issue is to get the same behavior to occur (e.g., "Get your shoes") while the contextual cues are gradually eliminated (e.g., putting on coats, holding car keys, and walking towards the front door of the house). For example, prior to putting on his or her coat, and with the keys not being present, the parent could walk to the front door of the house and then ask the child to get his shoes. If the child gets his shoes, reinforcement would be provided. If he didn't follow the instruction, a prompt may be necessary (e.g., gestural or partial physical) to help the child get his shoes. As he learns to get his shoes under this condition, the parent can then begin to remove the context of being at the front door. In this next step, the parent could place the child's shoes in a location near the rear exit of the house and repeat the same teaching strategy. At this point, the child is able to get his shoes without the parents going through the routine of putting on coats, holding car keys, and going to the front door.

The next step would be to remove the contextual cue of being near a door. Thus, the parent could place the child's shoes in a different room (e.g., his bedroom) and teach him to get his shoes when away from the doors leading out of the house. Once the child is able to get his shoes without all of the contextual cues, it will be obvious that he is able to respond when only given the verbal instruction itself.

Additional receptive responses can be taught by using the context of ongoing routines and reinforcing situations. Many children are simply led to the table to get food that has been placed there for them, or are guided into a sitting position so that their shoes can be put on prior to being allowed to go outside. If these typical events are reinforcing to the child, it is possible to build a response requirement into these routines. For example, prior to giving a plate of food (usually a reinforcer) to the child, with the plate in one hand, the parent could lead the child (i.e., gently physically guide) to the table with the other hand. When standing next to the chair, the parent can give the instruction to "Sit down," while gently physically prompting the child to sit, and then place the plate in front of the child. In this example, the key response is the child sitting down on the chair. Physical prompts to assist in teaching the child to sit when given the instruction must be gradually eliminated (usually over a series of trials) while the child does more of the work of getting into the sitting position. Similar teaching strategies can be used to get a child to learn responses such as "Get a diaper," "Give me the towel," "Throw it in the trash," etc.

Children need to be reinforced for coming when called!

When a child's name is called, will his situation be improved if he comes, or will he need to stop engaging in an enjoyable activity to do a non-preferred task?

Responding When Name is Called

Parents and teachers are often anxious to teach children to comply with the instruction to come when called (Beaulieu, Hanley, & Roberson, (2013). Unfortunately, children are frequently called at a time when they are already engaging in some reinforcing activity, or when the requested activity is undesired by the child. Hence, coming when called doesn't necessarily result in a reinforcing situation.

In order to teach a child to come when called, it is critical to consider what behavior is expected on his part. Specifically, the child should walk to the instructor when he hears the words "Come here" **(C 1)**. Many children will walk to take a reinforcer that is in view, or held out by another person (i.e., offered), and it is often relatively easy to teach the child to come under these circumstances. It is also possible to provide a gentle physical prompt (e.g., take the child's hand and lightly lead them closer), or to provide a beckoning hand gesture while repeating the instruction. As soon as the child moves to the instructor, it is important to immediately deliver the reinforcer and pair the delivery of the reinforcer with praise. Once the child has been successful in responding to the instruction when provided multiple prompts, the prompts should be reduced as soon as possible. However, the physical and gestural prompts should not be faded so quickly that the child doesn't come when called.

Once the child is approaching when the reinforcer is clearly present and with the instructor only a few feet away, the instructor should slightly increase the distance travelled to get the reinforcer. Once the child walks a variety of distances toward an adult with a reinforcer present, the next step is to gradually reduce the visual presence of the reinforcer. For example, if the reinforcer is a food or drink item, briefly show the child the item, give the instruction and then partially hide the item behind the instructor's back. When the child arrives, the item is immediately given to him along with praise for coming. As the item is being placed behind the instructor's back, it might be necessary to once again use the gestural prompt to help get the child to come. Eventually, the child should be able to come when called and when given a gestural prompt to come, while the reinforcer is completely hidden behind the instructor's back.

Next, the child should learn to come to different individuals in varying situations (e.g., different locations inside each room, and different places outside), for a variety of hidden reinforcers. Varying these conditions is important because if coming when called is only taught by one person, in one situation, using one reinforcer, the behavior may not occur when any of these conditions change. For example, if the child is not interested in a specific item or event that is characteristically used, he may not respond. Rather than only giving a specific item as the reinforcer for coming, events such as being picked up or tickled can be used as reinforcers. However, since the activity may not have an item that can be seen (i.e., a visual prompt) to get the behavior to occur, it will probably be necessary to use some specific hand motion to signal that the activity is likely to occur upon the child's arrival. For example, if the child likes to be tickled, the instructor could get his attention, and then while approaching, make a motion with her fingers (as if she were tickling the child's torso) immediately prior to tickling the child for a few seconds. After repeating this sequence a few times, the instructor could back away a few feet from the child, and say "Come here" while making the tickling motion, and tickle and praise the child when he steps forward to the instructor. The praise should be specifically related to the instruction being followed (e.g., "Thank you for coming!"). Training trials should be spaced throughout the day to avoid satiation (i.e., the reinforcer loses its value), and to make use of the varying motivational conditions during a child's day.

Lisa's Story

Lisa was a five-year-old girl who didn't enjoy being approached by adults. She couldn't communicate and was unable to follow simple instructions. Whenever an adult approached her, she would immediately try to get away from them. She had to be constantly watched very carefully so that she wouldn't leave safe environments. It appeared from talking with her parents that she had learned that when an adult approached her she would need to stop her preferred activity and be made to engage in a non-preferred activity. Lisa would often cry or scream, and sometimes scratch people when required to do those activities. Her parents and therapists were frustrated with her active refusal to do what was asked of her.

When I started to work with Lisa, I knew that my first task was to get her to enjoy interacting with me. Therefore, I had to pair myself with the delivery of one of her reinforcers. I noticed that when she wasn't being carefully watched, she would scan the room and grab certain unattended food items. She was very sneaky! She waited until she could get the items without having to interact with an adult. I decided to make sure that all the food items were removed from the room. If she wanted one of those items, she would need to get it from me.

My first attempt to get her to come to me was a failure. I had a piece of candy that I had previously seen her grab. I held it up so she could see it and asked her to come get it from me. Unfortunately, she just ignored my request. I then decided that when she was looking in my direction, I'd put the piece of candy on a table near her. When I walked away from the table, she quickly went over to the table and ate the candy. I then repeated placing a piece of candy on the table but this time I only stepped back a few steps from it. Once again, she watched me as she quickly moved and took the candy. After a few similar trials, I then sat at the table and placed a piece of candy on it so that it was between Lisa and me. I decided it was time to just hold a piece of candy on my flat hand that was extended towards her. She watched me carefully as she came towards me and took the candy.

The next day, I approached her by extending my arm in her direction while holding out a piece of candy. She immediately took the candy. I then stood several feet away from her and again extended my arm with the candy on my hand. She then took a few steps towards me and took the candy. Next, I started varying my location and the distances from her as I offered her a piece of candy. She quickly began to approach me whenever she saw the candy in my extended hand. I then started to call her name and motion with my other hand for her to come to me before extending the hand with the candy. After several trials, she started to come to me when I said, "Lisa, Come here," while I motioned for her to come before I extended my hand with the candy.

It didn't take very long after those initial interactions for Lisa to approach me whenever I was in her sight. I was now able to get her to come for other food items. She began to follow my simple instructions to participate in a variety of learning activities. At first, I only asked her to sit on a chair before being given a preferred food item. At other times, I would ask her to put a puzzle piece into an inset-type of puzzle board, or to put a block into a container. On other occasions, I would give her a reinforcer just for coming when called. Eventually, she would go along with multiple and varied requests prior to being provided with reinforcement. She was now learning many important new skills.

The reason I was able to get her to work for me was due to my first teaching her that she could get her reinforcers when interacting with me. At first she didn't need to do much to get the reinforcers; she merely had to take the candy I placed on the table. She then learned that just because I was near the candy didn't mean I was going to make her do something (what she had learned from her previous interactions with others). She next learned that I might ask her to do something simple to get the reinforcer. Once she had learned that it was desirable to approach me, and that it was easy to get reinforcers for doing simple responses, she started to learn many new skills.

Following Instructions to Perform Actions

One type of receptive language skill that needs to be evaluated is the ability to follow simple directions that don't involve objects, but rather involve performing a specific action (C 9). The skills involved include performing the correct action when directed to clap, wave, jump, sit down, stand up, and blow a kiss. Although these responses can be taught to the child in specific contexts, his ability to perform these actions can also be assessed outside of the context in which the skill was originally taught. For example, a child being taught to "Wave bye-bye" when he is leaving his classroom by being instructed to "Show me waving," or simply "Wave," can also be asked to do the same thing when leaving other locations. Once again, the praise statements that are given following the behaviors should be specific to the action performed by the child (e.g., "Nice waving," Good clapping!").

Following Instructions Using Imitative Responses

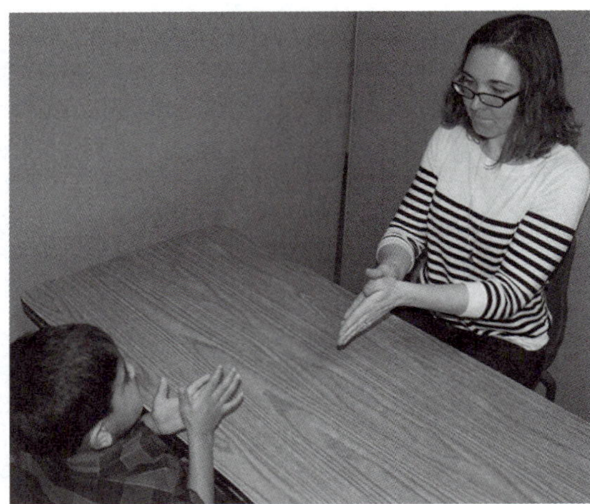

Boy imitating clapping hands.

If a child has acquired some imitative behavior, it is possible to use these skills to help teach him to follow directions to perform actions. For example, children who can imitate clapping or jumping can also learn to do these same actions when asked to "clap" or "jump" without the imitative model. In this situation, the instructor could say, "Clap hands" (instead of saying "Do this"), then get the child to imitate her clapping, and then reinforce his imitative clapping **(D 3)**. On the next trial, the instructor could say, "Clap hands" and present an imitative model of clapping. If the child claps, immediately reinforce the behavior and present the trial again with a slight delay in the adult's model (i.e., begin to fade the prompt). If the child does not immediately begin to clap following the imitative model, a slight physical prompt could be used to get the clapping to occur, and the child's clapping should be followed with the delivery of a reinforcer and a repeat of the trial.

After multiple trials, the child may start to clap his hands after the adult says, "Clap your hands," and before the adult models the response. When the child claps his hands without the model, he should be provided with big reinforcement (i.e., highly valued and in greater amounts than what was given for the responses that followed prompted responses) as he is now following the instruction. After the first response is acquired, repeat this process with a second response (e.g., "jump"), and then teach the child to discriminate between the two verbal stimuli by intermixing the two receptive commands. Once two responses are acquired, additional commands (e.g., "wave") should be used **(C 9)**.

Correcting Errors

Whenever a child correctly performs a requested action, that response should be reinforced with both praise and another reinforcer. However, as a child learns to follow instructions to perform an action, he will sometimes make an incorrect response. There are two basic types of errors: not responding to the instruction, and performing the wrong action (See Figure 3-1). In the case of the failure to respond after three to five seconds, the instruction can be presented a second time. If he then follows the instruction, reinforcement should be provided. If he still doesn't immediately begin to perform the action, he should then be provided with either partial or full physical prompts (if necessary) to help him perform the action. Next, he should be provided with praise for complying with the prompted response, but then be asked once again (without the prompts) to perform the action. Stronger reinforcement should then be provided for performing the unprompted action. A similar correction procedure should be implemented as soon as the child performs an incorrect action. That is, immediately after the incorrect action, repeat the instruction and prompt the correct action, then repeat the instruction without the prompts. Continue the correction procedure until the child is able to perform the correct response without prompts.

Figure 3-1.

Correction Procedure for Errors When Following Instructions to Perform an Action

Instruction	→	Child's Response	→	Consequence
Tell child to "Clap hands."	→	Child claps his hands.	→	• Reinforce with praise "Good clapping!" • Other reinforcer
	→	Child does different action (e.g., jumps).	→	• Repeat the instruction. • Provide imitative model and partial or full physical prompt if necessary to get child to clap. • Repeat instruction without prompts.
	→	Child does not respond.	→	• Wait 3–5 seconds. • Repeat the instruction. • If still no response, use model and partial or full physical prompt if necessary to get child to clap. • Repeat instruction without prompts.

Selecting the First Receptive Actions

Figure 3-2 provides a list of 50 common action words (i.e., verbs) that children usually learn early in life. The list includes three groups of verbs to help identify those actions that may be reasonable to attempt to teach the child. It should be noted that in reference to the ability to respond to words spoken by others, the child must be able to follow an instruction to perform (or demonstrate) a requested action and be able to select a picture representing an action **(C 35)**. Because motion is only implied in pictures of people performing an action, the receptive skill of selecting pictures of actions often doesn't develop until after a child has learned to demonstrate an action upon request and after he learns to receptively identify multiple examples of common items.

It is recommended that the words included in Group 1 be considered before those in Groups 2 and 3. The concept is that the words in the lower numbered groups are often easier to teach (e.g., easy to physically prompt) or more commonly used and required of a child prior to those listed in the higher groups. Note that it is easier to use simple physical prompts to teach actions such as clapping or waving than more complex actions such as crawling or catching. Because a child eats and drinks several times a day, the instructions to "Eat," and "Drink" are ones he will hear throughout his day. Individual circumstances make it necessary for a parent or instructor to consider teaching action words in an order that is specific to the child.

Figure 3-2. **First 50 Verbs List**

	Group 1	Receptive: Demonstrate	Receptive: Picture	Label: Ongoing	Label: Picture
1	Clapping				
2	Brushing				
3	Crying				
4	Drinking				
5	Eating				
6	Jumping				
7	Kicking				
8	Waving				
	Group 2				
9	Closing				
10	Cutting				
11	Dancing				
12	Drawing				
13	Opening				
14	Reading				
15	Rolling				
16	Sitting				
17	Sleeping				
18	Standing				
19	Swimming				
20	Washing				
	Group 3				
21	Blowing				
22	Bouncing				
23	Catching				
24	Climbing				
25	Coloring				
26	Combing				
27	Cooking				
28	Crawling				
29	Hanging				
30	Hiding				
31	Hitting				
32	Holding				
33	Hopping				
34	Hugging				
35	Kissing				
36	Playing				
37	Pointing				
38	Pouring				
39	Pulling				
40	Pushing				
41	Running				
42	Singing				
43	Swinging				
44	Tapping				
45	Throwing				
46	Tickling				
47	Touching				
48	Walking				
49	Writing				
50	Zipping				

As the child learns to follow instructions to demonstrate actions, his acquired responses should be transferred to the 50 First Verbs List (See sample data in Figure 3-3). Although a child can be presented with opportunities to be taught these skills throughout the day, the most significant demonstration of his mastery of any of the action words is his response to the first instruction of the day to perform the action. If he is able to respond correctly the first time he is asked that day, he will have remembered that response to the instruction throughout the night. If he is able to respond correctly the first time he is asked to perform the action for three consecutive days, that response should be considered acquired or "mastered," and a "+" should be recorded on the 50 First Verbs List.

Figure 3-3.

		Receptive		**Label**	
	Group 1	Demonstrate	Picture	Ongoing	Picture
1	Clapping	+			
2	Brushing				
3	Crying				
4	Drinking				
5	Eating				
6	Jumping	+			
7	Kicking				
8	Waving	+			

Teaching Receptive Discriminations Using Reinforcers

Eventually the child must learn to touch or point to specifically named items. Receptive identification of items usually results in considerable recognition and praise for the typically developing child. However, this outcome may not be a sufficient reinforcer for a child with language delays who often does not know what response is expected of him. In order to increase the motivation for the child to participate in this type of learning activity, it is often helpful to use a reinforcing item as the one to be touched, because children often have a tendency to reach for things they like. The critical response to teach the child is touching the item when given the instruction "Touch (reinforcer)" **(C 4)** and shown the item. At first, it may be necessary for the instructor to hold the item (e.g., a cookie) in one hand and after having presented the instruction "Touch cookie," use the other hand to physically guide the child's hand to touch the cookie. The child should be presented with praise for touching the cookie (e.g., "Yes! That's the cookie!") and given some to eat as well.

On subsequent trials, the goal is to fade all of the prompts used to teach reaching and touching the named item (Alberto & Troutman, 1999). Note that in this task, the child is not being required to discriminate between different items, which is a much more difficult task. In order to fade the physical prompt to touch the item, it is often necessary to use more subtle gestural prompts to get the response to occur. Moving the item slightly closer to the child and/or tapping the top of it with a finger often serve as an effective prompt to get the touching to occur. As these types of receptive trials are being conducted, it is important to generalize the reach and touch response to include reaching to a variety of positions in front of the child (i.e., on the right and left sides, above and below eye level). The child should also be taught to touch a variety of other reinforcing items (only one at a time). The outcome of this procedure is that the child will be able to reliably touch a named item on request. This skill will ultimately facilitate the ability to learn to receptively discriminate among a variety of items.

The next step in the procedure is to introduce a distracter item (stimulus) **(C 10)**. Often an empty hand can provide such a stimulus. The instructor should hold up the targeted item, a cookie for example, along with her empty and open hand and say, "Touch the cookie." There are several ways to increase the probability of success during this initial discrimination training. The item can be placed closer to the child, tapped on, or wiggled. Attempts to touch the open hand should result in the instructor moving her hand away from the child and moving the object closer to him. Once he can successfully touch a specific item on command, additional objects should be used as distractors along with the empty hand. If the child can discriminate between these two stimuli without errors, then additional objects should be slowly introduced. The initial presentation of additional items can be done in a manner similar to the introduction of the hand as a distracter (i.e., by initially providing prompts to ensure success before fading them out) **(C 12)**.

Teaching Receptive Discriminations of Objects

Children must learn to receptively identify many common objects **(C 11-13 & 16)** and pictures of those items **(C 14 & 17)**. Although they may be more interested in reinforcers than common objects, they must still learn to identify common items. The initial words chosen to teach a child to receptively identify should be for those items that he encounters in his daily life. It is generally desirable to use real objects as the first items, but pictures can be used for some children. Real objects may be more effective in developing labeling skills because they are three dimensional, and are present in the child's daily environment. The objects should be ones that are easy to identify, clearly defined, and talked about frequently in the child's environment (e.g., shoe, cup, spoon). As the child learns to receptively identify real objects, he can then also be taught to identify pictures of those items. There are several additional issues presented in Figure 3-4 that the instructor should consider before selecting specific words for training.

Figure 3-4.

How to Select the First Words to Teach a Child to Receptively Identify

1. Select words that are for important and relevant items for the child in his daily life (cup, shoe, spoon).
2. The words should be for items that the child sees or uses frequently in his daily activities.
3. The words should be for items that can be clearly identified, that is, the name of the item is consistent across all variations of the item (e.g., ball), and all adults can agree on what the item is called, and easily identify it with a single word (e.g., sofa vs. couch, coat vs. jacket or hoodie, etc.).

(Cont'd on next page.)

Figure 3-4. (Cont'd.)

4. The words should be for items that are easy to discriminate from each other (i.e., a hat and a tree are very different, but a truck and a car are quite similar).
5. The targeted words should occur frequently in the child's day-to-day environment (e.g., "cup" "spoon" "shoe" may be heard more often than "rug" or "microwave").
6. The words should be for items that are stable (nouns) not transitory (verbs), so the child can have more time to attend to and physically interact with the item.

How to Pick Words to Teach Using the First 220 Noun List

For the child who is unable to receptively identify many words, the First 220 Nouns Lists (See Appendix 1) can be very helpful in determining which words might be most important for the child to learn at any given time. The word list includes 220 nouns that children often acquire during their first several years of life.

The nouns list is broken into four groups. The first group of nouns is comprised of foods and other items that are frequently reinforcers for children. It also includes a couple of animals that are common household pets and a few vehicles. The second group contains some clothing items, common household items, common food items and some items seen outside the home. The third and forth groups include a greater assortment of items that are commonly seen or used by children, but are not seen as often or are not as easy to discriminate as the items listed in the earlier groups.

There is no exact order in which words should be taught to a child. However, the selection of words to be taught should be carefully considered. As specified earlier in this chapter, the main strategy is to select words that are important and relevant in a child's daily life. Therefore, a useful strategy is to consider selecting nouns from the first group (mainly reinforcers) before considering teaching words from the second, third or forth groups. Although each of the words on the list are important for a child to learn, it is important to teach him words that he frequently hears others say, are easiest to be learned, and are items that are seen or used by him on a daily basis.

As the child learns to receptively identify new words, it is important to record these new skills on the word lists (see Appendix 1: Data Collection Instructions on the bottom of the First Nouns list). The selection of new words to be taught can then be continued using the same strategy, selecting from the words that the child still has not acquired. Since every child is different, each program to teach labeling skills should be individualized by selecting words that are relevant to the specific child.

Standard Receptive Discrimination Teaching Procedure

When beginning the receptive discrimination teaching procedure, an instructor will usually place a small array of items (i.e., a display) on a table in front of the child. It is very common to start with only two or three objects in the display. As the child improves his ability to receptively identify items, the number of items displayed should be increased. Items should be placed the same distance from the child and there should be some space in between them. They should be placed in a manner that requires the child to actually move his arms and hands (at least six to eight inches) when reaching for an object in the array. This distance is important, because not only does it require an effortful response, but it also provides the instructor with the opportunity to intervene when needed by using prompts to teach the child to select the correct items.

However, when the receptive discrimination task is first introduced, the instructor will need to teach the child the response of handing an item to her. The instructor should have only one common item (e.g., shoe) on the table and say "Shoe, Give me shoe," while holding out a hand to receive the item. However, since the child has never engaged in this type of activity, it is important to use prompts to get him to select and give the named object. Thus, an errorless teaching procedure can be utilized that includes having the adult hold her open hand near the named item and use her other hand to physically guide the child to pick up and then release the object into her open hand. His cooperation with allowing his response to be physically prompted should be reinforced. This procedure should continue for several trials in which the item is placed in various locations on the table. The physical prompts should be quickly eliminated, followed by the elimination of the hand prompt (placing it near the object). The goal is to present the instruction and have the child visually scan the options, select the shoe, and then place it in the instructor's hand (that is held in a neutral position).

Array of objects for a receptive discrimination task.

Once the child knows how to follow the instruction to give the named item, the next step is to teach him to select a named item from an array of several objects. The goal is to have him receptively discriminate (i.e., hear the name of an item and select it from a group of items) each of the items in the array. In the procedure used to teach him to give the named object, he was not required to discriminate the object to be selected because there was only one item. Now, he must learn to scan a selection of items and pick only the one that is requested (Green, 2001).

Boy selecting a plate on request.

The skill of receptively identifying items can be taught using several different methods. The first method is using the Reverse-Matching-To-Sample transfer to Receptive Discrimination Procedure that is described in Chapter 7. That procedure is often very helpful in getting a child to learn his first receptive discriminations. The following procedure is a commonly used method of teaching a child to receptively discriminate objects. This efficient format is often utilized to teach many new discriminations once the first several items are learned.

Introducing the Receptive Discrimination Task

When the receptive discrimination task is introduced to the child, the instructor should first require him to look at each of the objects in the array. The instructor should then give an instruction to select one of the objects in the array such as "Shoe, Give me shoe," while holding out a hand to receive the item. However, since the child has never engaged in picking one of several items, it is important to use prompts to get the child to give the named object (i.e., the shoe). Thus, an errorless teaching procedure can be utilized that includes the use of both a positional prompt and a gestural prompt (Alberto & Troutman, 1999). The positional prompt involves strategically placing the "target item" (i.e., the one he is to select) so that it is closer to the hand the child uses to pick up the items, thus increasing the chances that he will select the correct item. The gestural prompt involves having the adult hold her open hand near the named item. This positioning serves as a prompt as to which item the child is to select. Reinforcement is then delivered after the child selects and hands the target item to the instructor. If he begins to reach for the non-target object (i.e., the wrong item), the instructor can most often stop him from selecting the non-target (if it is positioned so that he needs to reach for it), and then provide further prompts (e.g., partial physical prompt) to select the correct item. Only praise would then be given following this heavily prompted response (independently correct responses should be reinforced at a higher level than corrected responses).

Positional prompt: "Plate. Give me plate."

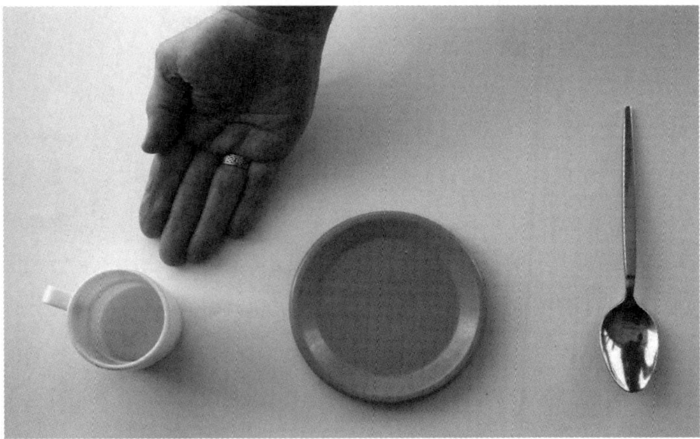

Hand prompt: "Cup. Give me cup."

Because it was necessary to increase the prompt level to get the child to correctly select the item on the last trial, it will now be necessary to repeat the same trial without extra prompts. Reinforcement (praise plus a stronger reinforcer than those that followed the prompted responses) can then be delivered following the correct response (that did not require the extra prompts). This process of increasing the prompt level to get a correct response following an error and then immediately repeating the original trial without the extra prompts is referred to as a "correction procedure" (Sundberg & Partington, 2013). This method of correcting errors can be used throughout all phases of the receptive discrimination training (See Figure 3-5). Additionally, correct responses that do not require any prompts should always be reinforced with a higher valued reinforcer than those responses that require additional prompts.

Figure 3-5.

Correction Procedure for Errors When Selecting Named Items

Instruction	→	Child's Response	→	Consequence
Tell child to "Give me shoe."	→	Child gives a shoe.	→	• Reinforce with praise "Yes. Shoe." • Other reinforcer
	→	Child selects different items (e.g., spoon).	→	• Replace spoon in array. • Repeat the instruction. • Provide gestural, partial or full physical prompt as necessary to get child to give the shoe. • Place shoe in a different location. • Repeat the instruction without prompts.
	→	Child does not respond.	→	• Wait 3–5 seconds. • Repeat the instruction. • If still no response, use gestural, positional, partial or full physical prompt as necessary to get child to give the shoe. • Place shoe in a different location. • Repeat instruction without prompts.

On some trials, the student may not respond immediately after the instruction to select an item is given. If he hasn't started to respond after about three to five seconds, he should again be prompted to look at each of the items and the instruction should be repeated. If he doesn't immediately begin to respond, the instructor should use a prompt to get him to respond (e.g., gestural or partial physical prompt).

It is very important that the position of the target and non-target items be systematically varied. The objective is to have the child locate and select the named item. Therefore, it is critical to move the target so that it isn't always on the right or left side. It is also important to eliminate the positional and gestural prompts as soon as the child is able to select the target item. Note that he must continue to respond correctly, so it is necessary to reduce the prompts slowly enough to avoid the child making errors. However, they should be removed as soon as possible so that the child will respond to the word that specifies which item he is to select, and not learn to respond to the prompts. Many children become dependent upon prompts ("Prompt dependency") due to a teaching error of not correctly fading the prompts.

Trial-by-Trial Data as Fading Prompts

The collection of trial-to-trial data can often be helpful to demonstrate the fading of prompts in the teaching process. On the sample data sheet that follows (See Figure 3-6), note that on the first and second day of teaching, a prompt was used on each trial to help the learner "errorlessly" learn how to select the shoe when asked "Shoe. Give me shoe." On the third day, only the first four trials were prompted, and the child was able to respond correctly without prompts on the last two trials. Note also that on this data sheet, there is no distinction about which types of prompts were used (positional, gesture, full or partial physical). Although the instructor was systematically decreasing the prompts (and those variances could also be recorded), in this case only the fact that the responses were prompted is indicated. On the fourth day, only the first two responses were prompted, and on the fifth day the child was able to select the item without any prompts.

Figure 3-6. Sample Data for Receptive Identification of Objects

Place 2 objects in front of the student and ask "(Item); give me (Item)"

Date	Item									
11/20	shoe	P	P	P	P	P	P	P	P	
	cup									
11/21	shoe	P	P	P	P	P	P	P	P	
	cup									
11/22	shoe	P	P	P	P	+	+			
	cup									
11/23	shoe	P	P	+	+	+				
	cup									
11/24	shoe	+	+	+						
	cup									

P	Prompted Response
+	Correct Response
-	Incorrect Response

Once the child is able to consistently select one named item (e.g., shoe), it is then necessary to complete the same process using a second item (e.g., a cup). Once again, positional and gestural prompts, and correction procedure can be used when the selection of the second item is now used as the targeted response.

When the child is able to correctly select the second item, it is then time to alternate having him select the first and second items (i.e., shoe and cup). Up until this point in the training, the child could have merely been correct by finding the one item that was presented repeatedly, (i.e., multiple successive trials). The child could just locate and select the same item that he did following the previous instruction. At this time, it is critical that he learn the word that specifies which item is to be selected based on the instructor's direction (i.e., "shoe" vs. "cup").

It is crucial that the trials be mixed so that the item requested and the position of the objects are varied. In this way, the child is able to respond correctly based on hearing the name of the requested item, rather than from knowing the pattern of presentation. Thus, it is important to ensure that he scans the items, and then attends to the instructor as she instructs him to select one of the items. The rationale for presenting the instruction "Cup. Give me cup," as opposed to "Give me cup," is that the key word necessary for responding correctly is highlighted, or made more salient, by having it be both the first and last word that the child hears before he responds. He has already learned from the teaching process that he is to give an item to the adult, so the "Give me" component isn't critical in determining which item is to be selected.

When the child is able to correctly select either of the two items upon request, it is then necessary to add another item to the array (e.g., a spoon). At this point in the training process, the third item is just an additional non-target item. If the child is still able to select each of the first two items in the presence of the third item, then that third item can be taught. Specifically, the adult can take one of the "mastered" items (i.e., shoe or cup), and then teach the child to select the "spoon" when put in an array with either the shoe or the cup. When he is able to consistently select the spoon and not the other item, the array of items can include all three of the items (i.e., the shoe, cup and spoon). If the child is able to correctly select any of the three items when located in any position and asked in any order, additional items can be taught using the same process.

The Importance of Working on Only a Few Target Words

When attempting to teach a child to receptively identify new items, it is important to make sure that he has many opportunities (i.e., acquisition trials) to learn the target words. Therefore, a useful strategy is to focus on only a few words at a time. Consider the problem that adults often encounter when they meet many new people at an event. After being introduced to several individuals in a short amount of time, it is difficult for most people to remember more than a few names. The same phenomenon is true for children who need to learn the names of many items. Rather than merely having a few "trials" to learn many words, a more productive approach is to involve the child in many acquisition trials on a few words at one time. If the child is able to intensely focus on a few words, there is a greater chance that he'll remember that item on the following day.

How to Confirm That a Child Already "Knows" Some Items

Teachers and therapists sometimes know—or suspect—that a child already knows some items when he hears them named. To determine those objects that he can receptively identify, the adult should place three or four objects in front of the child and ask him to give her one of those items. Because he could randomly select the correct object by merely grabbing any of the items, it is important to ensure that he actually can receptively identify the objects.

There are a couple of strategies that can be used to ensure accurate identification of objects. Watch to see if the child scans the objects and then makes a deliberate reach for the named item. It is also desirable to present the object with a second group of items, ensuring that the position of the object is different from the first time the child was asked to select it (e.g., on the right side of the array vs. on the left side). Because the item being requested is always included in the array of items, he has a one-in-three chance of picking the correct object (if there are three items in the array) even if he didn't look at the items before responding. If he can select the named object a couple of times without making a mistake, and can do so the first time he is asked on three consecutive days, it's reasonable to consider that the child has "acquired" or "mastered" the skill of being able to receptively identify that object. This information can now be indicated on the First 220 Nouns List (See sample of recording on Figure 3-7) by marking a "+" next to the word under the "receptive" column. (Note that a "+" will be placed under the "Generalized Receptive" column after the child can select multiple examples of each item.) A new "target" object can now be added to the items included in the teaching session to replace the newly acquired object, and the newly acquired object can be randomly included in the array of items used to teach other objects.

Figure 3-7. Sample Recording of Known Objects on the First 220 Nouns List

WORD	CATEGORY	Receptive	Generalized Receptive	Tact	Generalized Tact
Bird	Animal				
Fish	Animal				
Coat / Jacket	Clothing				
Hat	Clothing				
Shirt	Clothing				
Shoes	Clothing	+			
Socks	Clothing				
Swimsuit	Clothing				
Apples	Food				
Bananas	Food				
Fries	Food				
Hamburger	Food				
Hot Dog	Food				
Oranges	Food				
Sandwich	Food				
Bed	Household				
Bowl	Household				
Chair	Household				
Cup	Household	+			
Door	Household				
Fork	Household				
Garbage Can	Household				
Phone	Household				
Pillow	Household				
Plate-Dish	Household				
Refrigerator	Household				
Sink	Household				
Sofa-Couch	Household				
Spoon	Household	+			
Table	Household				
Toilet/Potty	Household				

Avoiding Confusion For the Child

Many parents would like to see their child develop a pointing response. They want him to be able to point to items he would like and to items when he hears people name them (e.g., "Point to the cat"). However, when a child is learning to receptively identify the first few items, it is important to not unintentionally make the task confusing for him.

In the receptive discrimination teaching procedure specified above, the child was required to select and give the named object from a set of items that were placed in front of him. Alternatively, the child could have been taught to point to the named item. However, with young children, it is possible to incorporate the identification of real objects as part of his daily activities. For example, when getting ready to go outside, the parent might ask the child to get his shoes. Therefore, asking a child to get named items (or "give me X") seems to be more likely to occur in normal daily activities than pointing to items.

Sometimes parents look at books with their child and may want him to point to the pictures. The child learning to point to the items in a book would certainly be a wonderful accomplishment. However, it must be remembered that many children have difficulty identifying three-dimensional objects, and many have even greater challenges in learning to identify those items in pictures. Furthermore, in addition to the child not knowing the names of the objects, he also doesn't know how to differentiate between the instruction to "point to" and "give me" the named object. Therefore, for the child who is just learning to receptively identify objects, it is probably best not to confuse him by varying both the instructions and the item that he is to locate.

However, it may not be confusing if he is required to give only one type of response in each of two totally separate conditions. For example, when looking at a book while sitting on a parent's lap, he may be asked to "point to" specific pictures of items (giving the named item isn't possible). When sitting at a table with an array of objects he could be asked to "give" the named objects. In the early stages of learning to identify items, while it is possible for the child to point to the named items while sitting at a table, this approach would not be recommended because now he would need to not only differentiate the named item, but also determine what he is supposed to do with it. While he also needs to be able to make these multiple component discriminations (differentiate both the item and the action), this approach may result in the child having difficulty learning even the names of the items. Once the child is able to receptively identify numerous objects, he can then be taught the specific response that the instructor would like him to do with the item (i.e., give it or point to it).

Extending Receptive Identification Skills

After the child has been successful in being able to consistently receptively identify any of at least 10 objects that are presented in an array of at least three objects, the receptive discrimination skills should be further developed along several dimensions.

Extending Receptive Identification Skills

1. More items in the array
2. Different examples of items
3. Matching objects to pictures
4. Selecting pictures of items
5. Adding more items
6. Change words used in task
7. Select items in everyday situations

1. More Items in Array

One of the first extensions involves increasing the number of objects in the array. The size of the array can be systematically increased until that there are at least six objects in the array. Another variation involves randomly placing the objects in a nonlinear arrangement; the child should be able to scan and locate items even when they are not in a neat row. Additionally, he should be able to select the objects when they are rotated (e.g., 45o, 90o, 180o) so that they have a slightly different appearance.

Non-linear large array of pictures.

2. Different Examples

Because the child can identify several objects, procedures should now be started to teach him to identify slightly different examples of those objects. For example, if the child learned to select a certain "cup" (e.g., blue plastic cup), he can now start to be taught to select other examples of cups (Becker, Engelmann, & Thomas, 1975). The other cups should vary in a variety of ways. (It doesn't matter if it is made of metal, plastic, ceramics, or paper, or it can be any color, shape, size, etc.) Note that these other examples of cups can be included in the ongoing receptive identification teaching procedure (as new items) or can be included in other teaching sessions that involve the matching non-identical items. (For more details, please see Chapter 7 regarding Matching-to-Sample.) As a child learns to receptively identify other examples of the objects, this information should be noted on the Generalization of Receptive and Labeling Skills Data Sheet (See Figure 3-8).

Figure 3-8. Generalization of Receptive and Labeling Skills Data Sheet

		Receptive						Tact					
	WORD	Object	Pict 1	Pict 2	Pict 3	Black & White	Different Person	Object	Pict 1	Pict 2	Pict 3	Black & White	Different Person
1	shoe	+											
2	cup	+											
3	spoon												
4													
5													
6													

3. Matching Objects to Pictures

For the first several objects that a child learns to select, it is important to ensure that he can also identify those items when he sees pictures of the objects. Once again, the Matching-to-Sample procedure can be helpful in teaching him that the object is the same as a picture of the object. Thus, it is possible to follow the matching object-to-picture procedure outlined in Chapter 7 **(B 4)**.

4. Receptive Discrimination of Pictures

It is also possible to start using pictures in the array. At first, a picture of one of the mastered/acquired items can be placed in an array with one or two other acquired objects. In this situation, the child already "knows" the two other objects, and is only required to select the picture of the target item. As he progresses and is able to select various pictures of an item when in an array with two other acquired objects, the objects can be gradually replaced with identical pictures of items. Finally, pictures of other examples of the items can be included in the training to facilitate the generalization of the receptive discrimination skills.

5. Continue Introducing More Objects

As training begins to include new examples of the original objects and pictures of the objects, it's also important to continue to introduce new objects in the receptive discrimination teaching sessions. Once again, it's desirable to ensure that each new word to be introduced is one that is frequently seen and used by the child. Ideally, the procedures for selecting new items from the First 220 Nouns List will be reviewed when selecting the new items to be taught.

6. Changing the Words of the Instruction

Now that the child is able to receptively identify named items, he needs to learn to follow instructions to use his skills when interacting with others. Unfortunately, if other people don't know the exact words to use, he won't be able to use his newly acquired skills with them. Therefore, it's important that as the child begins to expand his list of receptively known words, his instructors start to make slight changes in the words they use to get him to select named objects.

For example, if the original instruction that was used to teach him to select a shoe was "Shoe. Give me shoe," this request could be changed to simply "Give me shoe." Other instructions could include: "Get the shoe," "Find shoe," Where's the shoe?," "Can you give me the shoe?," etc. By increasing the variety of instructions to select a named item **(C 20)**, the chances are also increased that the child will be able to use his new skills with others.

7. Generalization to Natural Environment

Finally, the child needs to learn to use his receptive discrimination skills in his daily life. Therefore, those items that the child has learned in structured teaching sessions must also be used in his daily activities. Thus, if the child has learned to select a cup, a spoon and a shoe when these items are presented on a table, he should also be asked to hand these items to his parents and instructors when they are in various locations in his home or classroom. For example, when he wants a drink of juice, he could be asked to "Give me the cup" or "Get the cup" that is on a counter. When he is getting ready to go outside, he can be instructed to "Get shoes." Using these skills during his daily interactions will help to generalize his skills due to slightly different words being used when asking him to get the items, and he'll be able to use these abilities with different people and in different locations. But most importantly, it will also help to ensure that his newly acquired skills are maintained by the natural consequences of using them. After getting his cup or shoes when requested, he also then gets his juice and gets to go outside to play. He also becomes a more active participant in his daily routines and interactions with others.

Moving Beyond Initial Receptive Language Skills

In this chapter, the basics of how to teach a child to start listening to and following simple directions were presented. Once a child can follow some simple directions to perform several actions (e.g., clap, wave) and can receptively discriminate several common objects, he is able to respond to some of the words of others. The next step is to extend those skills so that he is able to listen to and respond to other words. It is necessary to increase his responses to core vocabulary words (e.g., learn the names of household items, animals, etc.) and to then learn to respond to more complex combinations of words (e.g., adjective and noun combinations, verb and noun combinations) **(C Section of ABLLS-R®)**.

Summary

The main goal in the development of receptive skills is to teach the child to correctly respond to the language of others. He must eventually learn to follow a wide variety of instructions, some of which require multiple and complex discriminations. Some of the earliest instructions require the child to follow instructions presented during routine situations (e.g., "Stand-up," "Come here," "Jump"). One of the most important considerations is that after following directions, the child immediately gains access to reinforcers for complying with the instructions. The child coming to an adult when called should result in a desirable outcome for him.

A child also needs to follow instructions to perform specific actions (e.g., wave, clap) and to identify items that are named by others. He should develop a core vocabulary that results in him being able to discriminate between a selection of items or pictures named by others (e.g., "Give me the ball."). The selections of the first items to teach a child to receptively identify should include common items that he sees and hears others talk about on a daily basis (e.g., shoe, cup, spoon). It is important to only attempt to teach him to receptively identify a few items at a time. Once he has learned to select items upon request, his new skill should be generalized so he is able to identify other examples of those items, and use his skills in a variety of contexts.

Potential Learning Objectives Related to the Development of Initial Receptive Language Skills

The following objectives are provided to assist a parent or teacher in targeting specific skills that may be appropriate for a child's intervention plan. Please see the ABLLS-R® to assess the child's skills and to identify additional objectives for further skill development.

Each child is a unique individual and requires input from a variety of people who know him and are familiar with effective programming strategies. Therefore, these learning objectives are not being prescribed for any particular child, but rather are being provided as examples of objectives that are consistent with the skills described in this chapter.

C 9 (Child's name) will follow instructions to perform at least 5 simple actions (e.g., clap, turn around, arms up).

C 16 (Child's name) will select a specified object for at least 20 common objects when the object is presented in an array of three or more objects on a table in any position in front of him.

C 17 (Child's name) will select a specified picture for at least 20 common objects when the picture is presented in an array of three or more pictures on a table in any position in front of him.

4 Teaching Motor Imitation Skills

Regardless of the conceptual analysis of human development, all theoreticians have recognized the importance of learning skills by observing the actions of others (Bandura, 1962; Bijou, 1993; Bijou & Baer, 1965; Novak & Pelaez, 2004; Piaget, 1962). However, the mere observation of others is not a sufficient enough factor to result in the acquisition of many skills. It is also important for an individual to be able to imitate actions (i.e., duplicate the behavior modeled by others) (Catania, 1972) and to discriminate the appropriate conditions for the use of those skills (Brown, Brown, & Poulson, 2008).

The ability to imitate the motor behavior of other people plays an important role in a child's verbal and social development. If a child can imitate the behavior of others, he can acquire a number of skills with only minimal training. A typically developing three-year-old child can imitate a wide variety of complex actions and sequences, and use those imitation skills to learn many additional skills (Partington, Bailey, Pritchard, Nosick & Doerr, 2010). Some children with developmental delays are able to imitate some simple motor actions, but have difficulty imitating fine motor movements, sequences of actions, and matching the dynamic characteristics (e.g., speed, timing) of certain models. However, many nonverbal children cannot imitate even simple actions.

Similar procedures are used to both develop initial imitative skills and extend existing imitation skills. However, there are different factors that need to be considered for a child who is not imitating any actions versus those who can imitate at least a few actions. Therefore, it's important to identify the elements involved in the process of teaching a child to imitate and in extending existing imitative skills.

Components of Imitative Responding

There are several critical components involved in imitation behavior. First, the instructor must be able to motivate the student to engage in imitative actions. The child must also pay sufficient focused attention to the modeled action so that he can see not only what action is being performed, but also how that action is being performed. He also needs to know that he is being asked to perform the action. Finally, the child must make his own actions match those of the model. Hence, there is a need to consider the motivation of the child to cooperate with an adult, the nature of the instruction, and the level of difficulty of the responses that are being modeled to the child.

Motivation

Some children will imitate a few actions they observe, but won't imitate those same actions upon request. It's important that a child be able to imitate actions when requested so that he can learn from the instruction being provided to him. A child who is able to watch what others are doing and do those same actions is clearly capable of imitating the actions of others. However, if that same child will not cooperate with an adult who requests that he imitate simple actions, the issue to be dealt with is that of "instructional control." In this situation, it isn't that the child fails to observe, or is incapable of making simple motor actions that match a model, but rather he is failing to cooperate with the instructor. The issues of concern include his ability to follow instructions that indicate that he is to copy the action, and his motivation to follow those instructions. In these situations, the instructor needs to present clear instructions (e.g., "Do this") and arrange the conditions so that the learner will be motivated to imitate. That is, she should have a clearly identifiable and powerful reinforcer available before modeling an action that is easy for the child to imitate.

Attending

In some cases, children simply haven't learned to carefully watch what others are doing. These children need to be taught to attend to the action of the adult. Once again, motivation is a key issue. Why should a child watch what others are doing? The answer is that there must always be reinforcement following the attending behavior. Therefore, it is critical that at first, the child be required to engage in only simple imitative responses (Baer, Peterson, & Sherman, 1967). Some responses are easier to imitate than others simply because they don't require the child to carefully attend to the details of the model, or they don't require the child to attend for a long period of time. However, it's important to "shape" the child's ability to more carefully attend to models by differentially reinforcing (i.e., more and better reinforcers for better attending) the child's careful attending to more intricate and lengthy models.

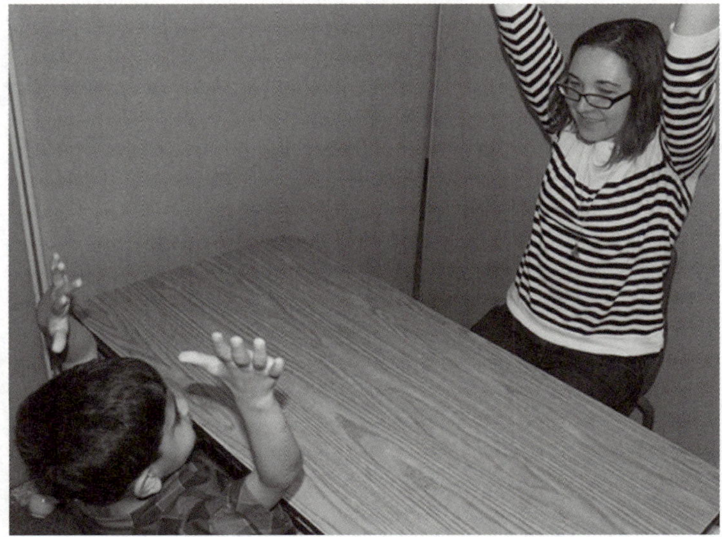

Child imitating teacher raising arms over head.

The Model

Some actions are difficult to imitate due to the transient nature of the model. When an adult models a specific motor action, the action has often ended when it is time for the child to make the same action. For example, consider a model of a single clap of the hands. The adult might say, "Do this," and then clap her hands. The clapping is no longer visible, but the child is required to make an action that he has just seen. Although the instructor may have had his attention when she began to present the instruction, he may not have been attending well when the model was actually presented. Another consideration is that he may have quickly "forgotten" the action that he was shown. Thus, these transient types of models may be difficult for some children who have fleeting attention.

In contrast, another type of model involves an ongoing demonstration of the model. When actions are continuous and ongoing, the child can still observe the action even if he doesn't attend for more than a brief period of time. Additionally, he can also compare what he sees himself doing in relation to the action of the model; he can observe that his behavior matches the action.

Consider a second type of clapping model in which the adult continues to clap as he asks the child to "Do this." In this situation, the child can begin his actions at any time the model is being demonstrated and can still be able to see the model even if he doesn't attend for a short period of time. Another benefit to the ongoing model of clapping is that the child can observe both his own clapping action and the ongoing model at the same time, and see that his actions actually match the model. Using these ongoing models is often a good place to start when beginning to teach a child to imitate actions.

The Instruction

There are many different ways to indicate that a child should imitate an action. An instructor might say: "Do this," "My turn...your turn," "Watch what I do.... Now you do it," "Let me see if you can do this," etc. Children who do not have well-developed imitative skills often also have poor receptive language skills (i.e., they can't follow instructions). Therefore, it is often best to start with a simple and clearly stated instruction (e.g., "Do this") to avoid any confusion as to what the child is expected to do (i.e., imitate). Once the child is able to follow one simple instruction to imitate an action, it's possible to generalize his imitative skills by teaching him other variations of the verbal instructions or gestures that others may use when asking him to copy their actions **(D 7)**.

Teaching Children to Follow Instructions to Imitate

Early imitation training can take several forms, but perhaps the most important elements in training involve making it fun for the child, and capitalizing on the child's ongoing motivation for specific activities or reinforcers. For example, children often enjoy hearing others singing songs (e.g., "The Itsy Bitsy Spider," "The Wheels on the Bus," "If You're Happy and You Know It," "Head, Shoulders, Knees, and Toes"). While singing these songs, adults usually perform actions associated with the lyrics. If children are encouraged to perform the actions with others who are singing, they'll often easily learn a few simple actions for each of the songs. Of course, the use of any prompts (e.g., verbal, gestural or physical) will need to be faded (i.e., gradually reduced and eliminated) as the child begins to be able to perform the actions. Note that in the beginning, imitative attempts, or approximations of the modeled actions will be reinforced. Over time, the reinforcement will need to be provided for increasingly more accurate imitative movements.

Other potentially fun actions can be included in the early imitation training if the instructor can make the actions seem like a game. Specific motivators and reinforcers can be used if the instructor can identify a strong motivator (e.g., the child likes playing with dried beans in a container). In this situation, the instructor could model scooping up and pouring out beans into the container **(D 1)**. She could first do those actions, and if the child is interested in watching the beans fall, she could encourage the child to copy her action. Similar types of actions associated with reinforcing items or activities may include tapping a drum, or pushing a button to activate a sound on a toy or "talking book." In these examples, in addition to praise, the child's responses produce a sound that may reinforce the child's imitation of the model. Please see an example in the next section, "How to 'Shape' Imitative Tapping of a Drum".

If the child will imitate at least some actions under these circumstances, then further training will probably be easy. However, if he doesn't imitate any actions associated with reinforcing activities, then more intensive training procedures will be required. In either case, the process of teaching the first few imitative responses involves specific steps.

Determining the First Few Imitative Responses

It is critical to select the first few responses to be easy ones for the child to imitate. The responses should be easy for him to see what to do, and easy for the instructor to physically prompt the action. Simple responses using objects such as tapping a drum with a stick, pressing a button on a "talking book," picking up and dropping a block in a can, and shaking a maraca or tambourine are often very easy to teach. The child can also be taught to imitate simple actions using his arms, hands and legs. For example, the child can be taught to raise both his arms over his head, to rub or tap one of his hands on a table or on his stomach, wave or clap his hands, or stomp his foot.

At first, an effort should be made to avoid teaching the child responses that require him to pay close attention to the more subtle aspects of the action. For example, it is difficult for many children to place their hand on their ear versus placing it on the top of their head. Similarly, it is sometimes difficult to teach a child to attend to imitations that require one hand versus two hands being placed on their head.

Early Imitative Skills

Using Objects	*Simple Motor Actions*
Tap drum with a drumstick	Clap hands
Press a button	Wave
Drop block in a container	Tap table
Shake a maraca	Tap tummy
	Raise arms over head
	Stomp feet

Once the child has mastered several of the easy-to-prompt responses, additional imitative responses can be selected from the Partington Imitation Skills Assessment (See Appendix 2). The list of skills in this assessment cover a wide range of skills that vary from quite simple ones that require very little focused attention to more complex responses that require the child to pay extremely close and extended attention to the modeled actions.

How to Teach the First Few Imitative Responses

When teaching a child to imitate...

- Have a clearly identifiable reinforcer
- Ensure the child is attending
- Use simple words for the instruction
- Model a simple action
- Prompt as needed and fade prompts

The procedure for specifically teaching any imitative behavior starts by asking the child to imitate a physical movement with the verbal prompt, "Do this." The instructor should immediately reinforce any correct responses or approximations of the target response. If the child does not respond, or emits an obvious incorrect response, then the instructor should repeat the request and the movement a few more times. If the child still fails to respond, then the procedure should be repeated with the use of physical prompts to guide the child's arms through the correct imitative action. (The physical prompt sometimes works better if a second adult does the prompting from behind the child.) The child should be reinforced immediately with praise and other reinforcers (See Figure 4-1).

The next imitation trial should occur within a few seconds, and the instructor should slightly reduce the physical prompt, and of course, immediately reinforce the child's correct behavior. This process of presenting a model, prompting and then fading the prompts, and reinforcing the imitation of the action should continue until the child is able to imitate the modeled action without physical prompts. It should be noted that, when possible, the physical prompts should be faded both from trial to trial within a session, and over the course of several sessions. Occasionally, it may be necessary to use a greater level of prompt for a trial (especially at the start of a new session to teach imitation), but the prompt level should always be minimized as soon as the child demonstrates the ability to perform the action on his own.

Figure 4-1.

Correction Procedure for Errors When Imitating

Instruction	→	Child's Response	→	Consequence
Tell child to "Do this" while demonstrating an action.	→	Child imitates the action.	→	• Reinforce with praise "Good job." • Other reinforcer
	→	Child performs different or non-accurate imitation.	→	• Repeat the instruction and model of action. • Use partial or full physical as necessary to get child to imitate. • Repeat the instruction without prompts.
	→	Child does not respond.	→	• Wait 3–5 seconds. • Repeat the instruction and model of action. • If still no response, use partial or full physical prompt as necessary to get child to imitate. • Repeat instruction without prompts.

Any trial should be presented only when the child is attending to the instructor. The model that an instructor uses should be presented clearly and concisely, and should not be accompanied by complicated verbal instructions. For example, the verbal prompt should simply be "Do this," while modeling a clap. The instructor should avoid saying additional words such as "Come on Fred, do this, you can do it, Fred. Look at me, Fred." For some children, no verbal prompts should be given; the instructor should just perform the action. The instructor should present the clap in exactly the same manner during each trial (e.g., same force, position, number of claps) and avoid engaging in additional physical behaviors such as head and body movements. It should be noted that each child is different, and these additional verbal and physical stimuli may actually help teach imitation in some cases.

Martin and Pear (2002) suggest that imitative "control can be developed much more effectively when the teacher attempts to minimize the possibility of errors on the part of the student." This suggestion of using "errorless learning" is derived from the works of Terrace (1963) and Touchette (1971), as well as several other basic behavioral researchers (e.g., Catania, 1998). The skillful use of prompts, and the careful fading of them, can help minimize errors. A child who cannot emit any imitative behavior has obviously had a long history of failure. If no response typically occurs after the "Do this" prompt, then the instructor should simultaneously give the student a physical and verbal prompt and immediately reinforce the behavior. The instructor should then gradually delay the delivery of the physical prompt. A teacher who skillfully uses prompts (by adjusting the delivery and removal of the prompts) and reinforces closer approximations of the target response, can greatly reduce a student's errors, thereby increasing the probability that the child will learn to imitate.

Requiring an Actual Response When Fading Prompts

The most important element in fading the physical prompts is the delivery of reinforcement following the actual action performed by the child. Remember that reinforcement strengthens behavior. At first, reinforcement may be delivered for the child merely allowing us to guide his hands through a specific (prompted) imitative action. However, it is then important to fade prompting, such as using only a partial physical prompt, or by delaying prompting (to see if he will begin attempting the action), and to reinforce the child's approximation of the desired action. To eliminate the prompts, it's necessary to begin reinforcing some level of effortful response performed by the child.

Imitation With Objects

Some children are able to imitate actions using objects before they are able to imitate motor actions involving only movement of body parts (e.g., clapping hands, rubbing tummy, etc.). Some children may have more success at imitating an action when the instructor uses an object such as a drumstick to pound a drum or a block that's placed into a container. In these imitative tasks, the instructor can easily ensure that the child has visually attended to the actions. She can watch him to make sure he's looking at the beating of the drum, and can wait to release the block into the container until he is clearly looking at the hand that's holding the block. When he's then given the same (or another identical) object, he can still see the items used in the modeled action. The actual model of the action may not be ongoing for all of the actions (i.e., the dropping of the block into the container), however, it can be there for some actions (e.g., both adult and child can hit a drum at the same time). Even if the model of the action isn't still present, the objects that were used to perform those actions are still present (e.g., the block and the container) and the sight of those items may facilitate the child's imitation of the previously modeled action.

How to "Shape" Imitative Tapping of a Drum

The process of "shaping" involves reinforcing a child's responses that are approximations that are becoming increasingly closer to the desired response. For example, if the desired response is to imitate tapping a drum with a stick, following a model of that same action (as will always precede each trial), the first trial might involve taking the child's hand and totally moving it to tap the drum (i.e., a full physical prompt with no independent action by the child). The behavior that would be reinforced is the child's loosening of his arm so that the instructor can move it to complete the action (i.e., cooperation). On the next trial, the instructor could move the child's arm so that the stick is a few inches above the drum. When the instructor releases the child's arm, it will likely fall downward so that the stick hits the drum. Reinforcement would then be provided for the stick hitting the drum. Even though gravity helped to make the response happen, the child still had to independently hold the stick until it struck the drum. After a few similar trials, the child's behavior of holding the stick and striking the drum will have been reinforced and it may now be possible to present the imitative model, give the stick to the child and lead his hand so that the stick is above the level and almost over the drum. If the value of the current reinforcer is still strong, there's a high probability that the child will extend his arm the little amount that is necessary for the stick to hit the drum and get the reinforcer. As he now starts to independently extend his arm a short distance to imitate the tapping of the drum, that distance can be increased by simply not leading the child's arm as close to the drum. Eventually, through the process of reinforcing the child's behavior that becomes closer to the desired response (i.e., "shaping"), reinforcement will only be provided when he imitates the drum tapping after seeing the model and being handed the drumstick.

Strategies for Developing an Imitative Repertoire

There are several strategies reviewed in the literature about how to teach the first few imitative responses to a child. One method involves teaching the first response, then a second, and then alternating between the presentations of the two responses (Risley, 1968). Additional imitative responses are then taught and then added to the mixture of the previously learned responses.

Another strategy involves teaching several distinctly different responses at the same time (Baer, Peterson & Sherman, 1967; Lovaas, Freitas, Nelson, & Whalen, 1967). In this situation, the child is presented with several different responses that are alternated on a random schedule. If the child is able to learn to attend to the mixture of several responses, it's likely that this second strategy will result in faster acquisition of the broad concept of "watch what the person does and then imitate." However, if the child has difficulty learning when several different responses are presented, the slower method of teaching responses in a sequential manner may help him begin to develop his ability to imitate.

Regardless of the method of introducing and teaching additional responses, the child needs to learn a variety of similar responses that require him to attend to the differences between them. For example, if he was taught to tap a drum with the drumstick, as soon as he sees the drumstick he will know that he is to pick it up and tap the drum. However, the sight of the drum and the drumstick should not be the only stimuli that indicate what the child should do. Remember that the main purpose of teaching a child to imitate is that he learns to focus on what someone is doing and become able to match that action. So in the presence of a drum and a drumstick, the adult might ask the child to imitate the action of picking up the drumstick and waving it in the air. The adult might also demonstrate the action of tapping the drumstick on the table instead of on the drum and perhaps the action to be imitated might be picking up the drum and tapping it with his hand **(D 2)**.

It is important to present a variety of imitative actions that don't involve using objects. For example, if a child was taught to imitate the action of tapping the table with his hand, he would also need to learn to imitate a model of rubbing a hand on the table **(D 5)**. Similarly, if he was taught to tap his head or stomach with one of his hands, he would also need to learn to imitate actions that require him to just place his hand on his head or on his stomach **(D 6)**. The most important part of developing a well-generalized imitation repertoire is to teach the child to carefully attend to the actions of others and imitate them, no matter what those actions might be **(D 4,5, 9-13)**. Although in the early stages of developing a child's imitation repertoire it's important to teach a variety of responses, it is also important to quickly begin to teach the imitation of similar, but slightly different responses. The goal is not to merely acquire a defined set of specific imitative responses, but to also develop the skills necessary to imitate the specific actions observed.

A final point presented by Martin and Pear (1995) is the importance of maximizing the number of training trials. Training should be conducted every day with as many trials, or learning opportunities, as possible each session. Some students may need several hundred trials every day in order to show improvement, while others require less intensive training. However, it is clear that sporadic training is not very effective for a child who cannot imitate motor behaviors, and imitation skills can easily be developed in many situations throughout the child's daily activities.

Interspersal with Requests/Mands

If a child is learning sign language as a response form to mand (i.e., request items or activities), those signs can also be used in the further development of the imitation repertoire. For example, if the child has learned to sign music by tapping his arm, present the child with a "Do this," prompt rather than a "What do you want?" or a "Sign music" prompt. Immediately reinforce correct responses or approximations with a strong reinforcer. Incorrect responses can be followed by a prompt such as holding up the music box. This procedure uses the variables that control mands (i.e., motivation) and tacts (i.e., the object) as prompts to teach imitation, and is often an immediately successful procedure if the child has already learned to mand with signs. The procedure can be repeated with the other signs that the child has learned.

Teaching Imitation Skills During Daily Activities

Imitative skills can be specifically taught in formal training sessions, but they can—and should be—developed during all daily activities. For example, when getting dressed, the child can be taught to imitate raising his arms over his head. While being bathed, he can learn to imitate rubbing soap on his arm **(D 5)**. While standing in line at the grocery store, he can learn to imitate tightening and loosening (e.g., squeezing the handle of the shopping cart). When walking to the park, the child can be taught to stomp on a sewer cover, to hop, or to jump off a curb **(D 4)**. The opportunities to teach children to pay attention to and imitate a wide variety of actions are endless. Thus, imitation skills can be easily taught, and should be incorporated throughout the child's daily life.

The teaching of imitation skills while walking to the park presents a great opportunity to make use of naturally occurring reinforcement. When a child enjoys the play activities at a park, and he knows from previous experience that he is on his way there, he will often be quite excited as he sees that he is getting closer to the park. Because his motivation to get there is very strong, it is possible to use this motivation to teach him to perform some imitative actions. For example, if the child has already learned to imitate a few actions, while walking to the park his parent or teacher could stop and ask him to imitate one of his known actions. Once he imitates the action, they can continue walking toward the park (a reinforcer). Although it would not be advisable to stop every few steps, if the child was requested to imitate an action perhaps three to five times during a ten-minute walk to the park, he would probably not resist these minor interruptions on the way to his major reinforcing activity. As the child becomes accustomed to stopping for imitation purposes, then novel actions could easily be introduced and taught using the standard prompting and prompt fading strategies.

Finally, it's important to remember that training should be as much fun as possible. If the child is forced to imitate, it's less likely that spontaneous or unprompted imitation will occur in the future. Additionally, remember to ensure that attending to others and copying what they do is an enjoyable activity for the child. Should the child ever spontaneously imitate a desirable action (e.g., exhibiting a new skill modeled by a peer or sibling), it is highly important to ensure that that imitation response is heavily reinforced **(D 26 & 27)**.

Trevor's Story

Trevor was a four-year-old boy who was receiving services from my staff at the STARS Clinic. He had regular sessions in which my staff was working on teaching him a variety of basic language and learning skills. One of the skills that we were teaching Trevor was to be able to imitate actions.

One day when his father came to pick him up, he indicated that he wished he could do more to help his son learn new skills. He went on to describe that unfortunately he had such a busy schedule that he found it difficult to make time to work with his son. I told him that there were a few simple things he could do that required little to almost no extra time. As I walked with them to their car, I told the father that it would be easy for him to start helping to develop his son's imitative skills. I then had them both stop walking and I demonstrated how to give an instruction and prompt Trevor to imitate knocking on a fence. I got down to Trevor's eye level, and when he was looking at me I said, "Trevor, do this," and I then knocked on the fence. He didn't respond, so I repeated the instruction and the model, and then took his arm and physically prompted him to knock on the fence. I praised him for "Good knocking" (praise was a reinforcer for him), and then repeated the instruction and model without a prompt. This time, Trevor knocked on the fence without me needing to provide any prompt. I gave him some enthusiastic praise, and then we continued to walk to the car.

As we walked, I explained the details of what I had just demonstrated to him. I then asked them to stop in front of a door we were passing. I then told the father that it was now "his turn" to get his son to imitate his knocking on a door. I provided Trevor's dad with verbal prompts and he was able to get his son to imitate his knocking. The father was excited that his son had watched his model and complied with his instruction.

We then walked a few more feet when I saw a man-hole cover (now known as a personnel access cover!) in the parking lot. I then demonstrated to the father how to get his son to look at my foot as I modeled stomping on the cover. Once again, I needed to use a physical prompt to get Trevor to stomp on the cover. I then repeated the sequence and he successfully imitated my stomping.

When we got to the car, I told Trevor's dad that before he opened the car door, I wanted him to get Trevor to imitate one of his actions. The father thought for a few seconds and said that he might try getting him to imitate his knocking on the door. I said that would be a great one to try. He then got at eye-level with his son, made him watch while he said, "Do this" and knocked on the door. Trevor quickly knocked on the door and the father excitedly praised his imitating and gave him a big hug. I praised the dad for following my lead and commented, "That wasn't too hard now, was it?" To which the father replied, "Actually it was pretty easy as long as I get him to really pay attention."

I told the father that he can chose almost any action that he wants to teach his child to imitate. The next time Trevor's dad came to pick up his son he was excited to show me several actions he had taught his son to imitate. He said he was surprised at how easy it was to teach the new skills to his son and that it really didn't take much time to do it. He also said that he now saw far more opportunities to get him to imitate than he had ever imagined.

Procedures to Continue Developing a Generalized Imitative Repertoire

Once a child has learned how to imitate at least 10 different responses (some of which would include the use of objects, while others are just imitation of motor actions) further development of those skills along several dimensions is critical. A young typically developing child can readily imitate a wide range of behaviors that have never been specifically taught, including complicated sequences of responses that involve a wide range of variations in how the specific actions are performed. This ability to imitate in such a precise manner makes it easy for these children to learn new skills just by watching others perform activities. Therefore, it is important to increase the variety of responses that a child with developmental delays can imitate, the complexity of the imitative responses, and the precision to which the modeled behaviors are imitated **(D 6, 15-17, 21-22)**. Having a well-developed generalized imitative repertoire (i.e., almost anything observed can be accurately imitated despite the setting, model, etc.) is critical for the learner to be able to develop a wide range of skills. The development of generalized imitation skills helps the child be better able to "learn to learn" a wide range of important skills.

The main issue in the further development of a child's imitative skill is to not get too bogged down in teaching any one specific skill. Many parents and educators will select a specific imitation action that they want to teach the child and put too much emphasis on teaching that one particular thing. The top priority should be to expand the number and variety of responses that the child can imitate, and to do so when asked to imitate using different instructions (e.g., "Do this," or "My turn...Your turn") **(D 7)**, and in a variety of situations (e.g., classroom, home, park). Other significant goals are to increase the child's ability to focus attention for longer periods of time and to attend to the various elements of how the model is being demonstrated (e.g., speed, timing, intensity and sequencing of the actions) in order for him to be able to replicate those actions. It is less important that any one skill be mastered (e.g., "arms up") than it is for the child to increase his ability to attend to and replicate many different types of actions (i.e., watching the model closely and imitating the nuances of her behavior). The same teaching procedures used to develop the initial imitative responses (i.e., prompt and then fade the prompts) should also be used in teaching the new responses. However, the types of actions presented each day should include a wide range of actions. If the child isn't able to imitate a certain response, the adult should work on teaching other ones and come back to the difficult one another day.

Variation in Instructions to Imitate

The child should also learn how to imitate actions when a variety of instructions are presented **(D 7)**. For example, many early training programs often give the instruction, "Do this" and then demonstrate a particular action. Although this type of instruction may be important in getting the child to learn how to imitate some actions, he should also realize that he is being requested to imitate when an adult or peer uses different words. Some examples of different ways of indicating that the child should imitate include statement such as, "Watch me, your turn," "Do what I do," "Watch what he's doing," or "Look, now you do it." The child must learn that all of these types of statements indicate that he should be watching a model and imitating the action or sequence of actions.

When shown actions with objects, the child should be able to imitate almost any action that might be used in a particular activity. For example, he should be able to imitate moving a toy car both quickly and slowly, have it make turns, go forward and backward, move to a location and stop, then turn and move to a second location. He should also be able to complete the actions at the same speed of a model **(D 15 & 16)** and—if he can imitate vocalizations—also make any sounds that are associated with the actions **(D 23)**. If he is shown a simple tapping pattern on a tambourine, the child should be able to not only imitate that action with the same speed, but also match the number and intensity of the taps both when performing the action along with the model, and following a demonstration of those actions **(D 20-22)**.

Imitation Involving Various Body Parts

One of the components of a good imitative repertoire includes the ability to imitate using different body parts. The child must be able to not only imitate actions that involve his arms, hands and fingers, but also his legs, head, mouth, tongue, and actions that involve movement of his entire body. He should be able to imitate a wide range of actions using his feet and legs (e. g., stomping a foot, spreading feet part, bending at knees, marching, hopping, making a kicking action, balancing on one foot) **(D 4)**. He should also be able to move his head in a variety of motions (e.g., twist head at neck as if to make a "no" action, moving head up and down as if to make a "yes" motion, moving head from side to side towards his shoulders, etc.) **(D 9)**, and be able to open and close his mouth, move his lips into a testing position, stick out his tongue and move it up and down and side to side) **(D 10 & 11)**. A child being able to imitate mouth and tongue actions in a mirror is often helpful in teaching him to vocally imitate sounds.

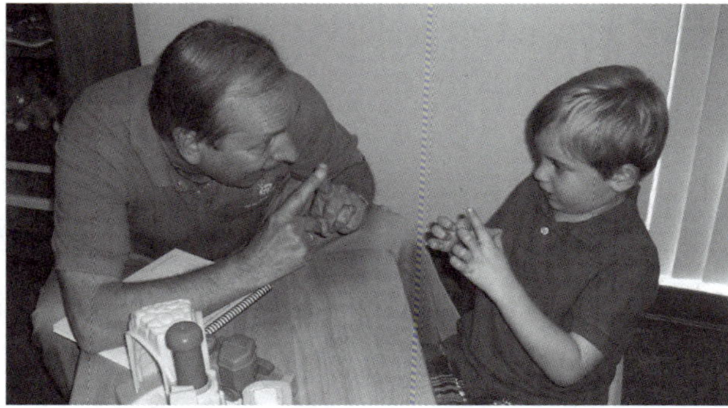

Teaching a child to imitate touching tips of fingers.

Development of Both Gross and Fine Motor Imitation Skills

Children need a well-developed repertoire of imitative skills that includes both gross motor and fine motor responses. For example, a child should be able to imitate a wide variety of action using his hands. Some of the responses could include clapping, rubbing hands together as if washing, rubbing hands together with palms and fingers kept in straight alignment, opening and closing the hand to a fist, waving "Bye" with the hands moving from side to side, as well as waving in a motion where the fingers bend towards the palm (in an open and close type of motion). He must also learn to imitate actions with his fingers including responses such as closing the fist and then extending the index finger as if to point, and a sequence of making a pointer finger, bringing it back to the fist position, and then back to a pointer position. He must also learn a similar action of moving his thumb into and out of the fist position. Additionally, moving his index finger in a curling motion (as if requesting somebody to come to him), touching thumbs together, index fingers together, and folding hands with fingers interlaced are just a few of the many actions which a child should be able to readily imitate **(D 12)**. Again, the specific responses are not as important as the child learning to observe a model and imitate a wide range of actions.

How to Teach a Child to Point & Make a Thumbs Up

To teach a child how to make a pointer finger, it is often helpful to hold his hand in front of his face in such a manner so that the only part he can move is his index finger. That is, the instructor should use her non-dominant hand to physically surround his dominant hand so that only his index finger can move. After getting the child to look at her hand, the instructor should then use her dominant hand to demonstrate the action of moving her index finger to a "pointer" position and then return it to a closed fist position. With the child's hand held next to the instructor's hand, he should be instructed to "Watch me", "Do this: finger up…finger down." The child's correct finger movements should be immediately reinforced. As the child sees that reinforcement is forthcoming for moving his finger, the instructor can then provide reinforcement after he matches the model of holding the finger in the extended and then closed position. If the child doesn't start to move his finger up and down along with the imitative model, the instructor should use physical prompts to assist the child in making the actions. The exact same procedure can then be used to teach him to make a "thumbs up" and return to a closed fist actions.

Movement and Static Motor Imitation

A child needs to learn to imitate actions that involve movement as well as those that require him to hold a static position. Many children with developmental delays are only taught a very few imitative responses such as clapping their hands, tapping their head, or knocking on a table. Sometimes children have never been taught to imitate actions involving holding their hands in a static position. For example, if a child is taught to imitate actions such as clapping hands, it is also important to make sure that he can move his hands to that same position and then hold them in that position (e. g., "prayer hands"). Similarly, if the child is taught to tap two hands to his head, he should also be taught to put both hands on his head and hold them in that position without tapping.

The child should also be taught to pay close attention to the position of his hands and to whether the model involves the use of either one or two hands. For example, when extending one arm or both arms in front of his body, the learner should be able to imitate those actions using either one or both arms (depending on the model), attend to whether the hands are held with the palms facing down, up, or facing each other, and whether the fingers are spread apart, closed together or held in a closed fist position. He should also be able to imitate moving either one or both extended arms (depending on what is demonstrated) up and down at his sides, or moving one or both arms from his side to reaching in front of him.

Movement Across Time and Space

As imitation skills begin to strengthen, it is important that the child learn how to imitate actions that involve the movement of his body across time and space. For example, he should be able to watch and then imitate actions such as getting out of a chair, walking over to a table, getting an object and moving it to a second location, and then returning to his seat **(D 26)**. The child should be able to accurately imitate not only the responses, but also the speed at which they were performed **(D 17)**.

Imitation of Sequences

Additionally, the child needs to be able to imitate sequences of responses at the same time as an existing model (i.e., switching movements when the model changes to a new action), and also to imitate those sequences of actions following a demonstration of a sequence of actions. Often, children will need to perform sequences of actions along with songs (e.g., "Head, Shoulders, Knees and Toes" song, or "The Itsy-Bitsy Spider"). When doing some sequences of actions, the child will often be doing it with a group of others, so he will need to learn to watch the speed and intensity of those actions and not only match those aspects, but also switch actions when the other children switch from one action to another.

Imitation at a Distance and in Mirrors

The child also needs to learn to imitate actions when the person providing the model isn't standing directly in front of him. He should be able to imitate actions when another person is standing beside him or behind him using a mirror to show him the action in the mirror's reflection. He should also be able to imitate actions that are modeled from across the room.

Teaching a Child to Imitate Mirrored Actions

When attempting to teach a child to imitate actions in a mirror, it is best to start with responses the child has already mastered versus a new imitative action. The goal is to teach the child to imitate the action when he is looking at the reflection, rather than looking at someone standing in front of him (**D 8 & 11**).

Therefore, the instructor should stand behind or beside the child and instruct him to look at her in the mirror. At first, reinforcement should be provided for only looking at the instructor's reflected face image (e.g., "That's nice looking at me!"). Then, the instructor should present a previously acquired imitative response that can be done using only one hand in relation to the upper part of the child's body (i.e., head or torso). Possible actions include touching the head, tapping or rubbing the stomach, and touching the nose. These examples make it possible for the instructor to provide an ongoing imitative action while also providing additional verbal prompts (e.g., "You do it....Tap your head.") and, if necessary, provide physical prompts. Once the child learns to look in the mirror to perform the first action, other similar previously mastered actions should be presented. As he learns to do several imitative hand actions in a mirror, other actions involving the head, mouth and tongue, and actions using the feet and legs can also be developed.

It is critical that the child develop an extremely well generalized imitative repertoire. With the exception of unusually talented motor movements (e.g., back flips), the child should be able to watch almost any example of actions that are performed by others, and be able to accurately replicate what they are doing or have done **(D 26)**. To develop this level of imitation mastery requires that the child develop sustained focused attention, an ability that is useful in learning many other skills. When the child has developed the ability to pay attention to the subtleties of what others are doing and is able to match those actions, he will then be able to learn a wide range of additional skills simply by being able to watch how others perform in a variety of situations. An extensive list of imitative skills (The Partington Imitation Skills Assessment) can be found at the end of this chapter.

Relationship Between Motor and Vocal Imitation

There are many specific skills that are developed when a child learns to imitate motor movements. Particularly, the child learns to attend to a model that is being presented to him and can accurately imitate that action. In the process, he learns that reinforcement is delivered only when he matches the actions of another person. He also learns through the process of "shaping" that he must pay close attention to his own response to make sure that it is accurate enough to result in the delivery of a reinforcer. That is, sloppy or inaccurate responses do not result in reinforcement. These same skills are also needed for him to learn to vocally imitate sounds, words, and phrases.

The difference between motor imitation and vocal imitation is that the motor imitation produces a visual stimulus (i.e., model) that needs to be copied, while with vocal imitation, the model is an auditory stimulus (Described in Chapter 5). In both types of imitation, the child must attend to the model stimulus and engage in a response that matches the model. During motor imitation tasks, there is a visual match between the modeled action and the product of the child's response. For vocal imitation tasks, there is an auditory match between the vocal model and the vocally imitative response.

However, there are several other factors that are unique to vocal imitation tasks. Specifically, most of the auditory models that the child is required to match are transitory in nature (i.e., they are no longer present when the child responds). Unless the adult makes a prolonged sound (e.g., holds the "O" sound for several seconds), the sound of the model ends before the child makes the matching sound. Additionally, in the case of prompting a child to make a matching sound or word, it is nearly impossible to physically prompt child to make the sound. Although certain prompts can be used to help signal to the child what sound is being requested (e.g., gesturing or touching a part of the mouth), or physically moving his lips in a certain position to make a sound (e.g., hold lips together to get an "mmm" sound), it is impossible to physically make the sound happen. Specific strategies for developing a child's ability to imitate vocalizations will be discussed in the following chapter.

Norman's Story

Norman's parents brought him to me so that I could assess his skills and make program recommendations. They had been receiving ABA therapy for several months, but were concerned that something was being missed in his program. He had made progress in several areas (including motor imitation skills), but they were concerned that he wasn't making progress in the development of his vocal imitation skills.

After my staff interacted with Norman, we did see that he was able to imitate numerous simple motor actions. However, the actions all involved his arms, hands and feet. He wasn't able to imitate any actions involving his head or mouth except moving his hands to the top of his head or to his cheeks. He wasn't able to imitate nodding or shaking his head, opening his mouth, sticking out his tongue, or closing his lips.

We decided to take Norman to the mirror, had him stand in front of us, and began to have him look at us in the mirror. After we had him looking at our reflections, we began to ask him to imitate the actions he could see us doing in the mirror. We started by having him do the actions that he could already do when he was sitting across from us and looking directly at our actions (i.e., putting hands on our head or on our cheeks). After a few prompted trials, we had him imitating those actions that he saw us do in the mirror.

Our next task was to get him to imitate a few head and mouth movements. We had him watch us as we presented a variety of actions and asked him to imitate them. At first, it took several full, then only partial physical prompts to get him to imitate the actions. After a several short trips to the mirror, Norman began to imitate several of the actions that we modeled in the mirror. Two of the actions included opening our mouths wide, and closing our lips tightly.

Now that he was imitating the mouth movements, we began to pair a vocalization with those two mouth movements. We made the "Ah" sound with our mouth open and an "MMM" sound with our lips closed tightly (both sounds we had heard him make, but not when he was asked to make them). He continued to imitate the movements and after several trials, he also began to make an approximation of those sounds. We reinforced his motor and vocal imitation combination with one of his preferred food items. It wasn't many trials before we had him consistently imitating those vocalizations while watching us in the mirror. After we had him solidly able to do a few of those vocalizations in front of a mirror, we then turned him away from the mirror and presented the same models. He then was able to imitate those two sounds when facing us.

Summary

The ability to imitate the motor behavior of other people plays an important role in a child's verbal and social development. If a child can imitate the behavior of others, he can acquire a number of skills with only minimal training.

In order to imitate, children need to learn to carefully watch what others are doing. It is important the child be motivated to watch the actions of others and be able to perform the same action. There must always be reinforcement following his attending to the actions and for reasonable attempts to replicate the actions. Therefore, it is critical that at first, the child be required to engage in only simple imitative responses that can easily be physically prompted by an instructor.

Some initial imitative actions often include manipulations of an object (e.g., pushing a car, tapping a drum, dropping a block in a container). Responses that can easily be physically prompted include raising arms over his head, tapping a table with his hand, and clapping hands. During the teaching process, the instructor can systematically reduce the amount of prompting so that the child is able to watch and then accurately imitate the actions or series of actions. At first, the child should only work on learning to imitate a few specific actions. As he masters a few imitative responses, the variety of tasks should be gradually increased until he is able to imitate almost any action that he is shown. The ability to watch and imitate known motor actions that are modeled in a mirror make it easier to teach a child to watch modeled actions involving the face and mouth. The ability to attend to what others are doing and then engage in matching those actions often make it easier to teach a child to also listen to, and then match, sounds and words spoken by others.

Potential Learning Objectives Related to the Development of Motor Imitation Skills

The following objectives are provided to assist a parent or teacher in targeting specific skills that may be appropriate for a child's intervention plan. Please see the ABLLS-R® to assess the child's skills and to identify additional objectives for further skill development.

Each child is a unique individual and requires input from a variety of people who know him and are familiar with effective programming strategies. Therefore, these learning objectives are not being prescribed for any particular child, but rather are being provided as examples of objectives that are consistent with the skills described in this chapter.

D 1 Upon request, (Child's name) will imitate at least 10 motor actions with an object (e.g., pretend to drink from a cup, roll a car down a ramp).

D 2 Upon request, (Child's name) will imitate at least 10 motor actions requiring a discrimination when using objects (e.g., when there is a pencil and a spoon and he is shown putting a pencil in a cup, he will do the same on request).

D 4 Upon request, (Child's name) will imitate at least five gross motor actions involving foot and leg movements (e.g., stomp foot, march).

D 5 Upon request, (Child's name) will imitate at least ten gross motor actions involving arm and hand movements (e.g., raise arms over head, clap hands, wave).

(Cont'd on next page.)

D 8 Upon request, (Child's name) will imitate at least five gross motor movements that he observes being modeled by others in a mirror.

D 9 Upon request, (Child's name) will imitate at leastthree gross motor actions involving head movements (e.g., nod head, shake head side-to-side).

D 12 Upon request, (Child's name) will imitate at least five fine motor actions (e.g., touch tips of index fingers together, make a pointer finger).

5 Teaching Vocal Imitation Skills

Developing Initial Vocal Imitative Responses

Although most children with autism or other developmental disabilities are able to say some words, some children have not developed the ability to control their vocal musculature sufficiently to be able to imitate specific sounds or words upon request. Producing vocal output in a specific pattern involves a complex sequence of actions on the part of the speaker. The child must be able to coordinate the position and movement of his mouth, tongue, and vocal chords with the muscles involved in moving air from his lungs in a controlled manner. The task of teaching him to echo specific sounds is difficult because these sounds can't be produced simply by someone moving all the involved parts of the child's body. It is possible to use certain prompts to help facilitate the output of certain sounds, but it isn't possible to physically make a child imitate specific sounds. However, because it is so important for children to learn to communicate by speaking, it is necessary to place a major emphasis on having the child develop the ability to imitate sounds, words and phrases. Therefore, vocal imitation training should be one of the first components of a language-based intervention program.

The ability to imitate sounds and words modeled by another person upon request is dependent upon several critical skills. Because of the complexity involved in reproducing sound patterns, the child must first be able to follow at least some directions to perform an action. It is important that he have an established history of reinforcement for complying with instructions to do something asked by others. He must also be motivated when attempts are being made by the instructor to have him imitate a sound or word. Assuming that the child's hearing is within the normal range, when a sound or word is presented for him to imitate, he must be able to fully attend to that particular sound or word. He must then engage all the body parts involved in making that sound in a controlled manner so as to match the sounds, and be able to attend to the similarity between his response and that of the model. For example, after an instructor has motivated him to attend, he may then be asked to say "mmm." He would then need to tighten his muscles such as to force his controlled breath through his vocal chords to produce a matching sound.

Despite parental attempts to get a child to imitate sounds or words, some children remain unable to imitate even simple sounds. Often, the child who has experienced failure in attempting to echo sounds will then attempt to avoid those types of interactions. Therefore, it is important for an instructor to maximize the child's reinforcement for attempting to imitate sounds. It is also critical that the modeled sounds are ones that have the highest probability of the child successfully producing, as some sounds are physically more difficult to make.

Is the Child Attending to Specific Auditory Stimuli?

Parents of children with language delays should always have their child's hearing evaluated to ensure that their son or daughter isn't hearing impaired. Although it may be difficult to have a child respond to some of the usual screening procedures, an audiologist who has experience evaluating children with developmental delays will be able to help rule out a hearing deficit as a potential factor in the child's speech and language delays. Additionally, because many individuals who have difficulty learning to speak have oral-motor deficits, it is beneficial to have a speech and language pathologist evaluate the strength, coordination, and mobility of the child's mouth, lips and tongue.

The skill of replicating a sound requires that the child actually attend to the sound he hears. However, there are many sounds that are present at any one given moment. Sounds come from a variety of sources and some of them are often just "background noise," while others are more critical for human interaction and performing daily activities. People are often talking, voices or music come from the television or radio, birds chirp, dogs bark, cars make sounds accelerating and honking, airplanes make noise taking off and landing, and appliances hum and beep: all are sources of a continuous flow of auditory stimulation. Most children respond differentially to the various sounds in that they ignore non-critical sounds, but do respond to sounds that are important to them in relation to their current motivation. For example, when a child is hungry and hears the noise of the refrigerator opening and closing along with the sounds of pans being placed on the stove, he may go to the kitchen because he knows that food will soon be ready. Hearing the theme song for his favorite TV program will usually result in the child running into the family room so he can watch his show. Sounds of the air conditioner turning on or a car driving by may simply be ignored because those sounds are not associated with his reinforcers.

Some children with developmental delays don't appear to respond to many of the sounds in their environment, and especially to sounds from adults who may require him to engage in non-preferred activities. There may be a few specific sounds that are associated with powerful reinforcers that result in a major change in activities. For example, the child who likes to play in the bathtub goes to the bathroom when he hears the sound of the water filling the tub, and the child who loves to swim runs to get his swimming suit when he hears the words "go swimming." In these examples, the child is highly motivated to engage in preferred (i.e., reinforcing) activities. However, when adults approach a child and attempt to get him to learn new skills, the motivation to attend to the words being spoken may be very low unless the adult has taken steps to both develop a history of providing reinforcement for the child going along with instructions, and is now approaching him with a clear indication that reinforcement will be provided for participating in the upcoming activity.

Now consider an interaction in which the adult is attempting to have the child replicate a difficult sound or word. If the child's previous history with this activity has not resulted in the successful replication of those sounds, the start of a vocal imitation session may result in the child attempting to avoid or escape from the adult's instructions. In this situation, he may not even be attending to the sounds being modeled by the adult, and his physical behaviors (i.e., attempting to avoid the interaction) may be interfering with the coordinated physical actions that are necessary to reproduce the desired sounds.

The research by Greer and Ross (2008) has suggested that for individuals who lack the ability to talk, it is important to develop their ability to discriminate different sounds. In essence, if we want a child to imitate sounds, it is important that he actually be able to hear the differences between the sounds that he is being asked to imitate. If he doesn't hear the difference between the sounds, how will he be able to learn to receptively identify items, and how will he be able to learn to vocally imitate sounds and words?

There are several methods one could use to help a child learn to attend to auditory stimuli. One method could involve starting a highly reinforcing activity when a specific word or sound is heard. After the reinforcer has been presented on several occasions following the specific word or sound, the child will begin to respond by starting to engage in the behavior associated with the reinforcing activity only when he hears that sound or word, but not when he hears other sounds or words not associated with the reinforcing activity. This type of conditioning (i.e., learning) accounts for the nonvocal child who reacts by going to the back door when he hears words such as "outside," or gets his swimming suit when he hears "go swimming." These words are clearly associated with highly reinforcing activities and hence hearing those sounds (words) results in the child engaging in behaviors associated with those activities.

For a child who has developed the ability to imitate simple actions with objects, there is another activity that can help to ensure that he is attending to auditory stimuli. There are several imitative tasks that involve objects that produce a specific auditory stimulus (i.e., sound). For example, shaking a maraca, tapping on a tambourine, and rolling a toy car on a table each produce a unique sound. If the child is able to imitate these actions, it is possible to teach him to attend to and engage in behavior that produces matching sounds without seeing the items, but rather by discriminating the sounds made by those items.

Replicating Sounds Using Objects

To teach the child to reproduce these matching object sounds, let's look at the several steps involved. The first step requires the child to imitate the specific action with each of the objects (i.e., shake maraca, tap tambourine, and roll toy car) when the adult shows the child what to do. The adult would have all three items on a table and the child would have his own matching set of items. She would then give the instruction to "Do this" and then perform one of the actions. The correct imitative action would result in reinforcement. Once the child has demonstrated that he is attending to the actions (each of which results in a unique sound), the instructor can then place a piece of cardboard in front of the child so that he can see his three objects, but not those used by the adult. The same instruction would then be presented (i.e., "Do this"), however, since the child is unable to see the action but can hear the sound produced by the action, his ability to replicate the action of the adult is solely based on his ability to hear the sound and discriminate the required action to produce the matching sound. Note that if the child is unable to replicate the sound, it is possible to use and then fade visual or physical prompts to teach this skill.

In essence, the skill of listening to a sound and then performing an action to replicate the sound is the same skill necessary for learning to vocally imitate sounds. However, with vocal imitation tasks, it is not as easy to prompt the child to engage in actions to produce specific sounds. It simply isn't possible to provide the full physical prompts necessary to have the child expel his breath with his vocal chords, with his mouth and tongue in a certain position so that they produce various sounds. However, the procedure does require the child to listen to the sounds and engage in behavior that produces a matching sound. Thus, attending to the sound (i.e., listening) and performing an action to produce a matching sound is reinforced, making it more likely that the child will attend to specific sounds and engage in other actions that result in the matching of sounds. Thus, this activity could be useful in learning to listen to sounds even for a child who is not yet able to imitate vocally.

Increasing Variability and Frequency of Spontaneous Vocalizations

To teach a child to talk, he must first learn to vocally imitate sounds and words. In addition to attending to sounds, he must be able to make the sounds needed to speak. As was described earlier, some children are very quiet and do not spontaneously make many of the different sounds used by others who speak. Thus, one of the goals for such children is to increase the variety of speech-related sounds and the frequency of those sounds made by the child **(I 1)**. In essence, it is desirable to have the child practice making speech-related sounds throughout his day (i.e., increase babbling). Once the child is making those sounds through babbling or vocal play, they can then be brought under instructional control so that he will be able to replicate them upon request. However, if the child doesn't make a certain sound, it is very difficult to get him to imitate it when produced by another person or object.

There are several techniques that can help increase a child's speech-related vocalizations. The first procedure involves the use of direct reinforcement for any vocalizations that the child emits. That is, when the child makes some identifiable speech sounds, the instructor should directly reinforce this behavior with attention, physical contact, or other effective reinforcers. The goal is to increase the frequency of vocalizations, and reinforcement is the main way to accomplish this objective. The intensity of this program depends on the individual child. If he almost never makes sounds, every effort to reinforce any sound should be made. If the child makes a variety of sounds, these different sounds should be reinforced. For example, if the child frequently makes an "ah" sound, but rarely makes other sounds (e.g., "mmm," "buh," "O"), stronger reinforcement could be provided whenever the child makes those less-frequently-heard sounds. Thus, differential reinforcement can be used to increase both the frequency and the variety of sounds made by the child.

Another example of directly reinforcing a child's spontaneous vocalizations is to provide reinforcement in the form of pushing a child on a swing whenever the child makes a specific sound. For example, for a child who enjoys swinging, when he is first put on a swing and given an initial push (for free—no response required), while positioned in front of the child, the parent can make a certain sound (multiple times) that he is heard to spontaneously make at least a few times per day (e.g., "E"). When the child makes any vocalization, the parent can give him a push (from the front) and praise him for "good talking." The parent should continue to say the targeted "E" sound. When he makes another vocalization, the parent can again give him a push while also providing praise. If the push and praise are actual reinforcers, the reinforcement will increase the child's vocalizations. It will then be possible to differentially reinforce the child for sounds that he makes that are closer approximations of the "E" sound. Slightly close approximations of the "E" sounds receive a little push (and the parent excitedly says "E, yes E"), while closer approximations receive a bigger push, but an actual "E" sound gets the biggest push (and perhaps even a couple of pushes). Again, the more desired or independent the response, the greater the reinforcement.

A second method of increasing a child's spontaneous vocalizations is to playfully engage with him while imitating his vocalizations (Palaez, Virues-Ortega, & Gewirtz, 2011). Often, a child enjoys interactions when an adult holds her face near the child's and makes funny faces while repeating the sounds the child is making. During these interactions, the adult may also tickle the child, or touch him in a preferred manner so as to make the interaction more reinforcing. An example scenario could be when a child is sitting on his parent's lap, facing the parent, and he spontaneously makes a sound (e.g., "buh, buh, buh"). The parent could immediately smile and bounce the child on her lap while repeating "buh, buh, buh" in a playful manner. If the interactions reinforce the child's spontaneous vocalizations, there will often be an increase in both the frequency and the variability of the child's vocalizations.

The third technique for increasing vocalizations is to take every opportunity to pair (associate) adult vocalizations with naturally occurring reinforcers (Sundberg, Michael, Partington, & Sundberg, 1996). For example, just prior to delivering tickles (a reinforcer) to a child, the adult should say a sound such as "baba" and then tickle the child (the sound should always slightly precede the delivery of the reinforcer by about one to two seconds). Repeat this pairing several times, and if tickles are reinforcers, soon that sound may become a reinforcer because it is associated with tickles. Repeat this procedure with a variety of different reinforcers, and eventually with a variety of different sounds.

If sounds become reinforcers to the child through this pairing process, then it is possible for them to become automatically strengthened when produced by the child. That is, some sounds may be heard "differently" by the child and take on reinforcing value because of this pairing. He enjoys hearing the sound that he now makes; it is the same as what he has previously heard others make while being presented along with other reinforcers. The sound he now produces has become a conditioned reinforcer (i.e., learned) that strengthens the behavior that produced the sound. Skinner (1957) has identified this effect as "automatic reinforcement" and he and others have suggested that it plays a critical role in the early establishment of speech in typical children (e.g., Bijou & Baer, 1965; Mowrer, 1950; Osgood, 1953; Vaughan & Michael, 1982). The use of this pairing procedure has also been effective for increasing speech for some children with language delays.

The purpose of reinforcing a child's vocal play is to increase the frequency and variability of his vocalizations so as to also increase the probability of establishing echoic skills (vocal imitation). Echoic skills play a major role in the teaching of new words, because if a child can repeat a word on command, then the transfer of control procedures described in Chapter 6 can be used to not only teach mands, but to teach other types of language as well (e.g., labeling and talking about items, activities, and experiences).

Identifying Initial Sounds to Bring Under Instructional Control

Before attempting to teach a child to imitate specific sounds, it is necessary to determine which sounds should be targeted for instruction. Certain sounds are often easier for a child to make than others. Generally, children learn to imitate vowels and perhaps a few consonants, often in a combination followed by one of those vowels. For example, "ah," "E," "mm," and "buh" are sounds that are easier for most children to make than are sounds such as "ch" and "th." Therefore, a careful review of sounds frequently heard from babbling infants will also help to identify sounds that are easiest to produce. Speech and language pathologists are aware of the complexity of producing certain sounds anc specific advice in the selection of appropriate targets for a child. Fc vocalization of consonants such as m, n, p, b, w and h often come befor… sounds such as the ones for f, y, t, g and k. The child's own spontaneous vocalizations can be surveyed to provide another source of input to identify sounds to teach him to imitate.

Children who are unable to vocally imitate still make certain sounds. Some children are unusually quiet, some make noises that are not useful for speech, while still others make a variety of speech-like sounds but are unable to make those sounds upon request. One of the first steps in selecting sounds to bring under instructional control is to conduct an inventory of the spontaneous sounds made by the child. While interacting with him and while merely listening to him when he is not engaged with others, it is helpful to write down the sounds the child makes. During these times, the frequency that those sounds are made should also be recorded. (See Figure 5-1 - Sample Spontaneous Vocalizations Data Sheet.) After several days of carefully listening to the spontaneous sounds made by the child, it will be apparent which of those sounds occur at the highest frequency. (In these sample data, "Ah" and "mm" are the highest.) Because it is known that the child is physically able to make those sounds, they are the best ones to attempt to bring under instructional control (i.e., teach him to make those sounds upon request).

Figure 5-1. Spontaneous Vocalizations Data

Record the spontaneously occuring sounds that you hear the child make.

Date	Person	Ah	E	O	MM	La	Buh				
11/20	Mom	IIIII	I	I	III						
	Dad	II	I		II						
	Susan	IIIIII	II		III	II					
11/21	Mom	IIIIIIII	II		III		I				
	Dad	III		I	II						
	Susan	IIIII			IIII	I					
11/22	Mom	IIIIIII	III	i	IIII	I					
	Dad	II	II		IIII		I				
	Susan	IIIII	I		IIIIII	I					
11/23	Mom	IIIIIIII	II	I	III						
	Dad	II			IIII	I	I				
	Susan	IIIIII	I		II		I				

The sample Spontaneous Vocalizations Data Sheet is used to record the sounds people hear the child make throughout his day. Each day, his parents and his instructor (Susan) record what sounds they hear and how often they hear him make those sounds. When the child makes a certain sound, they write the sound across the top of each collumn (e.g., Ah, E, O, MM, La). When new sounds are heard, they can be written at the top of the next collumn (e.g., Buh). Every time a person hears the child make one of the sounds, they record a "hash mark" (i.e., I) in their row for that particular sound. These data can then be used to deterine which sounds a child is able to make and which ones he makes the most each day. Those high-frequency spontaneous sounds may then be considered for development as ones he will be taught to make upon request.

Rachel's Story

I made a home visit to Rachel and her parents. She was a three-year-old girl who had very limited skills; she needed to develop all the skills included in this book! I noticed that Rachael was usually very quiet. On some occasions, when she was by herself, she would make some very low volume sounds. Others had attempted to get her to imitate sounds, but had been unsuccessful.

Her parents would often take her to the park to use the swings. She enjoyed being pushed by her parents. When I went with them one afternoon, I asked her dad to squat in front of her and push her from the front, rather than from behind her. I then told him to give her a few pushes to get her started. After she was moving, I would occasionally hear her make a vocalization. I told her father to get excited when he heard her vocalize and then give her a push. I also told him that he could talk with her while she was swinging, but to only give her a push when he heard her vocalize. He was instructed to get excited and talk as he gave her the push (e.g., "Yah! I heard that!") and repeat her vocalization. Rachel's rate of vocalizing quickly increased as a result of her getting pushes for vocalizing.

We noticed that many of her vocalizations sounded like approximations of the sound "E," so after a few minutes, her parents and I all started making the "E" sound. I told the father to now only give her a push when he heard her make an approximation of the "E" sound. I told him not to worry about her repeating after him (or us), but rather just give her a push any time she made that sound and say in a loud and excited manner "EEE!" If she made a weak approximation of "E" he was to still get excited but only give her a little push, but if she made a solid "E" she was to get a big push. In just a few minutes, her vocalizations of that sound increased dramatically. Rachel had learned that in order to get a big push, she had to say "E." It is important to note that while she was still not echoing the sound, that is making it upon request, but she was now learning to control her vocal musculature to make the sound—definitely a step in the right direction.

Developing Initial Vocal Imitative Responses

The procedures for strengthening a child's ability to echo an instructor are similar to those used for motor imitation, except vocal behavior is used, and the use of physical prompts is not as helpful. Note that the components and recommendations described for teaching motor imitation tasks are applicable when teaching a child to imitate a sound, except the child's response produces a sound (i.e., an auditory response product) rather than the sight of the action that matches a visual model (i.e., a visual response product).

The procedure consists of presenting the child with the verbal prompt "Say..." and reinforcing a correct response. At first, reinforcement may be provided for an approximation of a correct response. As the child continues to emit approximations, the accuracy of his vocalizations can be "shaped" by gradually reinforcing only those responses that more accurately match the sound being modeled. For example, an adult may shape a child's approximation of the word "ball" by gradually increasing the criterion for reinforcement as the child gains greater control of his vocal musculature. At first, the adult may start by reinforcing the response "buh," then requiring "baw," and finally requiring "ball."

There are several factors that can help this type of training be most successful. As with all teaching, it is important that the child can see that his cooperation with the instructions will lead to reinforcers being delivered. It is also important that the initial sounds to be brought under instructional control are ones that he has emitted frequently in the past. The objective is to get the child to make the specific sound he can already make when requested by the adult (e.g., "Say EEE") **(E 1)**.

It is also helpful if the initial sounds targeted for instruction are ones that may be somewhat prompted. For example, if the child can imitate moving his mouth to an "open wide" position and also move his lips to a pursed (i.e., tightly closed lips) position, the presentation of exaggerated visual models, along with the extended productions of sounds ("ahhhhhhhh" and "mmmmmmmmm" respectively), may increase the chances of the child making the desired sounds. Additionally, if he attends to the mouth of the adult when she makes exaggerated repetitive mouth movements that accompany the sounds "buh, buh, buh,

buh, buh," the child's vocally imitative response may be controlled by both the sound of the model and the visual stimuli of the instructor's mouth movement.

Other types of prompts such as modeling the sound "mmm" while gently physically prompting the child to purse his lips together may also be helpful in getting him to be able to successfully make that sound upon request. As with the use of any prompts to teach a new behavior, these exaggerated mouth positions and physical prompts should also be faded so that the child emits the desired sounds only when he hears the model. Examples of prompt fading include touching the child's lips, gesturing towards the adult model's lips, and merely modeling the sound.

It is important to note that speech and language pathologists have a variety of specific prompting methods that can be used to help develop other vocally imitative responses. Some of their methods involve having the child attend to and imitate positioning of the tongue and lip positions prior to and during the movements necessary to produce a sound or pattern of sounds. Another technique involves touching the child's face or neck in a certain way to prompt him to position his mouth or tongue in a certain manner to make a specific sound. Additionally, the use of an American Sign Language (ASL) sign paired with a specific vocalization can often help improve the ability to produce a particular sound.

How Far to Push When Shaping an Accurate Response

When attempting to get a child to imitate a sound, it is important to not push him so much that his attempts to imitate result in consistent failure. Often it will be necessary for the child to attempt to repeat the sound several times before he can actually make the response. Remember that for a child who hasn't learned to imitate sounds, the production of a specific sound upon request is a very difficult task (if it wasn't difficult, he would already be talking!). Therefore, because it is so challenging, and it is equally difficult to prompt him to be successful in making the response, keeping the child motivated to follow instructions is critical. Therefore, it is critical that reinforcement be carefully provided in order to gradually shape the accuracy of the child's responses.

What is "Close Enough"?

When teaching a child to say a particular sound upon request, the instructor will often hear him produce variations of that sound. Many instructors report being unsure as to which of those variations are "close enough" to the actual sound to be reinforced. There are two main issues that need to be considered: The first is the child's history of making that sound, and the second is the strength of the current reinforcer.

If the child is just starting to make the sound, almost all approximations of the target sound should be reinforced. The desired outcome of the reinforcement is to increase the child making approximations of that sound. As the child is consistently able to make an approximation upon request, the instructors should use a shaping procedure to improve the accuracy of the vocalization. This procedure involves the reinforcement of those responses that are closer to the targeted sound while not reinforcing sounds that are less accurate. Therefore, the accuracy or what is considered to be "close enough" should be constantly changing; as the child is able to make more accurate vocalizations, the reinforcement will only be provided following examples of his best responses.

The child may have started the day by making only a rough approximation of the sound. During the course of the day, only his best responses were reinforced so he was making more accurate sounds by the end of the day. The responses that were reinforced earlier in the day were no longer considered to be "close enough" to be reinforced. However, at the start of the next day, his responses may not be as accurate as they were at the end of the previous day. Therefore, it is sometimes necessary to go back to reinforcing a few of the lesser quality responses, but then immediately start to raise the criterion to require and reinforce his best responses from the previous day. As each day progresses, the overall accuracy should keep increasing until the child is able to clearly imitate the targeted sound on the first trial of each day.

It should be noted that on some occasions, the child simply will not be able to make the sound or a close approximation. Therefore, at some point, it will be necessary to stop attempting to get him to make the sound. This decision requires determining at what point the child's vocalization is "close enough" to be reinforced, and considerations as to the number of times a vocal model should be presented before giving up on trying to get him to make a good response.

When the learner is attending to a vocal model and is attempting to imitate that sound, he may be successful after a few attempts. However, if he isn't able to produce a reasonable approximation after several attempts, it's probably best to stop trying to get him to make that sound so that he doesn't "become frustrated" with the activity. (In behavioral terms, his attempted responses are "on extinction" in that no reinforcement is forthcoming, and his probability of making further attempts is decreasing.) Therefore, as a general rule, it is probably best to present the vocal model no more than three times before presenting the child with another (easier) instruction. In this situation, his behavior of complying with an instruction is still reinforced, but if he is able to imitate the vocalization following one of the models, the reinforcer will be delivered sooner. Note that it is also important that the reinforcer provided following the vocal responses be more powerful (or delivered in greater quantity) than the reinforcers that are provided following the easier responses (vocal or non-vocal). Thus there is incentive both to comply with instructions, and to correctly imitate the desired sound.

Maintaining Motivation to Vocally Imitate

There are a few ways to help keep the child motivated to participate in vocal imitation activities. The first is to have him imitate some well-established motor imitations prior to attempting to have him echo a sound. By presenting these easy to imitate actions, the child's behavior of matching the model will be reinforced. After receiving several reinforcers for matching the model, there will be "behavioral momentum" in that the child is already doing what is asked of him and he will be more likely to continue responding to get additional reinforcers (Dube, Ahearn, Lionello-Denlof & McIlvane, 2009). For example, if he has already learned to imitate some actions, he may be requested to "Do this" (imitate touching nose), "clap with me," and then "say 'mmm'." By presenting a few mastered responses before attempting the vocal imitation response, the child receives reinforcement for complying with the adult's requests before he is presented with the more difficult vocal imitation task. Professionals describe this approach as building "behavioral momentum" in that the child is already going along with the instructor (he's "on a roll") before the more difficult task is presented.

Research has demonstrated that mixing trials that include previously mastered responses with acquisition trial results in better performance by children (Winterling, Dunlap, & O'Neill, 1987; Volkert, Lerman, Trosclair, Addison, & Kodak, 2008). Thus, a second method to help maintain the child's motivation to respond involves interspersing the more difficult vocal imitation trials (i.e., echoic trials) with easier trials (e.g., mastered motor imitation responses, known receptive instructions), so that the child will maintain a high level of successful and reinforced responding.

During the process of shaping the accuracy of the response, it is important to remember that the child's motivation to make an accurate sound (or word) is dependent upon the strength of the reinforcer. If he isn't motivated to receive the item or activity that is being used as a potential reinforcer, there is no reason for him to make an effortful response to get it. In this situation, when adults recognize that the child isn't highly motivated, they should avoid the temptation to reinforce lesser quality responses. If the child learns that even lower level approximations will be reinforced, there is no reason for him to make a more accurate vocalization. This phenomenon of decreased accuracy in responding is often a result of what is referred to as "the law of least effort" (Whaley & Malott, 1968). This concept identifies that the child is only doing what is minimally necessary to receive the reinforcer. The best option is to stop trying to get an accurate response until the adult can find a more powerful reinforcer. Remember that it is always best to stop an interaction after the reinforcement of a high-quality response rather than trying to keep a session going as motivation wanes and the responding becomes less accurate.

Echoics in Mand Training

One of the most important methods of developing a child's vocal imitation skills is to prompt him to make the sound when teaching him to ask for reinforcers (See mand training described in Chapter 6). When teaching a child to ask for things he wants, there is always a strong motivation for a particular reinforcer. Some children cannot vocally ask for items or activities (e.g., to get something to eat, to be picked up, etc.) but can be taught to "mand" (i.e., ask for something) using nonvocal methods such as ASL signs or by using picture systems. As the child starts to successfully mand for these items and activities, he can also be gradually prompted and required to make vocal approximations for those items and activities. For example, when he is successful in using an ASL sign for "eat" to get another bite of food, the instructor can emphasize the "E" sound in the word "EEEEat," prompting the child to attempt to repeat that sound (as the bite of food is withheld for a second or two, but held directly in the child's view). The child's attempts at repeating the sound can be reinforced by the delivery of the food item along with the adult enthusiastically repeating the word "eat." If the child doesn't say "eat," (or "E" as an approximation), he should still be given his bite of food. However, if the child says the sound along with the sign, the delivery of the food will be more immediate, and he will receive more enthusiastic praise, and perhaps a greater quantity of food. Thus, not only does the vocal mand get faster delivery of the reinforcer, but it also gets a greater amount of the reinforcer than if he only uses the ASL sign to request the food.

A similar approach can be used as the child comes to the parent with his arms held in the "up" position to request to be picked up. The adult can acknowledge his request to be picked up (e.g., "You want "UP?""), and then delay picking him up far a few seconds as she says "UP.....UP.....UP." If the child should say "up" or make a sound similar to "up," the parent should immediately pick up the child and enthusiastically repeat the word "UP." If he has not previously said an approximation to "Up" or has only said it a few times, the child could still be picked after a few attempts to get him to say "Up" because he had made the sign for 'up.' However, by saying "Up" along with the sign results in him getting picked up sooner. Again, in this scenario, the adult is paying particular attention to when the reinforcer (i.e., being picked up) is delivered—ideally, immediately following a desired sign and vocal response from the child.

Sequence for Teaching Vocal Responses

When teaching a child to make his first few vocal imitations, it is often helpful to teach him to imitate each response separately. For example, when asking him to imitate the "Ah" sound, he can imitate that sound several times in a row. Similarly, if asked to imitate "mm," he can make that sound several times in a row. Once the child has mastered at least two separate sounds, it is then necessary to have him learn to imitate the sounds when the modeled sounds are alternated. The two sounds that he is able to make should then be presented to him in a random order so that he learns to discriminate which sound is being modeled, and he can make either of those sounds upon request. As the two sounds are now presented in a random order, it may be necessary to provide additional prompts (e.g., exaggerated mouth open, lips closed) to increase the chances of him making the correct vocalization. These prompts should then be eliminated so that the child matches the sounds only after hearing them. In fact, he should be taught to imitate those responses when he cannot see the adult's mouth.

After the child has learned to echo (vocally imitate) the first two sounds, new sounds should be targeted for training. New sounds can be prompted and shaped individually as were the initial sounds. Once he is able to consistently imitate these additional responses, they should then be included in the random presentation of the previously acquired "echoic" responses.

Collection of Data on Echoic Development

One of most important elements of effective teaching is to be aware of the changes in the learner's skills. When attempting to develop echoic skills, it is essential to know not only what sounds a child can reliably make, but also to document the development of the initial skills. There are many aspects to considering the sounds the learner can make. The first is his ability to make the sound in isolation **(E 1)**. The second aspect concerns his ability to make that sound in combination with other sounds **(E 7-12)**. Some sounds are easier to make when following certain other sounds, and some are more difficult when in the middle of a word or at the end of a word. The sound production process involves the flow of one sound to another (i.e., co-articulation). For example, the word "me" is made by making the "m" sound and then flowing into the "e" sound; the word is "me," not "m" "e" (two separate sounds). For the purposes of this book, the development of the isolated sounds and a few of the easier to develop sound combinations will be considered. As the child is able to imitate a variety of sounds and simple sound combinations, it will then be necessary to do a more complete evaluation of his ability to imitate sounds in the initial, medial (middle), and final positions within words.

For the child who is not able to imitate any sounds, or is able to imitate only one or two sounds, it's important to record his attempts to imitate a sound on a trial-by-trial basis. The main data to be collected includes both how often the child is able to imitate a sound, and how many attempts he made before he was able to produce the sound.

In reviewing the sample datasheet (See Figure 5-2), correct imitations of an "Ah" sound are indicated by a "+." A "|" specifies that a model was presented but the child did not correctly imitate the sound, and a "/" indicates that the child made a close approximation that was reinforced. A second attempt (a short time later) to get the child to make the sound is recorded in the next box in the row. Each box across the top of the data sheet (1-10) represents an instance of an attempt to get the child to imitate the sound. The next attempt may occur within a minute after the previous attempt, or after a longer period of time (e.g., 30 to 60 minutes or longer).

The collection of these data allows instructors to identify small, but significant, improvements in the child's ability to produce specific sounds upon request. These improvements will be identified as the child requires fewer attempts before being able to successfully make an approximation or an accurate response.

Figure 5-2. **Sample Echoic Data**

Imitation of the "Ah" sound | = SD (Model presented) / = Reinforced approximation + = Accurate Echoic Respons

<table>
<tr><th>Date</th><th>Instructor</th><th>1</th><th>2</th><th>3</th><th>4</th><th>5</th><th>6</th><th>7</th><th>8</th><th>9</th><th>10</th><th>Attempts</th><th>Total First Trial Correect</th><th>Percent of First Trial Correct</th><th>Total correct</th><th>Percent of Successful Attempts</th></tr>
<tr><td>11/24</td><td>Mom</td><td>|||</td><td>||/</td><td>|||</td><td>||/</td><td>|||</td><td>||/</td><td>|/</td><td>||/</td><td>|||</td><td>|/</td><td></td><td></td><td></td><td></td><td></td></tr>
<tr><td></td><td>Mom</td><td>||+</td><td>|||</td><td>||/</td><td></td><td></td><td></td><td></td><td></td><td></td><td></td><td>13</td><td>0</td><td>0</td><td>1</td><td>8%</td></tr>
<tr><td></td><td>Susan</td><td>||/</td><td>|||</td><td>||/</td><td>|+</td><td>||/</td><td>|||</td><td>|/</td><td>|||</td><td>|/</td><td>/</td><td></td><td></td><td></td><td></td><td></td></tr>
<tr><td></td><td>Susan</td><td>/</td><td>/</td><td>||/</td><td>/</td><td>|||</td><td>/</td><td></td><td></td><td></td><td></td><td>16</td><td>0</td><td>0</td><td>1</td><td>6%</td></tr>
<tr><td></td><td>Dad</td><td>|||</td><td>||/</td><td>|||</td><td>|/</td><td>/</td><td>||/</td><td>/</td><td></td><td></td><td></td><td>7</td><td>0</td><td>0</td><td>0</td><td>0</td></tr>
<tr><td>11/25</td><td>Mom</td><td>|||</td><td>|/</td><td>|||</td><td>||/</td><td>/</td><td>|/</td><td>/</td><td>|+</td><td>||-</td><td>+</td><td>10</td><td>1</td><td>10%</td><td>3</td><td>30%</td></tr>
<tr><td></td><td>Susan</td><td>||/</td><td>/</td><td>|+</td><td>+</td><td>||/</td><td>||+</td><td>+</td><td>||+</td><td>|+</td><td>|||</td><td></td><td></td><td></td><td></td><td></td></tr>
<tr><td></td><td>Susan</td><td>|/</td><td>/</td><td>|+</td><td>||+</td><td>+</td><td>+</td><td></td><td></td><td></td><td></td><td>16</td><td>3</td><td>19%</td><td>10</td><td>63%</td></tr>
<tr><td></td><td>Mom</td><td>/</td><td>||+</td><td>+</td><td>/</td><td>|+</td><td></td><td></td><td></td><td></td><td></td><td>5</td><td>1</td><td>20%</td><td>3</td><td>60%</td></tr>
<tr><td>11/26</td><td>Dad</td><td>||/</td><td>||+</td><td>|/</td><td>|/</td><td>||/</td><td>||+</td><td>|+</td><td>+</td><td>/</td><td>|+</td><td></td><td></td><td></td><td></td><td></td></tr>
<tr><td></td><td>Dad</td><td>+</td><td>||+</td><td>+</td><td></td><td></td><td></td><td></td><td></td><td></td><td></td><td>13</td><td>3</td><td>23%</td><td>8</td><td>62%</td></tr>
<tr><td></td><td>Mom</td><td>||/</td><td>//+</td><td>|+</td><td>+</td><td>+</td><td>/</td><td>+</td><td></td><td></td><td></td><td>7</td><td>3</td><td>43%</td><td>5</td><td>71%</td></tr>
<tr><td></td><td></td><td></td><td></td><td></td><td></td><td></td><td></td><td></td><td></td><td></td><td></td><td></td><td></td><td></td><td></td><td></td></tr>
<tr><td></td><td></td><td></td><td></td><td></td><td></td><td></td><td></td><td></td><td></td><td></td><td></td><td></td><td></td><td></td><td></td><td></td></tr>
</table>

By looking at the sample data sheet it can be seen that the child is developing the ability to vocally imitate the sound "Ah." On the first day his mother, father, and therapist each attempted to have him imitate that sound. There were 36 specific times he was presented with the instruction "Say 'Ah'." He was unable to repeat that sound the first time it was presented, but was able to make the sound on two occasions (6%) in which the instruction was presented several times. On day 2, he had 31 trials, and he responded correctly on the first presentation on five trials (16%), and was able to make the sound on a total of 16 of the trials (52%). By day 3, he had 20 trials, and he responded correctly on the first presentation on six trials (30%), and was able to make the sound on a total of 13 of the trials (65%). Over the course of several days, the child not only began to accurately imitate the sound, but also was able to imitate the vocalization for multiple individuals. His ability to imitate on the first presentation of the sound increased from 0% on day 1, to 30% on day 3.

Tracking the Development of Vocal Imitation Skills

For a child who can imitate some sounds on request, it is important to evaluate his existing echoic skills before attempting to teach new sounds. The sounds that he is able to imitate can be interspersed (i.e., mixed in with) among trials that are being presented to develop new sounds. This approach allows him to be frequently successful in imitating many of his easier sounds while working on learning to make the new sounds. The Echoic Evaluation Form (See Appendix 3) can be used to determine which sounds a child is able to make. Note that it is possible to present a variety of sounds and combinations to determine which ones he can imitate. If the child is able to clearly and consistently say a sound, a "+" should be entered next to the corresponding sound. (See Sample Echoic

Evaluation Data - Figure 5-3.) It should be recorded as a "-", if the child is unable to make an approximation of a sound. If the child makes a consistently good approximation of the sound, what his approximations sound like should be written in the approximation column. If he is making a good effort and can produce the sound sometimes, but is not consistent with imitating it, a "/" should be recorded to score his response as an approximation. The review of the child's echoic skills should help his intervention team (including his speech pathologist) identify reasonable targets to select for development.

Figure 5-3. **Echoic Evaluation Sample**

Sounds	As in the word	Sounds like	Dates of Assessment			
			11/12			
A	ape		-			
aah	hot		+			
ah	hat		-			
aw	awful		-			
Ah - Ah			-			
Ah - E			-			
B	bee		-			
bih	big		-			
bah	bah humbug		-			
buh	bubble		+			
bubble	(word)	buh-uh	/			

From these sample data we can see that the child is consistently able to accurately replicate the sounds "aah" and "buh," and that he is able to make an approximation to the word "bubble." He is able to make the initial "buh" sound followed by an "uh" sound.

Expanding the Initial Vocal Imitation Skills

For children who can imitate at least 10 sounds and possibly a few words on request, an emphasis should be placed on having them learn to imitate a wider range of sounds and combinations of sounds. The learner should be taught to quickly say each of his sounds in a random order **(E 2)**, and to say the sounds matching the speed of the model **(E 5)**.

For example, if he can make an "mm" sound, he should also be taught to listen and imitate a short "mm" sound as well as able to match a more prolonged "mmmmmmmmm" sound. As with the development of the initial sounds, a shaping procedure should be utilized to develop this skill (i.e., reinforce slightly longer sounds). The important skill that the child is acquiring is his ability to discriminate the variance of how the model sounds. Whereas before the issue was just making a sound, the next issue is how the sound is being made. To teach this discrimination, it is important to use prompts to get the child to make the new response (e.g., the prolonged "mmmmmm"). For this task, it's helpful to start by constantly providing the model while prompting the child to make the sound with the adult. As he learns to hold the sound for a longer amount of time along with the adult, the child should be taught to hold the sound following the model. Thus, the first step is to teach him to make a prolonged sound, and the second step is to teach him to discriminate when making each of the two variations of that response.

Once the child is able to hold a sound, it is then possible to start teaching him to roll from that held sound to a second sound **(E 7)**. The word "me" is not made by saying "mm"and then "ee" as was mentioned earlier in this chapter. Instead, the word is produced by making changes in the mouth that form the sounds, transitioning smoothly from an "mm" sound to the "ee" sound. Once again, the instructor can get the child to hold the "mm" sound and use exaggerated facial prompts to help him see the changes in the mouth's position, as well as hear the change in the sounds. Note that if he has learned to imitate motor actions that are modeled in a mirror, then it can also be used to facilitate the teaching of this skill.

Similar teaching procedures (i.e., shaping and discrimination training) should be used to teach the child to say sounds and words with variations in volume, pitch and speed **(E 15-17)**. It must be emphasized that there are two critical aspects for teaching these variances. The first is the ability to make the different responses; the second is to determine which of those responses is currently being required.

When teaching the child to make the discrimination between a loud and a quiet sound, it's important to get him to attend to the volume of the sound. It's often helpful to teach the child to make the quiet sound, as in whispering it, and then have him repeat the sound in his normal voice (or louder). Once he learns to imitate the whispered sound and the louder sound, it's then possible to teach him to match other volumes of the sound. Similar procedures can be used to teach him to then say sounds and words slowly or quickly, and to say them with a high- or low-pitched voice. It should be noted that teaching a child to sing songs can be helpful in developing these dynamic properties of vocalizations.

Further Extending of Echoic Skills

For a child who can say at least 20 words with reasonable accuracy that can be understood by most people, there should be a focus on having him learn to accurately say a larger number of words and phrases with a variety of sound combinations **(E 13)**. There should be a focus on improving his ability to articulate, produce phrases, and expand the dynamic properties of his speech.

Keep in mind that many typically developing young children often have difficulty producing certain sounds in certain positions in words. Depending on the age of the child with a developmental delay, he should be able to easily repeat words and phrases at a clarity level expected for his chronological age. By the time a typically developing child is approximately four years of age, he should be able to repeat phrases with a wide range of dynamic properties (e.g., loud or soft, fast or slow, high- or low-pitch) and should be able to deliver messages to others.

A child who is able to vocally imitate at least a three-word phrase (that can be understood by most individuals who are unfamiliar with him) can be taught many critical language skills (e.g., describing objects, talking about experiences).

However, if he is unable to match other vocal characteristics of children his own age (e.g., speak as if he were "the big bad wolf" or a "Goldilocks"), there should be a component of the intervention plan that will work on developing these vocal production skills to match those of his peers (E 16-20).

Special Note Regarding Children From a Bilingual Household

It should be noted that many children now grow up in a household in which English is not spoken or where it is the parent's second language. Often, these children hear many other sound combinations associated with their parents' native language. It is not uncommon for these children to be delayed in their ability to imitate many of the sound combinations unique to the English language. If the child is to learn to communicate in English, he will still need to learn how to produce those sound combinations. However, it may result in a slower rate of development due to the child not hearing those same words and sound combinations as frequently as a child who lives in an English-speaking household.

Summary

Because the most effective way of communicating with others is by speaking, it is important for children to learn to imitate sounds, words and phrases. Therefore, it is necessary to include vocal imitation tasks as one of the first components of a language-based intervention program. To vocally imitate, the child must learn to coordinate the position and movement of his mouth, tongue, and vocal chords with the muscles involved in moving air from his lungs in a controlled manner. The task of teaching him to echo specific sounds is difficult because these sounds can't be produced simply by someone physically moving all the involved parts of the child's body. As the child learns to imitate motor actions (e.g., clapping, raising arms over head), his ability to observe and match the actions of others can facilitate the development of his ability to match the sounds that are modeled by others.

For a child who does not spontaneously make a variety of speech sounds when babbling, it may be necessary to increase the frequency and variety of sounds he makes during the day. Direct reinforcement of his vocalizations of speech-related sounds and pairing of enjoyable activities with certain sounds are methods to accomplish this result.

When selecting the first sounds to teach him to imitate on request, consider those sounds that he already frequently makes on his own when engaging in vocal play (i.e., babbling). Because he is already making these sounds, the major task is to teach him to make those same sounds upon request (i.e., bring the responses under instructional control). It is important to ensure that attempts to get him to vocally imitate do not lead to failure. If the child isn't able to imitate a sound after several presentations of a modeled sound, he should be presented with other tasks that he has already mastered (e.g., simple motor imitation tasks). By interspersing easier tasks among the more difficult vocal imitation tasks, the child will be able to receive reinforcement for complying with instructions from his instructor. As he begins to imitate a few simple sounds, he should also be encouraged to attempt other sounds and a variety of sounds in combinations. He should work on the development of his vocal imitation skills for short periods of time, many times each day.

Potential Learning Objectives Related to the Development of Vocal Imitation Skills

The following objectives are provided to assist a parent or teacher in targeting specific skills that may be appropriate for a child's intervention plan. Please see the ABLLS-R® to assess the child's skills and to identify additional objectives for further skill development.

Each child is a unique individual and requires input from a variety of people who know him and are familiar with effective programming strategies. Therefore, these learning objectives are not being prescribed for any particular child, but rather are being provided as examples of objectives that are consistent with the skills described in this chapter.

E 1 (Child's name) will imitate at least ten sounds when you say, "Say ___" (e.g., "ah", "buh", "o", "e").

E 2 (Child's name) will be able to repeat at least five separate sounds in ten seconds when presented with a series of individual sounds presented in quick succession (e.g., "may", "moe", "me", "ah", "buh", "ee", "oh").

E 4 (Child's name) will be able to repeat a variety of separate pairs of sounds in combination in which the student must attend to both the starting and ending sounds (Says "ma" "ma" vs. "ma" "me" vs. "ma" "moe"; says "ee" "o" vs. "ee" "ee" vs. "ee" "ah"). He will be able to repeat at least 3 pairs of sound combinations for at least 2 starting sounds.

E 5 (Child's name) will be able to repeat at least two sounds matching the approximate length of the presented sound (e.g., short and fast vs. long/held sound--says "mm" vs "mmmmm").

E 7 (Child's name) will be able to repeat sound combinations in which the model requires the student to hold or elongate the first sound and smoothly transition to a second sound — not merely say two separate sounds. He will be able to smoothly switch between at least two held/elon gated sounds to at least two other sounds (e.g., says "mmmeeeee" smoothly transitioning from the "mm" sound to the "eee" sound, "aaaaammmm" as in an elongated "am").

E 8 (Child's name) will be able to repeat at least three vowel-consonant and 3 consonant-vowel sound combinations without breaks between the two sounds (e.g., "eat," "up," "go," and "me").

E 9 (Child's name) will be able to repeat at least three conso-nant-vowel- consonant-vowel sound combinations without breaks between the sounds (e.g., "mama," "dada," "peepee," and "meme").

6 Teaching Manding/ Requesting Skills

The Importance of Mand Training

The first type of expressive language skill to teach a nonverbal child should be a mand (i.e., a request for a reinforcer). This skill is taught first because the mand is a unique type of language that directly benefits the child by letting his caretakers know exactly what he wants at that particular moment. Mands are typically the first type of communication that humans naturally acquire (Bijou & Baer, 1965; Skinner, 1957). Infants cry when they are hungry and as a result they receive food. They also cry when they are uncomfortable and receive comfort, and cry when they want attention, and they receive attention. Early in life, different forms of crying begin to emerge for each type of motivation; infants even develop "fake crying" to make their needs known (Novak, 1996; Wolff, 1969). Crying quickly becomes a way to communicate with adults, or more specifically, a way to mand (request reinforcers, or to remove aversive stimuli). Most of an infant's first forms of language are mands for reinforcers that are caused by different types of motivation (i.e., motivational operations). Eventually (around 12 months of age), the young child learns to say words to ask for the different things that he wants—or let others know what things he doesn't want.

Every child must be able to use his language skills to be able to ask for things that he needs or desires. Whether the item is present or out- of sight, the child should be able to get access to those items or activities. He also must learn to be able to request that others stop undesired activities or to be removed from unpleasant situations. Furthermore, when the child needs information about the location of people who are momentarily important to him or about activities that may occur in the future, he should be able to request information about those individuals or activities. He also needs to be able to ask where an item is located and when an activity should occur. He also needs to be able to use a variety of adjectives, adverbs, pronouns and prepositions to delineate the specifics of the items and actions he would like to receive.

The mand occurs early in language development for typical children because of the direct benefit they receive (e.g., food, comfort). The nonverbal child also desires reinforcers and direct benefits. Regardless of the extent of their disabilities, they still get hungry, need attention, need aversive stimuli removed, and so on. In the early language training for a nonverbal child, it is possible to capture these ongoing forms of motivation as an opportunity to conduct language trials, and often the child is very willing to participate in this training because of the direct benefits he receives. For example, when the child is hungry (the motivation for food is strong), that is the time to work on teaching the child the word, sign, or picture point/exchange for "food."

Besides the child directly benefiting from being able to ask for specific reinforcers, there are additional benefits derived from teaching him requesting skills (i.e., manding). The parent of a nonverbal child who cannot ask for specific items is often at a loss as to why the child may be upset. Since he can't tell the parent what is bothering him, the parent often attempts to guess what might be the problem (i.e., What is the motivation for the child acting in this manner?). If he or she believes that the disruption is due to the child wanting some unknown item or activity (e.g., he is hungry, wants to watch a movie), the parent will often offer items to him in order to see if he wants one of them. Two benefits occur when the child is able to ask for specific items and activities. First, he is able to tell the parent what he wants, eliminating the source of confusion for the parent. Therefore, he no longer needs to become disruptive to alert the parent that he desires something.

Additionally, because the parent can deliver the requested reinforcers to the child, the presence of the parent or other adult is "paired" with delivery of those reinforcers. Hence, the parents themselves become stronger conditioned reinforcers for the child's behavior. This pairing usually results in an increase of his approaching and interacting with the adult.

Benefits of Learning to "Mand"/Request

1. Works for the direct benefit of the child.
2. Allows others to identify sources of the child's motivation.
3. Decrease in behavior problems.
4. Pairs instructor with delivery of reinforcers.

The Response Form

Before beginning a formal language training program, the assessment of the child's motor and vocal imitation skills should be conducted (see Chapters 4 and 5), and a decision should be made as to what response form will be used (i.e., speech, signs, or pictures). Remember that the initial decision regarding the best form of communication can change depending on the child's progress (e.g., increased ability to say sounds and words) or lack of progress. If a child cannot echo a word, or even a give a close approximation of a word, it will be difficult to immediately teach him vocal language. If he can imitate some actions, but can't echo sounds or words with reasonable accuracy, then sign language (ASL)* may be the most appropriate response form. If he cannot imitate any actions, then signs may be difficult, but clearly not out of the question and perhaps still a better choice than pictures.

Sign language is very similar to speech in that in both types of topography-based communication (Sundberg & Partington, 2013), the child must engage in a sequence of muscle movements to produce a unique response (e.g., say "shoe" or make the ASL sign for shoe), and the response is not limited by a set of pictures from which he may select an answer or make a response.

* American Sign Language (ASL) is being used in a general manner that does not make a distinction between the various types of sign language such as Signing Exact English.

In short, with both speech and ASL, the child must independently make his own responses, and each unique sign may also serve as a prompt for the corresponding spoken word.

However, if vocal imitation (i.e., echoic) and physical imitation are equally weak, then signs should be selected as the initial response form because it is usually easier to teach someone to imitate actions than to echo words. Although it may be easier to teach a child to make an ASL sign to request an item, the goal is to teach him to talk. Hence, it is important to continue to develop the child's control of his vocal musculature while using sign language to teach him to communicate. (See Chapter 5 regarding methods to develop control of the vocal musculature.) However, it should be noted that because a child isn't able to vocally imitate at present, this fact doesn't necessarily indicate that he should use a selection-based communication system.

For a child who has severe physical impairments, a selection-based picture system may be most appropriate. In these types of programs, requesting skills are developed by teaching him to either point to an item, or give a picture of it to another person. These systems are now available using electronic pads or actual pictures. The most researched of these systems is the Picture Exchange Communication System (PECS) (Frost & Bondy, 1994).

Disadvantages of Selection-Based Systems

Unfortunately, the selection-based systems do not share one of the important characteristics of speech (Sundberg & Partington, 2013; Sundberg & Sundberg, 1990; Wraikat, Sundberg & Michael, 1991). In selection-based systems, the child must scan the available pictures and then select one of them. Every response involves the same pattern of motor movement, and the child is not required to independently remember and then make a unique response as the answers are always present (i.e., the pictures contain all the possible options for the selection response).

In speech and sign language, the child must remember and then make a unique response for every word or request. Thus, sign programs have the advantage of pairing a specific motor movement with a unique spoken word (Sundberg & Partington, 2013). This fact makes it more likely that as the child gains control over his vocal musculature, that his making of the sign will prompt him to also make the corresponding vocalization (i.e., say the word that he is signing). Additionally, like speech, signs do not require the child to have pictures or electronic communication devices to be able to communicate. When signing, as with vocalizing, the actions he makes with his own body are all he needs to communicate.

One last form of communication involves writing or typing. Although it's rare to consider either of these options as an initial form of communicating, it should also be noted that some children could benefit from learning to communicate by these methods.

Motivational Considerations

Regardless of which response form is selected for the initial training, there are several variables that will increase the chances of successfully teaching a child to request items or activities (i.e., mand). First, strong forms of reinforcement should be used. Most children are reinforced by various sources such as food, drinks, toys, and some forms of attention. However, each child is different, and individual reinforcement surveys must be conducted. Also, the value of reinforcers may change many times throughout the day, week, or month. Hence, language training should be conducted when the motivation for a particular reinforcer is strong (Michael, 1988). If a certain toy is being used as a reinforcer, then trials and sessions should be conducted when the motivation for that toy is strong. For example, if a child does not emit any echoic or imitative behavior, but likes to listen to music in the morning before breakfast, then some training trials to teach him to request "music" should be conducted at that time. The motivation is strong, and music as reinforcement is the most potent, thus at this point in time, an instructor would have the best chances of successfully teaching a requesting response. In addition, a variety of prompts can be used (e.g., physical, imitative, verbal) to ensure immediate success.

Where to Start: What to Teach as the First Mand

By carefully observing a child's behavior, it is usually easy to quickly identify items or activities that he can be taught to request (i.e., mand). Almost all children like to eat some food items and drink certain beverages. Additionally, children often enjoy certain activities such as listening to music, watching a movie, being tickled, being pushed on a swing, or playing with a favorite toy. It's important to select words for reinforcers that can be controlled so that the child can only get these items or activities from an adult; if he is able to gain access to these items by himself, there is no reason for him to ask for them. (It is often beneficial to limit the child's access to certain reinforcers.) Some of the best first mands to teach are for consumables (e.g., food and drinks), those ending on their own (e.g., bubbles), or are easy to stop without physically taking something away from the child (e.g., tickles and songs). The items should be readily available and easily delivered on multiple occasions (e.g., sips of juice from a cup rather than a whole glass of juice). It's important for consistency to teach the child to ask for reinforcing items or activities that he wants on a daily basis, rather than items that are only desired every once in a while (See Figure 6-1).

A child's behavior will help identify his strongest reinforcers. For example, consider a child who frequently goes near the refrigerator, or pulls the parent to it when he wants something to eat or drink **(F 1)**. Another young child may approach and pull at his parent's legs when he wants to be picked up, and an older child may often attempt to get the parent's electronic tablet so he can watch a movie. Frequent actions such as these may point the way towards teaching the child his first mand (e.g., "eat," "juice," "up," or "movie") **(F 2-6)**.

Figure 6-1.

Issues to Consider When Picking the First Several Words as Mands

1. Select words that are for reinforcers (existing motivation), especially for those that adults can easily control the access to, and have the ability to use as reinforcers. Such as those that:

- are consumable (e.g., food, drinks)
- easily allow for short a duration of contact (e.g., bubbles, tickles)
- are relatively easy to remove from the student (e.g., music, video)
- are easy to deliver (e.g., books, cars, dolls)
- can be delivered on multiple occasions (e.g., small candies, sips of juice)
- always seem strong (e.g., "stim" toy, outside)

Many items might be reinforcing, but are difficult to manage for training purposes. These include car trips, board games, blocks, bike rides, long movies, walks, gum, hard candy, a bowl of ice cream, etc. These items can still be used as reinforcers, but perhaps for extremely high quality responding, or at the end of training sessions.

2. Select words that are already familiar to the child as demonstrated by an existing receptive, echoic, or imitative skill. For example, when the parent asks, "Do you want to go outside?" the child goes towards the door.

3. For vocal children, select words that involve a relatively short and easy response for the child to make. For example, many speech sounds are easier to produce than others, such as "aa," "ba," "mm," and "da"; "la" and "rrr" may be much harder. Also, words should be selected that match the child's existing echoic repertoire.

(Cont'd on next page.)

Figure 6-1. (Cont'd)

4. For signing children, select words that are iconic, that is, the signs look like the objects that they stand for, as in the sign "book," which looks like the action of opening a book, or the sign "eat" which looks like putting food in the mouth. Also, signs should be selected that match the child's existing imitative repertoire.

5. Select words that are for salient and relevant items to the child in his daily life. They should be items that the child sees or uses frequently in daily activities. It is also preferable to use items that are stable and clearly identified stimuli, that is, the name of the item is consistent across all variations of the item (e.g., ball), and all adults can agree on what the item is called. The selected words should occur frequently in the child's day-to-day environment (e.g., "eat" may be heard much more often than "spaghetti").

6. Select a set of words that will eventually be associated with a variety of motivators (e.g., foods, toys, video, physical play). For example, don't select all foods for the first several words or signs, or progress will stop when the child is not hungry.

7. Avoid selecting words or signs that sound or look alike (rhyme). It will be much harder for the child to differentiate between similar response forms (e.g., don't select the signs "eat" and "drink" as the first two signs because the look very similar).

8. Avoid words and signs that might have a negative or aversive history for the child (e.g., bed, toilet, no).

9. Avoid words such as "more" and "please" that do not clearly identify the nature of the motivation for a mand or the type of reinforcer being requested (e.g. something to eat, listen to music).

There are a couple of other important considerations for selecting the first mand to teach. One factor includes the ease with which the child can make the requested response (e.g., say the word or make an ASL sign for the item or activity). For the child who is capable of speaking, he must be able to say at least an approximation of the word (e.g., "uh" for "up") or be able to make an approximation of physical movement necessary to make an ASL sign (e.g., tap his left arm with his right hand as an approximation to the ASL sign for "music"). Furthermore, it is important that everyone who interacts with the child consistently use the same words for those reinforcers when interacting with the child. When required to use ASL sign (i.e., "sign") for "eat", a child will often become confused if one parent says, "eat" while the other parent says, "food". Everyone should agree on what specific words are used or not used (e.g., "eat," not "Oh, you want some food?").

Picking the Next Few Words as Mands

Once the child has learned to request one specific item or activity, the second item or activity to be taught should then be carefully considered. In addition to the criteria used for the first mand, the next several items or activities need to be carefully selected so as to avoid confusion on the part of the child. If he is only able to make a few vocalizations that approximate the word, it's important that the next item to teach require the child to make a sound that is both within his current capability and is different from the first mand (e.g., "uh" for "up" and "e" for "eat").

If the child is child is learning to "sign" for his reinforcers, then the motor movements associated with the signs should be significantly different from the previously learned mands. For example, the ASL sign for "eat" involves moving the fingertips of a hand to the mouth. The ASL sign for "drink" requires the child to move his hand towards his mouth with his fingers formed as if he were holding a glass and then tip the hand as if pouring the liquid into the mouth. In this example, there are two sources of potential problems. The first is that both signs require the movement of the hand to the child's mouth. The second issue is that both reinforcers involve consumption of a food item (i.e., both are swallowed). Therefore, it's usually prudent to only teach one of these responses (usually "eat"), until the child has learned to mand for other reinforcers that are associated with different types of motivational conditions (e.g., visual, auditory, olfactory, or tactile stimulation).

Remember that the main concept is to teach the child to request his specific reinforcers. The child will only mand for things that he wants and only when he wants them. Therefore, it is not appropriate to try to teach the child to ask for items or activities that the parents want him to ask for (e.g., to ask to use the bathroom, or go to bed)!

What NOT to Teach as First Mands

There are several requests that are not desirable to teach a child for his first mands. Many parents and professionals attempt to teach certain requests that seem to be functional for the child, but often cause unanticipated problems. One such problem occurs when the child is taught to request a "break" or "no" to stop an interaction. Keep in mind that it's important to establish a positive working relationship with the child so that he is motivated to participate in learning activities that will allow him to learn with others. If he's engaging in behavior that indicates he doesn't desire to maintain the teaching interaction, then the instructor must consider why he isn't motivated to participate in the activity and make appropriate adjustments to her approach (see Chapter 2). Specifically, it's counterproductive to teach the child to tell his instructor to stop interacting with him when those interactions are critical for his development. Unless he's older and has a significant history of physically hurting himself or others, it's not desirable to teach others to leave him alone (Carr & Durrand, 1985).

Another mistake that instructors often make when selecting a first mand to teach is in the attempt to teach a child "yes" and "no." Although most typically developing young children learn at an early age to indicate that they do or do not want something using these words, they have also developed many other specific requests (e.g., "up," "juice") prior to using "yes" and "no" to respond to offers from others. The child will often indicate through his actions that he either is interested or not interested in a specific item by either reaching for or pushing away the item. However, it's often very difficult to teach a child to listen to and answer questions as to whether or not he wants a specifically named item or event. Besides, it must be remembered that we want the child to learn to ask for specific items or events, not just use a word to describe what should be obvious from observing his reactions of interest or disinterest to items and events. As indicated above, we also don't want to reinforce a child for telling us "no" so that we allow him to avoid activities that are necessary for him to acquire skills that are critical for his development.

Another common mistake is to attempt to teach the child requests of "more," "please," or "want." These non-specific requests may be easy to teach in a certain context, but they do not specify the particular item or activity desired by the child. As a result, both the instructor and the child will often become very frustrated when the child attempts to gain access to a reinforcer outside of the context in which that response was originally taught.

Reasons Not to Teach "More," "Please," or "Want" as a First Mand

Many parents and professionals have attempted to teach children who don't have control of their vocal musculature to use signs such as "more" or "please" as a first mand (i.e., request). For example, while sitting at a table eating a snack, a child may be prompted to make the sign "more" and then is reinforced with a small amount of a preferred food item. After 10 to 15 of such mands for the food item, he continues to make the sign "more" without any prompts. In addition, that same sign may also be used for other reinforcers (e.g., when the child is being tickled). The instructor is usually very excited to report that the child quickly learned the response and began to spontaneously use it. However, the initial excitement is often followed by some very serious complications.

(Cont'd on next page.)

The major issue of concern is that the child has only learned that making the particular physical movement (i.e., the sign we call "more") will result in the continued receipt of the item that is currently being delivered. The child with such limited language skills is not likely to "understand" that he is requesting a greater amount of the item. As such, the major problem that often arises is that the child will use the sign in different locations and at times when the desired reinforcing item or activity can't be determined by the caregiver (e.g., food item or tickle). For example, when the child is in a different situation (e.g., not at a table where he was eating a snack, on the floor where the child was being tickled) and makes the sign "more," the caregiver would be unable to identify the motivation for the mand. Additionally, because the child has learned to do that movement (i.e., the sign we call "more"), he often continues to use that sign despite efforts to teach him other more specific mands. In essence, his history of being reinforced for that movement makes it a strong response that interferes with the acquisition of new signs for other specific items and activities (e.g., "tickle," "music," "open").

Consideration of Specific Items vs. Specific Motivation

As was previously discussed, it's crucial to teach a child to ask for a specific item or activity (e.g., "balloon," "push") rather than teach non-specific mands (e.g., "more"). However, when attempting to teach the first few mands, it's necessary to make a decision as to just how specific the request should be. For example, when a child is unable to ask for something to eat when he is hungry, he could be taught to ask for "eat." This response is both simple to say and is a relatively easy ASL sign to make (i.e., moving fingertips of one hand to the mouth). Although it identifies the motivation for the child's response (i.e., he's hungry), it doesn't specify the exact food item that he wants at that moment (e.g., a cracker, an apple, pizza).

There are several advantages for teaching the mand "eat" rather than teaching each specific food item. The first advantage is that when a child is hungry, he can make a request and get something to eat. Once his parents know that he wants something to eat, they can offer him one or more of the items he frequently eats and he can then select from the available options. Thus, one request gains access to one or more options associated with the motivation of hunger. On the other hand, if he only learned to request "apple," he wouldn't be able to gain access to other food options until he learned to request those specific items. In short, he may be hungry but may not want an apple. Similarly, teaching a child to mand for a "movie" versus asking for a specific movie (e.g., a specific "Mickey Mouse" movie or a specific "Dora the Explorer" movie) can be problematic. If he can request "movie," he can then select from the available options, whereas, if the specific movie wasn't available, he could still get to watch something else. Once he has learned several mands related to a variety of motivators (e.g., hunger, activities that include visual, auditory, and tactile stimulation), it then is appropriate to teach him to request specific items and activities associated with those motivational conditions (e.g., " 'Dora' movie").

It should be noted that some clinicians argue that it's better to teach the child very specific requests (e.g., "apple") rather than those associated with the general motivation associated with the request (e.g., "eat"). Even when provided with the highest quality interventions, children vary considerably in their ability to acquire language skills such as manding for their reinforcers. While some children will quickly acquire a variety of specific mands, others with significant delays have been observed to never learn more than a few. If a child can receptively discriminate a variety of different specific items (e.g., point to or get a variety of movies or food items) he might very well be able to quickly learn to mand for those specific items. However, some children who are learning to mand are unable to select specific items on request, and may have greater difficulty acquiring the specific mands. If a child isn't able to learn more than a few mands, his access to a broader range of reinforcers would be limited.

However, if he were to successfully learn mands associated with a variety of motivational conditions (e.g., "eat" for hunger, "movie" for visual stimulation), he would also be more likely to be able to learn to mand for more specific items associated with those motivational conditions. Thus, until research is conducted to identify which children should be taught more specific mands from the beginning, it seems that it is most prudent to teach children to make requests related to the motivational condition prior to teaching mands for very specific items.

Specific Procedures for Various Response Forms

The procedures to teach requesting skills (i.e., mand training) described below will be divided into four sections based on the child's entry level:

(1) Procedures for teaching requesting skills (i.e., mands) to a child who has no, or only very limited, vocal and motor imitation skills

(2) Procedures for teaching signed requesting skills to a child who has some motor imitation skills

(3) Procedures for teaching vocal mands to a child who has some vocal imitation skills (i.e., echoics)

(4) Procedures for teaching pointing to pictures as mands for a physically involved child who cannot echo sounds or imitate actions.

1. Beginning Mand Training for Children Who Cannot Echo or Imitate

For children who don't cooperate with instructions from adults, including those that don't require him to understand spoken instructions (e.g., resists even being physically prompted to walk with the adult), it will be necessary to initiate a "pairing procedure" and start to develop some initial instructional control. One of the easiest ways to get the child to start to go along with the instructor is to identify one of his strongest reinforcers (e.g., a grape), hold the reinforcer so that the child clearly sees the item, and begin to reinforce him for merely approaching and taking a small amount of the reinforcer from the adult **(A 1)**. Because the child's approach behavior is reinforced, he will continue to approach the adult to gain access to the reinforcer as long as the motivation to receive that reinforcer remains strong.

After the child has experienced several reinforcers for merely approaching, the adult can slowly begin to shape additional behaviors **(A 5)**. Now that the child will come to the adult, the delivery of the reinforcer can be delayed for a second or two. For example, the child approaches and reaches to get a grape from the adult, but now while the child is looking at the adult, she says, "Eat" and models the ASL sign for "eat" before giving the grape to the child. After a few similar trials, the child will have learned that he'll receive the grape—but only after looking at the adult while she says and signs "Eat." The next step in the shaping process includes the adult taking the child's hand and then saying and signing, "Eat" with her other hand prior to delivering the grape. Thus the child has now learned that the taking of his hand and the model of the sign and word precede him getting a grape. The final step involves taking the child's hand and physically prompting him to make the ASL sign following the adult's model of the sign. Once the child is allowing the adult to physically prompt the imitation of the ASL sign **(A 5 & 6)**, it is then possible to continue with the mand training procedure that follows.

Mand Training Utilizing ASL Signs with a Somewhat Cooperative Child

If a nonverbal child is somewhat cooperative and has some identifiable reinforcers, but cannot echo or imitate, then procedures to teach the first mand should be implemented. Several variables can be manipulated that will increase the probability of successfully teaching a child who fits this description to mand.

The most important teaching tools are:

- The use of strong forms of reinforcement
- Relative motivation (specific times when the reinforcers are especially strong)
- The behavioral techniques of prompting and fading

In addition, the use of sign language will probably result in faster acquisition of an understandable mand (i.e., request), because the trainer can physically prompt the response, which can't be carried out with speech. This basic training procedure will be described below.

Teaching the First ASL Mand Using Physical Prompts

The teaching procedure for a non-imitative child consists of using physical prompts (along with other prompts) to assist him in making a successful response. This prompted response will allow the child to immediately come in contact with a reinforcer (e.g., eating a cookie, watching a movie). The first step is to select a sign to teach (Figure 6-1). This sign should be for a strong reinforcer (e.g., food, book, music), or for a highly desired activity (e.g., a push on a swing, being lifted up), and training should be conducted when the motivation (establishing operation) for the reinforcer is strong. Also, the sign should be physically easy for the child to make, easy for the instructor to physically prompt, and relatively iconic (i.e., resemble the item or activity it stands for).

Mand training is more likely to be successful if the procedure involves the simultaneous use of a number of different prompts and consequences. The top panel of Figure 6-2 contains a diagram of eight potential (independent) variables and their relationship to the signed response (the dependent variable). Six of these variables precede the response and are technically referred to as antecedent events, and two follow the response and are termed consequent events. Although this chart lists many types of prompts and reinforcers, it should be noted that an instructor should use only the fewest prompts (i.e., variables) necessary to get the response to occur. In addition, it may be that some children have a unique history that makes a specific type of prompt inappropriate for that child. (Some children are tactilely defensive so physical prompts would be contraindicated; others may have a defective history in relation to specific verbal prompts such as "What do you want?" so this verbal prompt should not be used.) However, the goal of the procedure is unprompted (spontaneous) communication, therefore all prompts should be eliminated as soon as possible.

Teaching the sign "eat," for example, should begin in the following manner. When the child is hungry (motivated) show him the item of food (nonverbal stimulus) and say "What do you want?" or "Sign eat," (two different verbal prompts), and model the sign "eat" (imitative prompt). It is unlikely that the child will correctly respond at this point (since the child has not been able to imitate in the past), so the instructor (or a second adult) should then physically prompt the child by moving his hand to his mouth (as in making the sign for eat). This fully prompted interaction should then be reinforced with praise (e.g., "Eat!") and the food item (e.g., a grape). It should be noted that whenever the child does sign "eat," or provides an approximation of the sign, without the physical or verbal prompts, he should be immediately reinforced.

Teaching a Request (Mand) Using Sign Language

Figure 6-2.

Teaching to Request (Mand) Using Sign Language

Panel	Example	Antecedent →	Behavior →	Consequences	Example
1	**Hungry**	**Motivational Operation**	**Signs 'Eat'**	Food Item	Given food item
	"What do you want?"	Verbal Stim. to Respond		Praise	"Eat, Right, Eat!"
	Food Item	Nonverbal Stimulus			
	Sign "Eat"	Intraverbal Stimulus			
	ASL sign for "Eat"	Imitative Stimulus			
	Guide Hands	Physical Prompt			
2	**Hungry**	**Motivational Operation**	**Signs 'Eat'**	Food Item	Given food item
	"What do you want?"	Verbal Stim. to Respond		Praise	"Eat, Right, Eat!"
	Food Item	Nonverbal Stimulus			
	Sign "Eat"	Intraverbal Stimulus			
	ASL sign for "Eat"	Imitative Stimulus			
	Guide Hands	*Physical Prompt*			
3	**Hungry**	**Motivational Operation**	**Signs 'Eat'**	Food Item	Given food item
	"What do you want?"	Verbal Stim. to Respond		Praise	"Eat, Right, Eat!"
	Food Item	Nonverbal Stimulus			
	Sign "Eat"	Intraverbal Stimulus			
	ASL sign for "Eat"	*Imitative Stimulus*			
4	**Hungry**	**Motivational Operation**	**Signs 'Eat'**	Food Item	Given food item
	"What do you want?"	Verbal Stim. to Respond		Praise	"Eat, Right, Eat!"
	Food Item	Nonverbal Stimulus			
	Sign "Eat"	*Intraverbal Stimulus*			
5	**Hungry**	**Motivational Operation**	**Signs 'Eat'**	Food Item	Given food item
	"What do you want?"	Verbal Stim. to Respond		Praise	"Eat, Right, Eat!"
	Food Item	*Nonverbal Stimulus*			
6	**Hungry**	**Motivational Operation**	**Signs 'Eat'**	Food Item	Given food item
	"What do you want?"	*Verbal Stim. to Respond*		Praise	"Eat, Right, Eat!"
7	**Hungry**	**Motivational Operation**	**Signs 'Eat'**	**Food Item**	**Given food item**

In Figure 6-2, the top panel identifies all the critical elements that could be used (antecedent variables) to help the child make the response "eat." The dashed lines in the second panel illustrates the fading of the physical prompts that were used to initially develop the child's sign for the word. The additional panels suggest a sequence for eliminating the other prompts and the presence of the items that were used to develop the mand response.

How Much of the Reinforcer to Provide

When delivering a reinforcer following the child's mand, it is important to consider how much of the reinforcer to deliver. The amount should be sufficient to have a strengthening effect so that he will want to repeat the request (i.e., actual reinforcer). However, it shouldn't be so great that he doesn't want to request it again for quite some time. (i.e., satiation occurs). In general, the reinforcer should be the smallest amount necessary to have him continue to mand for that reinforcer. For example, when a child requests something to eat (i.e., mands "eat"), he can be given a few raisins or a half of a potato chip. He will quickly consume the food, but still be sufficiently hungry to continue to make more requests for something to eat. If however, he is given a bag of raisins or potato chips, he could simply make the first request and not be motivated to ask for something to eat for quite some time. Remember that the process of teaching him to mand for reinforcers depends upon him being able to practice this skill.

Fading the Physical Prompt

The next step is to fade out (gradually remove) the physical prompt (Figure 6-2, Panel 2). The entire sequence should be repeated (i.e., all prompts and the grape presented), but this time the instructor should try to give slightly less of a physical prompt (for more information on fading physical prompts the reader is referred to Martin & Paer, 2002). This procedure may need to be repeated many times to see any reduction in the physical prompt needed. However, for some children a response without physical prompts may occur very quickly. The main objective here is to eliminate the need for physical prompts as quickly as possible, while insuring that the child is successful in obtaining reinforcement. Once the child can make (i.e., emit) an approximation of the sign for food (e.g., independently moving a finger toward his mouth), physical prompts should be dropped. However, the prompts may be needed later to get the behavior going again when there has been a time lapse between correct responses or training sessions. The instructor should try to conduct as many teaching trials as possible each session, and each day. The critical feature of this procedure is the careful shaping and fading of the prompts necessary to develop the sign. Hence, this particular procedure is most effective when carried out by individuals who have some experience in prompting, fading, and the reinforcement of successive approximations.

Approximations That Are Shaped

Note that the child's sign can be an approximation of the sign being modeled by the instructor. Although it's desirable to have the child make an accurate sign, remember that the most important issue is that he's able to make a specific response that lets others know what he wants. At first, it's okay to accept a response that is somewhat close to the one desired. As he starts to regularly use that approximation to gain access to the reinforcer, the instructor can "shape" a more accurate response by gradually increasing the requirement for the child to make a more accurate sign before delivering the reinforcer. If the response is not "accurate enough" to warrant the delivery of a reinforcer, it should not be reinforced. If the child is allowed access to reinforcers following a "sloppy" response, then his accuracy will not improve.

Error Correction When Fading Prompts

When any type of prompt is being faded, there will often be some errors made when the child responds after being given a lower level of prompt. When an error occurs, it is important to implement a correction procedure. Following the incorrect manding response (e.g., made the wrong sign, said the wrong word, gave a partial response), the instructor should immediately re-present the trial using a higher level of prompt to get the child to make the correct response. The child should be praised for making the correct response, and then he should immediately be presented with the opportunity to respond to the initial level of prompt. The child's mand should be reinforced if he is able to respond correctly. If he still doesn't respond correctly at the lesser prompt level, the correction procedure should be repeated again (See Figure 6-3).

Figure 6-3.

Correction Procedure for Errors When Requesting/Manding

Motivational Operation	→	Child's Response	→	Consequence
Hungry	→	Child says or signs "eat."	→	• Give food item with praise "Eat."
	→	Child says or signs "movie."	→	• Tell child to say or sign "eat" and use necessary prompts to get him to say or sign "eat." • Then ask, "What do you want?" without any additional prompts.
	→	Child makes a poor approximation to the word or sign.	→	• Use necessary prompts to get the child to say or sign a more accurate response. • Then ask, "What do you want?" without any additional prompts.

Beginning to Fade the Imitative Prompt

Once the child can emit the sign without physical prompts, the instructor should begin working on fading the imitative prompt for the sign (See Figure 6-2, Panel 3). The sequence of prompt fading will now be described for the child who can imitate signs.

2. Mand Training With Signs for an Imitative Child: Fading out the Imitative Prompt

If a child has some motor imitative skills (or has reached the point of not needing physical prompts with a sign), then the mand training procedure should begin without the use of physical prompts, but may include any or all of the other variables previously mentioned and outlined in Figure 6-2, Panel 2. That is, training should occur when the child is hungry, reinforcers are present, and verbal and imitative prompts are given. If he started with physical prompts, then the following procedure is the next step for him. Several trials should be given at this point (before attempts to fade the imitative prompt) to allow the child to be successful with the training procedures. The instructional task at this point is to teach him to make the sign without the imitative prompt (see Figure 6-2, Panel 3).

The instructor should hold up the food item and ask, "What do you want?" Or say, "Sign eat." (Note that for some children both verbal stimuli may be unnecessary, or verbal stimuli needs to be limited. If this is the case, use only the "Sign eat" prompt, or even just the specific word "eat" along with the imitative prompt.) By increasing the delay (by as little as three to five seconds) between the presentation of the question (or when the food item is held up in front of him) and the delivery of the prompt, the imitative prompt can be faded out (Halle, Baer, & Spradlin, 1981; Martin & Paer, 2002). The imitative prompt can also be faded out by decreasing the intensity or physical characteristics of the prompt (e.g., only give part of the sign), or a combination of both fading procedures. For example, to fade the imitative model for the sign for "eat," the instructor can first move her hand so that her fingers come to within two inches of her mouth, then only come to within four inches, and finally, only make a slight upward motion of the hand. Correct signs or approximations should be immediately reinforced with praise (e.g., "Eat!") and the food item. Hence, the next time the food item and the verbal prompt "Sign eat" are presented, the child is more likely to emit the sign without the imitative prompt.

The elimination of the imitative prompts is the primary objective of this phase of mand training. Therefore, greater amounts of reinforcement should be provided following unprompted responses than prompted responses. The elimination of the imitative prompts may occur in a few trials if the motivators and reinforcers are strong, and the child has a reasonable imitative repertoire. If the child mands for the reinforcer several times in a row, it may be possible to quickly fade out all of the prompts within that one series of interactions. The next time the opportunity for the child to mand for that reinforcer is made available, it may be necessary to use some prompts to get the child to make the correct response. However, the prompts should be faded faster with each successive opportunity to mand for it, and the prompt level needed to get the first mand (in a sequence of mands) should be less over time. Sometimes, if the child has multiple opportunities to mand for a reinforcer throughout his day, by the end of the day, he will be able to spontaneously mand for the item as the opportunity is presented.

Once the behavior occurs without the imitative prompt the child is making, the request is still controlled by multiple variables. These include the fact that he wants to get the item (i.e., motivational variable), the presence of the item (i.e., a nonverbal stimulus), and partially by the remaining verbal prompts. Eventually, it is important that the child be able to independently (spontaneously) sign "eat" under the control of each of the above variables when they are presented independently.

When to Fade the Remaining Prompts

It's a major accomplishment when a child no longer requires either a physical or imitative prompt to request an item or activity. At some point, it will be necessary to eliminate the remaining prompts. He should eventually be able to ask for things even when they are not present and nobody is asking him if he wants anything.

It should be remembered that when teaching a child to request an item, only the minimum prompts necessary should be used to get him to make the response. Whenever possible, these prompts should even be eliminated between successive requests. Therefore, the prompts "What do you want?" and "sign _______" may no longer be needed except on an occasional basis. However, if these prompts require additional procedures to eliminate their use, those procedures are described in greater detail later in this chapter (See the section "Fading Out the Verbal Prompts").

At this point in the training, the item may still need to be present in order for the child to request it. Until he is taught that he can ask for items when he can't see them, the child may simply not know that he can get those items. (The procedures to fade the items associated with the request are described in the section "Fading Out the Object".) However, before starting to fade the presence of the item, there is often much work that can be done to improve other components of the child's requesting skills.

Continued Development of Imitation and Echoic Skills

The process of teaching a child to mand presents a great opportunity to improve his ability to imitate both motor movements and vocalizations. Because the child is responding to obtain a highly desired reinforcer, it is possible to use his motivation to "shape" those skills (i.e., reinforce successively closer approximations of the modeled actions and sounds). As has been discussed earlier, an instructor should always be attempting to teach the child to pay attention to not only the actions of others, but to attend to exactly how those actions are being performed. By withholding reinforcement for those responses that are not as close to the original model, and by reinforcing the more accurate responses, the child will develop more precision in his imitative responses.

Because speech is the desired response form, the child can also be prompted to, and reinforced for, including a vocalization along with the signed mand (Ross & Greer, 2003). Echoic skills (i.e., vocal imitation) should always be a part of a nonvocal child's overall programming. As he is working to develop his echoic skills, vocalizations that are approximations of the word being taught as a mand should also be required before reinforcement is delivered. If the child has extremely weak echoic skills, rather than requiring the vocalization, instructors can merely provide greater amounts of praise and the specific reinforcer when the child spontaneously imitates an approximation of the instructor's vocalizations (e.g., the child says "EE" after the adult has said "eat"). However, once the child is consistently able to make that sound, it can be required to be made along with the sign for the reinforcer.

As the child is able to make a vocalization along with the sign for the reinforcer, it is important to continue requiring him to make the sign until his vocalizations are accurate enough to be understood by others who are not familiar with him. One mistake that instructors sometimes make is dropping the requirement for the sign too soon. There is often excitement that the child is now "talking." However, if his speech is still not clear, his use of the sign along with the vocalization will increase the child's success in obtaining reinforcers.

Adam's Story

After two years of intensive ABA intervention, Adam still had not developed the ability to vocally imitate any sounds or words, was able to imitate only a few simple gross motor responses, and was unable to mand for items. His team had unsuccessfully tried to teach him to mand for items using both signs and pictures.

While participating in an intensive program at our clinic, Adam approached me while I was holding a bag of potato chips. As he reached for the bag (indicating that he would like one), I said "Eat" and handed him a half of a chip. After he finished eating it, he reached toward the bag again (speech and language pathologists refer to this action as "communicative intent"). I then said "Eat" and modeled the ASL sign for "eat," then quickly took his hand and totally physically prompted him to do the sign "eat" and again said "Eat," and gave him another half of a potato chip. He did not resist my physical prompting. Each of the next three times he reached for the bag of chips, I repeated that sequence. On the next trial (when he reached for a chip), I said, "Eat" as I modeled the ASL sign for "eat" then partially lifted his hand toward his mouth. Adam independently finished moving his fingers to his mouth. I immediately and excitedly said "Eat!" and handed him a whole potato chip because he had made the desired response. On the very next trial, I just said, "Eat" and modeled the sign, and he independently imitated the sign without me providing any physical prompt. I repeated that same sequence on the next trial and he successfully imitated the sign and received a half of a chip. The next time he reached for the bag, I just said, "Eat" and he immediately and independently made the sign for "eat." I excitedly said, "Eat!" and gave him two potato chips because he now did not require either a physical or an imitative prompt. The next time he looked toward me with my bag of chips, I just looked at him for about two seconds and he independently made the sign for "eat." Once again, I excitedly said "Eat!" and gave him two potato chips because he had now spontaneously manded for the food. He had several more independent mands (now only giving him one chip per mand) before I stopped giving him chips. The whole process to teach his first independent mands took only 10 minutes of instruction.

Adam's mother had watched the teaching session and was quite excited. I told her not to get too excited just yet, because he was just repeating a simple motor movement that resulted in him getting the chips. I told her that we might need to do the same teaching process the following day. The next morning when Adam and his mother entered the clinic, the mother said, "I didn't know that Adam liked corn." I asked her what she meant by her comment. She told me that on the previous evening, Adam approached her as she was preparing some corn on the cob and spontaneously made the sign for "eat." It was exciting that he used the new sign to request a different food. Much to my surprise, when I pulled out the bag of chips for the first time that morning, Adam immediately walked to me and spontaneously made the sign for "eat" without me saying anything to him! Not only did he quickly learn the sign, but also he was also able to use it for other food items. Over the following four weeks, he learned to mand for five other items and activities.

Dealing with a Child's Refusal to Respond

When teaching a child to mand for reinforcers, we are teaching him a new way of getting items and activities that he may have previously received without having to do a specific response. Because he is now being required to produce a specific response, he may attempt to engage in behaviors that have previously worked to get the reinforcer. For example, he may walk away from the instructor to see if he can get the reinforcer when the adult isn't paying attention, or he may engage in disruptive behavior. Because the child currently wants the reinforcer and the instructor has control of it, it's crucial that the old behaviors not be reinforced. If the child walks away, perhaps the motivation to do something to get the reinforcer isn't strong enough at that moment. The solution is to maintain control of the reinforcer until the motivation to obtain it is stronger.

A child may have previously learned that he actually gains access to reinforcers following engagement in disruptive behavior (e.g., crying, fussing, tantrumming). During a teaching session, if the child begins to engage in disruptive behavior, the adult should make sure that the disruptive behavior is not reinforced. If the behavior is only a little fussing, this behavior can easily be ignored, and the child can be given greater amounts of the reinforcer when calmly manding than he would receive when he fusses. If he engages in more significant disruptive behavior (e.g., grabbing at the adult, falling to the floor and crying), the adult should stop trying to get the child to mand until he is calm. When he is calm, training can resume, and when it does, the adult should ensure that the level of prompts provided are sufficient to ensure that the child is likely to be able to give a mand response that can be reinforced.

Multiple Sessions per Day/Limiting Access

Remember that a child should only be taught to ask for his reinforcers when the motivation to receive that reinforcer is strong (i.e., when he wants it), and instructors must limit the child's access to that reinforcer. If he has free access to the reinforcing item, there's no need for him to learn to ask for it. By limiting the child's access to toys or other reinforcing activities (e.g., electronic pads, videos, books, music, preferred food items) the adult will increase his motivation to get them. Therefore, the reinforcer should only be made available at times when the child is being taught how to mand for it. For example, he will only be hungry after he has not eaten for a while. Thus, after a few hours without having access to food, the child will be hungry, and that is the time to attempt to teach him to mand for something to eat. The child can then be given a small amount of a preferred food item each time he is prompted to mand "eat," either by using the sign for "eat" or by saying, "eat." After the child appears to be not as interested in obtaining more of the food item as indicated by not giving an accurate or effortful response, the session should be stopped, and training can be resumed at a later time in the day when the motivation to respond for that reinforcer is strong. There should be several sessions conducted each day that are specifically devoted to teaching the child the mand "eat."

Introducing the Second Sign

As the child is able to mand for the first reinforcer without the need for any physical or imitative prompts, a second sign should be introduced. The new sign should also be related to a strong form of reinforcement, be iconic (the sign resembles the object or an action associated with it), and be easy to produce. It should also look very different from the first sign, and involve a different motivator and type of reinforcement (e.g., if the first sign was "eat" perhaps "book" could be a second sign, but only if the child enjoys looking at books). If the two signs look alike or rhyme, or if they both involve hunger and the delivery of food, then they will be harder to acquire. Training on the two signs should alternate, and be interspersed with other responses that are strong in the child's repertoire (e.g., receptive instructions, matching-to-sample). The same training procedure described above should be used for establishing the new sign, and the procedures described later should be used to further develop the first sign.

Error Correction for Wrong Sign

When a second mand is introduced, it's not uncommon for the child to use the wrong response for the desired reinforcer (e.g., signs for "eat" while reaching for a book). Following an incorrect manding response (e.g., made the wrong sign, asked for the wrong item), some instructors may want to give the child what he asked for anyway. However, when it's obvious what the child wants, the instructor should just ignore the incorrect response and prompt him to make the correct response (the sign for "book"). The instructor should state what the child is wanting and prompt him to make the correct response (e.g., "Book, you want 'book'…sign 'book'" along with an imitative model of the sign). The child should be praised for making the correct (prompted) response, and then he should immediately be presented with the opportunity to mand for the item or activity without the prompts. His mand should be reinforced if he is able to respond correctly. If he still doesn't respond correctly without the prompts, the correction procedure should be repeated again.

Solving a "Scrolling" Problem

Sometimes a child will engage in what is commonly referred to as "scrolling" in which he starts to make the signs in a one-after-the-other manner that has been used in the past to get various reinforcers. This type of error is usually a result of attempting to teach too many mands prior to developing at least two strong mands that consistently occur only under the appropriate motivational condition. When "scrolling" of mands is observed, instructors must ensure that the child doesn't receive a reinforcer immediately after a sequence of two or more different mand responses. Instructors should consider these multiple responses as an error and begin the standard error correction procedure. That is, prompt the correct mand response and after the child makes the prompted response, immediately ask him, "What do you want?" and reinforce a correct unprompted response. If the problem continues, a procedure for teaching each response within a specific context is often effective in reducing the scrolling behavior.

Teaching New ASL Mands in Specific Contexts

An additional procedure can be used for a child who continues to have difficulty learning which sign to use to mand for each of the two or more reinforcers. One method that has helped children learn which sign to use involves teaching him to mand for each of the reinforcers in significantly different contexts. For example, for the child who isn't always using the sign "eat" when food is present and "book" when a book is the reinforcer, instructors can ensure that the mand for book is (at first) always available only in the family room, and that food is only available in the kitchen. Basically, each of the two responses is only used in one specific context (different rooms). As a result, the discrimination of which sign to make is multiply controlled by both the presence of the reinforcer and the room where the child is manding for the item. When the child learns to mand for the book only when in the family room and mand for food only when in the kitchen, the contexts (i.e., locations) where he is able to mand for the reinforcers should be gradually varied until he is able to mand for those reinforcers in any situation.

How to Collect Mand Data

The data sheet in Figure 6-4 provides a simple method for measuring the child's ability to mand for reinforcers, recording each instance in which the child mands for a reinforcer. Note that during the process of learning a new mand (i.e., requesting a specific reinforcer), he will often require some prompts to make the desired response. If the adult is required to totally physically prompt the response, then the child has merely allowed the adult to move his hands and arms. Because the response didn't require him to do anything other than cooperate with the full prompt, it really isn't necessary to record those events. However, if the child did finish a partially prompted response, his actual response could be recorded with an "|" to indicate that he did some actual responding on his own. If he was able to mand for the item by imitating a sign modeled by an adult, his datasheet could be marked with a "+" for each of those imitatively prompted mands. Whenever the child is in the presence of the reinforcer and either independently uses the sign to mand for the reinforcer, or mands for it when asked, "What do you want?" an "S" could be recorded to indicate that he spontaneously manded for it (i.e., no physical or imitative prompts were needed). In addition, if he spontaneously manded for the item and also said the word or a sound associated with the reinforcer, a "W" should be recorded (indicating the child said the (W)ord or an approximation of it).

As the child's use of the mand continues to develop, additional methods of recording data may also be desired. For example, it is possible to record instances in which the child approached an adult and then manded for an item or activity. In this situation, the child made the request when he was not actively engaged in a session to teach the skill. It might also be beneficial to record the number of times that the child mands for various reinforcers at home or at school, or to record the instances in which he mands for an item that is not in his presence. Each of these types of data can be used to track the development of the child's manding skills.

Figure 6-4.

Date	Eat	Up	Tickle			
5/1	I I I I					
5/2	I I I I I I I I +					
5/3	I I + I I I + + +					
5/4	I I + + + I + +					
5/5	+ + + S + S S + S S					
5/6	+ S S S S + S S	I I I I I +				
5/7	S S S S S + S S S S	I I I + + + I + +				
5/8	S S W S S S S W S	I + + I I + + + I +				
5/9	S S S S W S W W S	+ + + S + S				
5/10	W S W W W S W	S S S S W S				

I	Partial physical prompt
+	Imitative
S	Spontaneous
W	Word or Sound & spontaneous

Collecting Mand Data

One of the easiest ways to collect data on the acquisition of a mand is to simply record the number of responses each day. Although one could collect data on all the times the child was prompted to make the sign, it is not necessary to record all of the responses that were totally physically prompted as the instructor did all the work for those trials.

The data in this sample only include those trials in which the child completed at least a part of the response by himself (only a partial physical or an imitative prompt). It is possible to record all trials, but the method presented in this sample demonstrates the child's own responses.

Placement of the data sheet on the family's refrigerator makes it convenient for both parents to record the data!

Fading Out the Verbal Prompts

Once the child has been successful with the first two signs, and can accurately use them to mand for those reinforcers (without imitative or physical prompts), it is necessary for instructors to begin to fade out the specific verbal prompt (i.e., "Sign eat," or "Sign book."), and only provide a general verbal prompt such as "What do you want?" when necessary. The selection of new signs should follow the criteria previously described, and the training procedures for the third sign should be similar to those for the previous two signs. Note that the acquired signs need not be perfectly executed (the responses can be reasonable approximations while the child continues to develop his motor and vocal imitation skills), or independently provided under each source of control before moving on to additional signs. However, the responses should be strong under a combination of motivation, nonverbal, and verbal control (i.e., reliably occurring without any imitative or physical prompts).

In order to further develop the first two signs, the next step is to carefully begin to fade the verbal prompts, "Sign eat," and "Sign book." The child should be able to emit these signs without physical or imitative prompts, but the other four antecedent variables may still be present (i.e., the motivation, the object, and the two verbal prompts). It is now important to free the response from these multiple sources of control because they will not always occur together in the natural environment (see Figure 6-2, Panel 4). For example, if a child responds only when verbal prompts are given, his verbal abilities will be greatly limited. In order to fade out the verbal prompt "Sign eat," and transfer stimulus control to the motivation, the object, and the verbal prompt "What do you, want?" the instructor should present the child with the object (when the motivation is strong) and say "What do you want?" and simply wait a few seconds. If an appropriate response occurs, immediately reinforce it. If a response fails to occur within five to10 seconds, give the verbal prompt "Sign eat," and reinforce a correct response. Repeat the trial within a few seconds, and wait. Often, after a few trials, the child will begin to respond prior to the verbal prompt (i.e., transfer of stimulus control). When he does so for the first time, he should receive extra reinforcement.

Adding More Signs For Reinforcers

New signs can be added at this point, but the instructor should proceed with caution, making sure that the early signs are strong before adding too many new signs. The number of new signs should not exceed five to 10 until the next step in the training is complete (fading out the object, producing the sign with only the verbal prompt "Sign...").

The child's communication abilities are rather fragile at this point and introducing many signs too rapidly can weaken previously established signs. A common problem with early signers is that new signs are often added to the training program too quickly (imitative prompts are not sufficiently eliminated), and the child's signs become mixed up (i.e., appears to be guessing or "scrolling"). Think of the thousands of times a toddler emits his first few words before other words develop. Instructors should provide a sufficient number of training trials to insure that the initial responses will remain strong when new signs are introduced. The new signs should be those for strong forms of reinforcement for the child (e.g., music, ball, book, bubbles, car, boat, cracker, drink, candy, milk), and added one-by-one in the manner described above.

Fading Out the Object

The next step with the previously established signs is to teach the child to ask for the item (e.g., food) in the absence of that item (Figure 6-2, Panel 5) **(F 6)**. The instructor should show the child that she has the reinforcer and then place the food behind her back, or in a bag, and ask the child "What do you want?" The instructor should then wait for at least three to five seconds before presenting a prompt, which should consist of bringing the food item out in front of the child. Since he can already mand for "eat" when a food item is present, the response should quickly occur. Reinforce his response with food and repeat the trial. Place the food item out of sight and ask "What do you want?" Usually, within a few trials, the response will occur under the control of the motivation and the verbal prompt.

Eventually, the verbal prompt also should be faded out (Figure 6-2, panel 6) in the same manner as described above. When this occurs, the child has emitted a "pure" mand, that is, the response is controlled solely by the motivation (e.g., hunger) and the specific reinforcement (e.g., receiving the desired food item). (Note that the fading procedures need not occur in the order suggested here: fading the two verbal prompts, then the nonverbal prompt. The opposite order may be more effective and appropriate for some individuals; however, it is important at some time to fade out all of these prompts in order to establish "spontaneous" requests [See Figure 6-2, Panel 7]. In addition, it isn't necessary that all signs occur as pure mands before additional training on the other types of language training are conducted.)

Pure Spontaneous Mands

Ideally, the child will be able to ask for items and activities when he wants them, even when the items or activities associated with them are not present. As mentioned above, a "pure mand" is one in which the response is controlled solely by the motivation (e.g., hunger) and the specific reinforcement (e.g., receiving the desired food item). Some clinicians wouldn't consider the child to be "spontaneously manding" for items unless his responses are "pure mands." That is, the item should not be present when the child asks for the reinforcer. However, many times in life, we do see items or come in contact with other associated stimuli (i.e., see items, hear others talk about items or events) that remind us that a certain reinforcer could be available. These stimuli may increase our tendency to ask for that reinforcer. If the reinforcer is present, and the child requests that item or activity without having been asked or otherwise prompted to mand for the reinforcer, it may still be appropriate to consider that response (that was not prompted by another person) as a spontaneous mand, even though it is not technically a "pure mand."

From a strictly technical perspective, in order to be a "pure mand," the response should only occur in the presence of the "motivational operation" and be reinforced by the delivery of the reinforcer. Thus, praise that usually follows the response would not be delivered. However, when interacting with a child, there is really no need to eliminate the excitement and acknowledgement that usually accompanies the delivery of the reinforcer that he requested. When any child mands for a reinforcer, an adult's typical reaction usually includes a comment such as "Eat, here's a grape." As was described in Chapter 2, the presentation of the reinforcer along with the words spoken by the adult help to establish the reinforcement value of both the words and the adult. Thus, from a practical perspective, there is really no need to eliminate the praise that is provided along with the actual reinforcer.

Training in the Natural Environment

To further build the child's communication skills for future real-life application, the training procedures from specific training sessions must be carried over to the child's natural environment. These teaching procedures can be easily conducted during his normal day and will most likely increase the speed of acquisition. The child should be required to use his new mands whenever the motivation for the reinforcer is strong. Parents, staff, and friends should all encourage him to mand using the signs when appropriate and reinforce his attempts to do so. It is important that these other individuals also provide the child with opportunities to sign when their motivation is strong, and to watch out for satiation (e.g., they are no longer hungry or interested in a certain toy). Language is maintained by the verbal community (i.e., the people around the child who communicate with him) and if he leaves a training session and goes to an environment where the signs are not used or required, and the previous inappropriate behavior gets reinforced (e.g., whining to get food), progress will probably be much slower. Parents and staff are often concerned about themselves having difficulty in learning signs, but in this early stage of training they should be able to learn the signs at least as fast as the child. In addition, if the child is successful, it often motivates the adults to acquire more signs.

Teaching a Child to Approach and Then Mand

It must always be remembered that the goal of mand training is to get the child to request items and activities when the motivation for them is strong. Because the teaching of the responses necessitates that an adult be near him, it's important to teach the child that he can mand for reinforcers even when the adult does not initiate the interaction. In short, the child can learn to approach the adult and then mand for a reinforcer. To help him learn this process, the adult can stand away from the child (e.g., across the room) and show him an item that is likely to currently serve as a reinforcer. The child will usually approach the adult to get the item. As he approaches, the adult could use a prompt to get the child to use his new sign to mand for the item (e.g., "What do you want?). After he is reinforced for approaching and manding for the item, the adult should then move to another location that is still within sight of the child and again show him that she is holding his reinforcer. After several such interactions, it is possible for the adult to also start fading out the object using the procedures described above (e.g., show him the reinforcer and as he gets close, move the reinforcer behind the back).

Teach a Child to Mand to Peers

A child should also be taught to use his manding skills to obtain reinforcers from his peers **(L 18 & 19)**. Because mand training is usually conducted by adults, the child has a history of being reinforced for manding to adults. A history of successfully manding to the child's peers also needs to be established. Although under normal free-play circumstances, peers may not be as likely to give up a reinforcer to the child, it is important that adults prompt other children (most often typically developing children including classmates and siblings) to deliver reinforcers when the child mands for items. It is an important part of the development of both social skills and manding skills to be able to request items from one's peers.

3. Mand Training For a Child Who Has Some Echoic Skills

Speech is the most desired way of communicating, and if a child has some echoic responses, then efforts should be made to teach him vocal words as mands. Children who have some developing echoic and imitative skills may benefit from a combination of vocal mands and signed mands. The training procedure is diagrammed in Figure 6-5 and is essentially the same as that used for sign language training, except words versus signs are used, and there are two less prompt levels available. As with sign training, the first word should be for a strong form of reinforcement, and training should be conducted when the motivation for that reinforcer is strong. The word should also be one that the child can echo or reasonably approximate so that most individuals would be able to understand him.

All the considerations that were described for teaching mands using sign language also pertain when teaching a child to vocally mand. It is equally important here to eventually fade all the prompts, teach the skills in multiple sessions each day, and develop strong mands that occur only under the correct motivational conditions (i.e., no errors). The correction procedures for errors when prompts are faded and when the child gives the wrong response are almost identical except the required responses are vocalizations rather than signs. Programming is necessary to ensure that the child is able to mand for reinforcers to a variety of adults and peers during his normal daily interactions. The child should also be taught to approach individuals and spontaneously mand for reinforcing items and activities even when the items are not present. Additionally, any disruptive behavior or other refusals to respond should be approached in the same manner as described in the teaching signed mands section of this chapter.

Teaching the First Vocal Mand

The transfer of the echoic response to the motivational variable is the main focus of this intervention. Training should begin with all the antecedent variables present (Figure 6-5, Panel 1). Specifically, if the targeted response is "eat," the child should be hungry, and the desired food item should be present. The instructor should hold up the food item and say to the child, "What do you want?" (a general verbal prompt to respond), and "Say eat." or simply "Eat." (echoic prompt). *(Note that the echoic prompt "Eat" is the most important variable that must be presented. When starting to teach a specific mand, it is not always necessary to ask the child, "What do you want?")* If the child says "eat" or an approximation of the word, immediately deliver praise and an item of food along with praise (e.g., excited "Eat!" or "Eat, yes eat!"). An incorrect response, or no response, should be followed by a re-presentation of the original trial (Panel 1). The child should respond since his echoic skill is strong (at least for the target word) and there is some current motivation for the food item. If he continues to fail to respond, try a different food item or a different time of day when his motivation may be stronger. If he continues to fail to respond, consider the procedures described in the cooperation sections above, or possibly consider the use of sign language in this early stage of training (only if the child has some motor imitation ability).

Figure 6-5.

Teaching to Request (Mand) Using Speech

Panel	Example	Antecedent →	Behavior →	Consequences	Example
1	**Hungry**	**Motivational Operation**	"Eat"	Food Item	Given food item
	"What do you want?"	Verbal Stim. to Respond		Praise	"Eat, Right, Eat!"
	Food Item	Nonverbal Stimulus			
	Say "Eat"	Echoic Stimulus			
2	**Hungry**	**Motivational Operation**	"Eat"	Food Item	Given food item
	"What do you want?"	Verbal Stim. to Respond		Praise	"Eat, Right, Eat!"
	Food Item	Nonverbal Stimulus			
	Say "Eat"	*Echoic Stimulus*			
3	**Hungry**	**Motivational Operation**	"Eat"	Food Item	Given food item
	"What do you want?"	Verbal Stim. to Respond		Praise	"Eat, Right, Eat!"
	Food Item	*Nonverbal Stimulus*			
4	**Hungry**	**Motivational Operation**	"Eat"	Food Item	Given food item
	"What do you want?"	*Verbal Stim. to Respond*		Praise	"Eat, Right, Eat!"
5	**Hungry**	**Motivational Operation**	"Eat"	**Food Item**	**Given food item**

Fading the Echoic Prompt

The procedure for actual training of a vocal mand begins in Panel 2 of Figure 6-5 where the echoic prompt is faded out. The fading procedures are similar to those described above for sign language. The instructor could use a delay procedure or a partial prompt procedure. The combination of these two techniques may also be effective. For example, the instructor could show the food item, ask the child, "What do you want?" then wait two or three seconds. If he didn't respond during the delay, the instructor would then give a partial echoic prompt (e.g., "Say E…" as a partial prompt for the word "eat"). The objective at this point in the training is to get the child to say, "eat" prior to the delivery of the partial echoic prompt. When this occurs, he should be immediately reinforced (perhaps with a larger piece of food if it is the first time, or a high quality response).

The main objective of this current instruction is to eliminate the need for echoic prompts as quickly as possible while insuring that the child is successful in obtaining reinforcement. For some children, a response without echoic prompts (i.e., vocal model) may occur very quickly within a session (i.e., he asks for "eat" multiple times in a short period of time). However, when there has been a time lapse between those unprompted responses in an earlier session, it may be necessary to use some prompts to get the behavior going again.

The overall desired outcome is for the child to be able to independently mand for that reinforcer (i.e., no partial echoic prompts necessary) whenever he wants it. Therefore, the instructor should try to conduct as many trials as possible each session, and each day. The critical feature of this procedure is the careful shaping and fading of the prompts necessary to develop the vocal mand. This particular procedure is most effectively carried out by individuals who have some experience in prompting, fading, and the reinforcement of successive approximations.

Error Correction When Fading Prompts

Whenever any type of prompt is being faded, there will often be some errors in the child's response when given a lower level of prompt. When an error occurs, it is important to implement a correction procedure. Following the incorrect manding response (e.g., said the wrong word, gave a partial response), the instructor should immediately re-present the trial using a higher level of prompt to get the child to make the correct response. The child should be praised for making the correct response, and then he should immediately be presented with the opportunity to respond to the initial level of prompt. The child's mand should be reinforced if he is able to respond correctly. If he still doesn't respond correctly at the lesser prompt level, the correction procedure should be repeated again.

Introducing a Second Vocal Mand

The next step is to introduce a second word. The criteria for selecting additional words in the early stages of mand training is similar to the criteria recommended for selecting new signs. These first words should be for items that are strong forms of reinforcement, and involve sounds that are already established in the child's echoic repertoire. The words should not rhyme with each other and should be for very different types of reinforcers. Training on the second word should be alternated with the training on the first word, as well as interspersed with trials on other types of language related skills such as echoic, imitation, and receptive trials (see Chapters 3, 4, and 5).

Once the child is successfully manding for two or three items, procedures should be implemented to fade out the object as a source of control (Figure 6-5, Panel 3). Procedures to fade out the object are similar to those used to fade out the object for the signer. The object could be placed behind the instructor's back, or placed in a box or bag. Correct responses should be immediately followed by the presentation of praise and the object. Incorrect responses should be followed by a repeat of the procedure and only partially hiding the item (e.g., leave it sticking out of the box). Eventually, the child must be able to ask for things when they are not present (a pure mand). However, for some children the removal of the object may result in the complete loss of interest in manding. While the ultimate goal is to eliminate the object, for these children it is probably best to continue to add new words and to keep the objects in view. However, this procedure should not last too long (e.g., 10 words) before the child is required to ask for items that are out of view, otherwise there is risk of becoming prompt bound (i.e., a prompt will always be required to get the response to occur). If the verbal prompt "What do you want?" has been used to teach the mands, the last step in the early mand procedure is to fade out that prompt (Figure 6-5, Panel 4). This last step is less important than the previous three, but if the goal is to obtain spontaneous requesting (a pure mand) then this step must be completed.

Error Correction for Saying the Wrong Word

When a second mand is introduced, it's not uncommon for the child to use the wrong response for the desired reinforcer (e.g., saying "eat" while reaching for a book). Following an incorrect manding response, some instructors may want to "give him what he asked for." However, when it is obvious what the child wants, the instructor should just ignore the incorrect response and prompt him to make the correct response (e.g., "Say book"). The child should be praised for making the correct (prompted) response, and then he should immediately be presented with the opportunity to mand for the item or activity without the prompts (i.e., "What do you want?"). The child's mand should be reinforced if he is able to respond correctly. If he still doesn't respond correctly without the prompts, the correction procedure should be repeated again.

Teaching New Vocal Mands in Specific Contexts

As was described for children who are learning to mand with signs, vocal children sometimes have difficulty saying the correct word when manding for one of two or more reinforcers. One method that has helped children make this discrimination is to teach the child to mand for each of the reinforcers in significantly different contexts. For example, the child who is not always saying "Eat" when food is present and "book" when a book is the reinforcer, instructors could ensure that the mand for book is (at first) always available only in the family room, and that food is only available in the kitchen. Basically, each of the two responses is only used in one specific context (e.g., different rooms). As a result, the discrimination of which word to say is multiply controlled by both the presence of the reinforcer and the room where the child is manding for the item. When he learns to mand for the "book" only when in the family room, and mand for "eat" only when in the kitchen, the contexts (i.e., locations) where the child is able to mand for the reinforcers should be gradually varied until the child is able to mand for those reinforcers in any situation.

Specific Issues Related to the Establishment of Vocal Mands

Shaping the Accuracy of Vocal Mands

When starting to teach a child to vocally mand for reinforcers, it's often necessary and desirable to reinforce the child's vocalizations even if they are only approximations of the word being modeled by the instructor. In fact, because he is momentarily highly motivated to receive a specific reinforcer, this moment presents a great opportunity to shape his vocal imitation skills. A child who may not be highly motivated to practice saying certain sounds under other conditions (e.g., sessions to develop echoic responses), is often much more cooperative when conducted as a part of mand training procedures.

Although it's desirable to have the child say the word with good articulation, remember that the most important issue is that he is able to make a specific response that lets others know what he wants. At first, it's okay to accept a response that is somewhat close to the desired response (e.g., "Moo" for movie). As the child starts to regularly use that approximation to gain access to the reinforcer, the instructor can "shape" a more accurate response by gradually increasing the requirement for the child to make a more accurate vocalization before delivering the reinforcer (e.g., "Moo-EE" for movie). When he says "Moo-EE" for "movie" within a certain context, most adults would recognize the word as being "movie." As the child develops greater control over his vocal musculature, he should eventually be required to accurately say the word "movie". However, at any point in the process of learning this skill, if a child's response is not "accurate enough" to warrant the delivery of a reinforcer, it shouldn't be given. If he is allowed access to reinforcers following a "sloppy" response, then his accuracy will not improve.

What is a "Close Enough" Vocal Mand?

When teaching a child to say a particular sound upon request, the instructor will often hear the child produce variations of that sound. Many instructors report being unsure as to which of those variations are "close enough" to the actual sound to be reinforced. There are two main issues that need to be considered. The first is the child's history of making that sound, and the second is the strength of the current reinforcer.

If the child is just starting to make the sound, almost all approximations of the target sound should be reinforced. The desired outcome of the reinforcement is to increase his ability to make approximations of that sound. As he is consistently able to make an approximation upon request, the instructors should use a "shaping procedure" to improve the accuracy of the vocalization. This procedure involves the reinforcement of those responses that are closer to the targeted sound while not reinforcing sounds that are less accurate. Therefore, the accuracy or what is considered to be "close enough" should be constantly changing; as the child is able to make more accurate vocalizations, the reinforcement will only be provided following examples of his best responses.

The child may start a mand training session making only a rough approximation of the word. Because his best responses are reinforced, he will be most likely making more accurate sounds by the end of that session. However, at the start of the next session his responses may not be as accurate as they were at the end of the previous session. Therefore, it's often necessary to initially go back to reinforcing a few of the lesser quality responses, but then immediately start to raise the criterion to require and reinforce his best responses from the previous day. As each day progresses, the overall accuracy should keep increasing until the child is able to clearly imitate the targeted word on the first trial of each day.

During this process of shaping the accuracy of the response, remember that the child's motivation to make an accurate sound (or word) is dependent upon the strength of the reinforcer. If he isn't motivated to receive the item or activity that is being used as a potential reinforcer, there is no reason for him to make an effortful response to get it. In this situation, when the instructor recognizes that the child isn't highly motivated, she should avoid the temptation to reinforce lesser quality responses. If the child learns that even lower level approximations will be reinforced, there is no reason for him to make a more accurate vocalization. The best option is to stop trying to get an accurate response until the motivation to gain access to that reinforcer is strong. Remember that it is always best to stop an interaction after the reinforcement of a high-quality response rather than trying to keep a session going as the responding becomes less accurate.

How Far to Push

As discussed in Chapter 5 (Teaching Vocal Imitation Skills), when attempting to get a child to more precisely imitate a sound or word, he shouldn't be pushed so much that his attempts to imitate result in consistent failure. The main considerations regarding vocal mands are how many times a vocal model should be presented and at what point the child's vocalization is "close enough" to be reinforced. When a child is attending to a vocal model and is attempting to imitate that sound, he may be successful after a few attempts. However, if he isn't able to produce a higher quality vocalization after several attempts, it's probably best to stop trying to get him to make that sound so that he doesn't "become frustrated" with the activity. (In behavioral terms, his attempted responses are "on extinction" in that no reinforcement is forthcoming, and his probability of making further attempts is decreasing.) Therefore, as a general rule, it is probably best to present the vocal model for a mand no more than three times. In this situation, because he continues to attempt to make the desired higher quality vocalization, his compliance with an instruction to vocally imitate should be reinforced. However, there is still motivation to make a more accurate vocalization because if he is able to imitate the vocalization following one of the earlier models, the reinforcer will be delivered sooner. Note that it is also important that the reinforcers provided following the best vocal responses should be more powerful (or delivered in greater quantity) than the reinforcers that are provided following the less accurate vocal responses. Thus, there is incentive both to comply with instructions and to accurately imitate the desired sound.

You Can't Always Get What You Want!

As a child is learning to mand for a variety of items and activities, it is important to reinforce his mands as often as possible. The lesson being taught is that he is able to receive reinforcers when he uses his signs or vocalizations to ask for them. However, once he has mastered the ability to mand for several different reinforcers, he'll also need to learn that not all of those mands will be reinforced.

As was mentioned earlier in this chapter, there is often a decrease in instances of frustration and disruptive behavior that occurs when a child learns to request items and activities. In the past, some disruptive behaviors may have been due to the child's inability to let others know what he wanted. He may exhibit fewer instances of these behaviors now that he has learned how to gain access to his reinforcers by simply manding for them. However, he also must learn that he is not able to get those reinforcers every time he asks for them.

Not receiving requested items is something that every child experiences in life. He must learn that even if he engages in disruptive behavior he still will not get what he has requested (Foxx, 1982; O'Neill, Horner, Albin, Sprague, Storey & Newton, 1997). For example, if a child asks for a movie at bedtime, he shouldn't be allowed to watch a movie, but rather should be made to go to bed. This lesson of not getting everything he asks for is an important one in the child's development.

Parents sometimes are concerned with the re-emergence of problem behavior. In reality, the current disruptive behavior is actually much different than the earlier behavior, and presents as a "better problem" rather than not knowing what is bothering the child. When a child engages in disruptive behavior because his mand didn't get reinforced, parents now know exactly why and are able to deal with it as if the child was typically developing. Specifically, they will not "give in" and let him have what he asked for because they know that he just needs to "get over" being upset. (In technical terms, his current mand is on extinction.) However, when it is an appropriate time for him to gain access to the reinforcer, his mands will be reinforced. (As the Rolling Stones song suggests "...but if you try sometimes, you just might find, you get what you need.") Through this process of reinforcing some mands, but not others, the child experiences the same learning experiences as every other child.

4. Teaching Manding to a Physically Disabled Child Who Cannot Echo or Imitate

Some children do not have the manual dexterity to produce signs, or the vocal control to emit words. For these children, who may have cerebral palsy or a traumatic brain injury, the response for mand training should consist of pointing to a picture or an object. Other children who cannot echo sounds or imitate actions but can do exceptionally well on matching-to-sample task, may also benefit from a pointing system. (A word of caution is warranted here: many children who cannot imitate or echo can still be taught words or signs with the procedures described in this chapter, and due to the many advantages of speech and signs [topography-based vs. selection-based systems], every attempt should be made to teach them to communicate with these less restrictive types of communication).

The pointing response in a picture communication can be made in a number of different ways depending on which muscle group the child can control (e.g., a head pointer, a mouth pointer, eye movements, or hand movements). The selection of the first pictures to teach, and the conditions under which the teaching should be conducted, would be exactly the same as those described above for signed and vocal mands. Start with pictures that represent highly reinforcing items or activities, and only conduct training when the motivation for those activities is strong. A correct response, or an approximation of a correct response should be immediately reinforced with praise and access to the reinforcer.

The types of prompts available for training this type of mand are similar to those described for signs and words. Pointing has some advantages over speech in that physical prompts and imitative prompts can be used (but obviously not echoic prompts). To start training, the instructor should place a single picture representing the reinforcing item on the table or the tray of the child's wheelchair. Then the instructor should hold up the reinforcing item (e.g., a radio) and prompt the child with the verbal prompts, "What do you want? Point to radio," and provide the imitative prompt of pointing to the picture. If the child does not respond, then physical prompts should be used. A fully prompted response should be reinforced with access to the reinforcer (e.g., a minute or two of listening to the radio). The procedure should then be repeated. On the next trial, the instructor should attempt to fade out the physical prompt (See Figure 6-2, Panel 2). Approximations of the correct responses should be successively reinforced (i.e., shaped), with constant effort on the instructor's part to give fewer and fewer physical prompts.

The next step in training is to eliminate the imitative prompt (Figure 6-2, Panel 3). The instructor should again present the object when the motivation is strong along with the verbal prompts, "What do you want, point to radio," and the imitative prompt. Approximations should be immediately reinforced and incorrect responses followed by repeating the verbal and imitative prompt. On each successive trial, the trainer should attempt to fade out the imitative prompt. Once the child can point to a picture without physical or imitative prompts, then new pictures should be introduced. The criteria for introducing new pictures and the fading of verbal prompts are similar to that described for signs and speech. Choose only reinforcing items for the first five to10 words, alternate mand responses with each other, and intersperse with the different types of language trials (i.e., receptive, echoic, imitation).

The picture exchange communication system (PECS) may be more beneficial for some students than a picture pointing system. PECS has the advantage of requiring the child approach and give a picture to the instructor. Thus, the adult must interact with the language system by actually receiving the pictures in her hands. This element may have substantial advantages over a pointing system that does not require adult interaction with the communication system. The procedures for the use of PECS also involve early mand training and have been described in detail by Frost and Bondy (1994).

Summary

The first type of expressive language to begin teaching a nonverbal child should be the mand (i.e., request). This type of language directly benefits the child by allowing him to gain access to desired reinforcers. It allows him to let others know what he wants, and makes the individuals who give him those items and activities more important to him.

The method by which he learns to ask for items depends on his ability to control his vocal musculature. Speech is always the most preferred method of communication. If a child is able to repeat words or say reasonably close approximations, he can be taught to ask for items by speaking. If his vocal imitation skills are not adequate, he can learn to request items initially using sign language until he is able to say words.

Training also begins by identifying and then teaching the child to request specific items. Non-specific requests such as "more" and "please" should be avoided as they often hinder the development of requesting skills. The specific procedures for teaching early mands effectively require a number of important considerations, and the careful use of prompts and reinforcement. After the child learns his first request, additional requests need to be carefully added so as to avoid causing confusion for the child. As each request is learned, the accuracy of the child's sign and word is always being developed using a behavior shaping procedure.

Potential Learning Objectives Related to the Development of Requesting/Manding Skills

The following objectives are provided to assist a parent or teacher in targeting specific skills that may be appropriate for a child's intervention plan. Please see the ABLLS-R® to assess the child's skills and to identify additional objectives for further skill development.

Each child is a unique individual and requires input from a variety of people who know him and are familiar with effective programming strategies. Therefore, these learning objectives are not being prescribed for any particular child, but rather are being provided as examples of objectives that are consistent with the skills described in this chapter.

F 5 (Child's name) will ask for at least 10 items or activities that he wants using a specific response (spoken word or with an American Sign Language sign) when the items are present.

F 7 (Child's name) will make eye contact when asking a person for items or actions at least 80% of the times that he makes requests.

F 8 (Child's name) will be able to ask others to perform at least 6 specified actions (e.g., ask others to "come" with him, "stand up," "sing," "open," "push," "(pick) up").

F 29 (Child's name) will spontaneously request objects or actions at least 20 times per day.

7 Teaching Visual Performance Tasks

One important set of skills involves a child being able to look closely at items, and especially those that he is asked to manipulate to complete a task. He must be able to pay close attention to the items that he sees in his environment. For example, he needs to be able to identify his jacket and backpack among those that belong to others. He also needs to be able to pay close attention to the different characteristics of a dog and a cat to be able to learn to name each animal. If a child is to learn common daily activities such as matching socks or putting away silverware, he must also be able to "match" or sort identical items. He must learn to watch what he is doing while he is manipulating various objects. For example, if he is to learn how to use a zipper to close his coat, or to pour juice into a cup without spilling, he must pay attention to his actions with the items involved in those tasks.

Thus, one of the important sets of skills a child needs to learn includes what professionals often refer to as "visual performance" tasks. These tasks require the child to carefully look at items as he performs actions involving them. It is important he can be directed to look at specific items, and be able to maintain focused attention on them while they are being manipulated by others (C 3-5). These skills are critical to be able to learn many more advanced tasks involving the manipulation of objects.

There are a variety of everyday tasks that require a child to attend to objects as he manipulates them. These tasks include such activities as completing puzzles

(B 1, 10-11, 14-15), matching objects **(B 3-7)**, sorting objects by categories **(B 8, 17-19)**, replicating block designs **(B 9, 12 & 23)**, and arranging items in order (e.g., smallest to largest) **(B 25)**.

Visual performance tasks require the development of several critical skills. In order to perform such activities, the child must be able to scan displays of items. He needs to be able to focus his attention on multiple items and must attend to the similarities and differences among them. He must also be able to pay attention to his actions as he engages in the coordinated motor movements necessary to adjust the positioning of items. Furthermore, he must be able to identify when his actions have been successful in completing the desired outcome.

There are several types of tasks that are often used to teach these visual performance skills. These tasks include using single-inset-piece puzzles **(B 1)**, putting pieces into shape-sorter boxes **(B 2)**, matching identical **(B 3-7)**, and non-identical objects and pictures **(B 8)**.

Developing Focused Attention to Objects

Many children with language delays have deficits in their ability to maintain focused attention on the manipulation of objects. In order for a child to learn a wide variety of tasks, it is important that parents and instructors be able to direct his attention to specific objects. Once he is able to attend to items that are shown to him, he must maintain focused attention while those objects are being manipulated. There are two procedures that help facilitate the development of these skills. The first is following directions to look at objects held in various positions, and the second is to track the movement of items.

Following Directions to Look at Items in Various Positions

Children need to be able to follow instructions to look at items that the instructor holds in any of a variety of positions in front of them. The adult should be able ask a child to look at an item that is held in his field of vision whether it be on the left or right side of him, or whether it is above his head, or held so that he is required to look downward to see it. He should be able to quickly look at the object (e.g., within three seconds) without requiring any additional prompts.

To teach a child to follow such directions, it is often helpful to start by asking him to look at one of his reinforcers. Because the child likes the item, he is more likely to look at it than an object that is not one of his reinforcers. Thus by using his interest in reinforcing items, it is often fairly simple to get him to comply with the instruction to visually locate the held item. When the child quickly follows the instruction to look at the item, his looking can be reinforced with that reinforcer. For example, if the child likes raisins, he can be asked to look at the box of raisins held by his instructor. She can sit across a table in front of him, and then ask him to "look" as she moves the box to a position on her right side. If he looks at the box, she can reinforce his looking by saying, "Good looking" and then give him a few raisins. After he has finished eating the raisins, she could then tell him to look at the box that she is now holding out to her left side. Reinforcement for his quick looking should be provided when the reinforcing item is held to either side at his eye level, or above or below his eye level.

Regardless of the position in which the reinforcer is held, he should be able to look at it within a few seconds. If at first he doesn't look at the item within a few seconds, the instruction can be re-presented along with a prompt. The prompt may involve saying additional words such as "over here" as the instructor also points to it with her other hand or taps the item with the fingers of the hand that is holding it. These initial responses that require prompting can be reinforced with access to the item (e.g., raisins). However, as with the use of any prompt, it must be faded as quickly as possible. Once the child has followed directions without prompts to look at the item on multiple occasions, it will then be necessary to withhold reinforcement when the child doesn't look quickly or requires additional prompts. Thus, the child will learn that he gains access to the reinforcer only when he responds quickly to the instructions.

After the child quickly and consistently looks at reinforcers held in a variety of positions, he can also learn other related skills. For example, he could be taught to attend to reinforcers held in successive positions prior to reinforcement. He would be provided with praise for looking at it in the first position and, then instructed to look again when it is moved to a second location. Another extension of the skill would be to reinforce his looking at the reinforcer in an initial position and continuously watching it as it moves from that position to another (i.e., tracking its movement). The same prompting, fading prompts, and reinforcement of quick looking procedures would be used to develop these additional skills. Additionally, this process can also be used to teach the child to look at common objects (e.g., a shoe, a spoon), except that now his quickly looking at the object will continue to be reinforced with praise (e.g., "Good looking") and an existing reinforcer (e.g., raisin).

Teaching to Track the Movement of Objects

As was just described, the child can also be taught to track the movement of items. This skill is important because many of the skills a child needs to learn will require that he maintain his attention on items and how they are being manipulated. Tracking the movement of items for short periods of time requires that the child maintain focused attention on an object.

Similar teaching procedures can be used to teach the child to track items. As with looking at items, it is often helpful to start by instructing a child to watch a reinforcer. One such method to develop this skill is to place an existing reinforcer (e.g., a raisin) on a paper napkin under an overturned transparent plastic cup. In this manner, the child is able to see the reinforcer that is covered by the cup. He should then be instructed to "watch" as the napkin, reinforcer and cup are moved on the table. At first, the child's watching the movement for a few inches should be reinforced with praise and the reinforcer under the cup. The behavior that is being reinforced is the child's tracking the movement of the reinforcer. As the child is successful in tracking the reinforcer for a few inches, the length of time he must track it can be slowly increased (e.g., by a second or two at a time), and the movement of the cup can also involve changes in direction. Once he is able to track the movement of the cup when the reinforcer is present, it is also possible to teach him to watch the movement of a non-see-through cup after he has observed the reinforcer being placed under it.

How to Teach a Child to Do Inset Puzzles

Figure 7-1.

Several types of inset puzzles.

One activity that requires a child to attend to his manipulation of objects involves inset puzzles. Completion of these types of puzzles requires the placement of uniquely shaped pieces into their counterpart cutout sections on a board. (See Figure 7-1 for examples of inset puzzles.) Sometimes these boards use puzzle pieces of different shapes (e.g., square, circle and triangle) or different sizes of a specific shape (e.g., all triangles). Other inset puzzles may have pictures of an object (e.g., a car, an apple, or a cat) with a matching picture of the item in the cutout section of the puzzle board so that the child can match the puzzle piece to the picture on the board.

There are several skills involved in being able to position objects in an inset puzzle board. The first skill involves being able to scan the board to see the potential places where a piece can be inserted. The child must also then look at the puzzle pieces that are in front of him and determine which of the holes in the board will accommodate each of the pieces. He must then be able to pick up the pieces and physically place them in their corresponding positions on the board. The main requirement is that the child "looks and places" the piece in the correct hole. It is not sufficient for him to move the piece and let it drop into the correct position without watching what he is doing. Although many typically developing children can quickly learn to complete such puzzles, any or all of the steps involved in the task may need to be specifically taught to a child with developmental delays.

Figure 7-2.

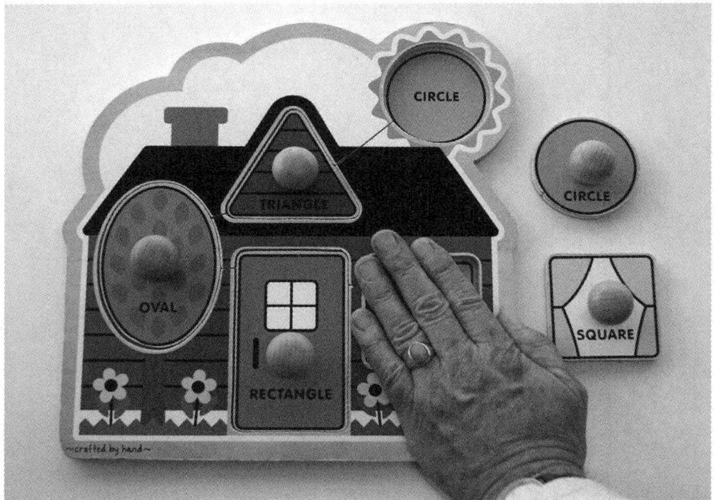

Teacher covers other holes with hand to help child select the location to insert the puzzle piece.

At first, it may be necessary to only remove a single piece from the board and then teach the child to pick up and manipulate that piece into its opening. Some children may require numerous prompts (e.g., physical, verbal, gestural) just to pick up the piece and move it to the open hole in the board while the instructor covers the other pieces with her hand (See Figure 7-2). However, once the piece is over the open hole, the child may not be able to turn it so that it slides into the board. Once again, the instructor may need to prompt the child to "turn it" or "look" so that it drops into the opening. If the child has picked up the piece, but isn't looking at it or at the location where it is to be placed, he must be stopped and the task should be re-presented. He should then be given whatever prompts are necessary to get him to attend to each of the critical factors involved in the task.

Figure 7-3.

Circle removed from inset puzzle.

One method for simplifying the task is to carefully select the first few pieces to be taught. It is often beneficial to select a circle as the first piece to be taught as circular pieces will drop into the board regardless of how they are turned (Figure 7-3). Pieces in other shapes (e.g., a square, triangle) that require the child to attend to how they are oriented can then be taught. Squares or triangles with sides of equal sizes are easier than rectangles or triangles with varying sized sides as those shapes require manipulation into the specific positions that allow them to fit into the board.

With the easier types of pieces, the child may be able to readily position them without being required to closely watch what his hand is doing. However, it is important that as he continues to develop these skills, the child learns to look at the pieces as he manipulates them to fit into the holes in the board. Reinforcement should be provided for his watching his hand as he places the piece into the corresponding hole. He should not be allowed to use a mere "trial and error" method of placing the pieces. When he is able to look at both the pieces and the openings, other variations such as those that have pieces with other unique forms can be taught.

Figure 7-4.

Two pieces removed from inset puzzle.

Another factor that can be adjusted is the number of pieces the child is asked to insert. Initially, it is desirable to give him only a single piece to place. When he correctly positions the piece in its hole on the board, he can be given a reinforcer for his action. After he is able to place a few pieces when there is only one open hole and each piece is handed to him one at a time (while the other pieces are in their place), it would then be appropriate to remove two of the pieces and then teach him to locate the corresponding holes and place those items. This additional step will make the task a little more difficult because the child will be required to pay greater attention to pieces and the available openings (See Figure 7-4).

Keep in mind that the child will be learning several important skills throughout the inset puzzle process. Putting individual puzzle pieces into a frame that accommodates pieces of differing shapes or sizes requires him to scan the board and the pieces in front of him. He must also stay focused while moving each piece to its corresponding hole, and must persist on manipulating the puzzle pieces so that they drop into the corresponding holes in the board. He must also learn to make the determination of where each piece goes and continue to place all the pieces until the entire task is completed.

William's Story

William's parents were concerned about his failure to learn many basic skills. He was in a school program, but he hadn't acquired any meaningful skills. He was nonverbal, was unable to imitate and didn't follow any directions. The staff had told his parents that he was severely globally delayed and they were not optimistic about his future progress.

When I started to work with William, I noticed that he seemed to be waiting for me to prompt him to do something for me. He was very passive. His parents told me that in order to get him to do anything, they pretty much had to totally prompt him to do the actions. I surmised that his previous teaching interventions had not focused on getting him to make independent responses. I explained to his parents that it looked like he was always waiting for someone to "help him" do desired actions. The problem of "being prompt dependent" is not a trait of the child, but rather it is a result of the failure of his instructors to eliminate their prompts. In essence, why should he do anything for himself when others would do it for him?

I then proceeded to place a few small wooden blocks and a small bowl on a table in front of him. I took one of the blocks and made sure he was watching when I said, "Do this" and dropped the block into the bowl. I immediately grabbed his hand and physically prompted him to pick up a block and moved his hand over the bowl. I gave him a partial physical prompt (i.e., moved his fingers) so that he dropped the block into the bowl. He was praised and given a small food item for a reinforcer. I repeated the task a few times and he was eventually able to release the block after I had moved his hand over the bowl. After a few similar successful trials, I merely had to model the action and he would do the whole sequence of picking up and dropping the block in the bowl by himself.

We then took out an inset puzzle and removed a wooden circular piece. I told him to "Put in" the piece as I physically guided his hand so that the piece slid into its hole on the puzzle board. He was given a preferred food item and praise when the circle slid into the hole. I was very careful not to allow the circle to slide into the hole unless he was watching the movement of the circle. On the subsequent trials, I would place the circle on the board so that all he had to do was push the piece forward into the hole. But again, I wouldn't allow him to move the piece unless he was looking at it. After about four or five trials, William began to push the piece into the hole without assistance.

The mother was so excited that she asked to be able to have him do it for her. Not only did he consistently place the circle piece into the board, but she also got him to slide a triangle into the board. His parents both commented that they had never seen him focus his attention on what he was doing like he did with that activity. I told them that the reason he was able to do it was that we had carefully selected an easy task that required minimal attention and effort for him to be successful, and we had systematically reinforced his independent actions as we gradually eliminated our prompts. The behaviors of looking at what he was doing and moving the pieces into the corresponding hole were the behaviors that resulted in reinforcement. In order to get independent responding, those behaviors need to be reinforced. I explained that doing tasks for him, and then allowing access to preferred items (i.e., reinforcers) only reinforces the behavior of passively letting others move his arms and hands and doesn't teach him to attend to the task and do the necessary actions.

How to Teach a Child to Do Form Boxes

The same "look and place" skills involved in inset puzzles are necessary to be able to place various shaped objects into a shape sorting can or cube (See figure 7-5). The pieces used for this type of task are often slightly more difficult for children because they must be more precise in the manipulation of the pieces to get them to pass through an opening. With inset puzzles, the pieces are flat which makes it possible to just slide the pieces into the desired position. However, form boxes require that not only the correct hole be identified, but also that the shape be turned to the specific angle that will allow the piece to slide into the hole. Once again, the child will only be able to complete this task if he is able to maintain focused attention and persists in manipulating the pieces until they slide into the container. As with inset puzzles, it may be helpful for the instructor to cover some of the holes with her hand so as to prompt the child to locate the correct hole (See Figure 7-6).

Figure 7-5.

Form box.

Figure 7-6.

Hand prompt.

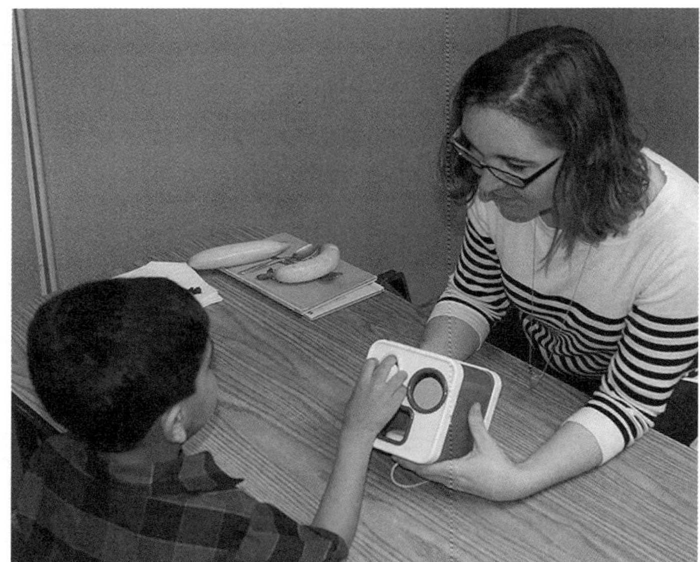

Child inserting a triangle piece in the correct hole of a form box.

Matching Objects to an Identical Object

The matching of objects is another visual performance task that requires a child to attend to and manipulate objects. This activity is often referred to as a "Matching-to-Sample" procedure by professionals. In this activity, the child is presented with a display of several items. He is then given an object that matches one of the items in the display (often referred to as an "array") and is told to put it with the matching item. He must then look at the item he was given, scan the items in the display, and then place the item next to, or on top of, the matching item.

Figure 7-7.

Sample display for matching objects to identical objects.

How to Teach Matching-to-Sample

There are several critical details involved in teaching a child to match items (real objects or pictures). The details include the selection of identical or similar objects or pictures of objects, the number of items used in an array (i.e., a display), the positioning of those items, the order of presentation of items to be matched, and the responses of the child.

When selecting items to include in a matching to sample procedure, it is often best to start with common objects that the child encounters in his daily life. Some examples would include items such as a shoe, cup, a plate, and a spoon (See Figure 7-7). When beginning such a procedure, it is often beneficial to use real objects **(B 3)**. As the child learns to match real objects, he can then also be taught to match objects to pictures of that same object **(B 4)**. The same procedures are used to teach a child to match pictures to identical and then non-identical pictures **(B 5 & 8)**. Most often, a therapist will begin by having the child match identical objects, and once he's able to match numerous identical objects, he will be taught to match non-identical items (e.g., spoons that vary slightly in size or pattern).

When beginning the matching to sample procedure, an instructor will usually place a small display of items (i.e., an "array") on a table in front of the child. It is very common to start with only two or three objects in the array. As the child improves his ability to match items, he will need to learn to match items in a larger array.

These items should be placed the same distance from the child and there should be some space in between the items. This clear separation of objects is important in the early process of developing this skill. If they are too close together, it may be difficult to determine if the child actually made a correct response if he should place the object in between two of the items in the display. The items should be placed in such a manner that the child is required to actually move his arm and hands (at least six to eight inches from the child) when placing an object with its matching counterpart in the array. This distance is important because not only does it require an effortful response on the part of the child, but it also provides the instructor with the opportunity to intervene by using prompts to teach the child how to correctly place the items.

When the matching to sample task is introduced to the child, the instructor should first require him to look at each of the objects in the array. He should then be given a matching object, be required to look at it, and then instructed to put it with the matching item in the display. When handing the item to the child, the instructor should say the name of the item, have the child repeat it (if the child can imitate the word or say an approximation of it), and then tell him to put the item with the one matching it in the display.

A specific example would be the instructor saying "Shoe," requiring the child to say "shoe", and the instructor then directing him to "put with shoe." As the child places the shoe with its match, the instructor can also say something such as, "Shoe, nice putting shoe with shoe." In this manner, the name of the item is being paired with the sight of the actual item allowing the child to hear the word with the item, and say the word as he holds and places it. In essence, the word for the item is being paired in a manner that is similar to what is required for him to receptively identify and name the item. In some instances, this matching-to-sample procedure that incorporates the child hearing and (possibly) repeating the name of the item (i.e., if he is able to vocally imitate the word) results in the child learning to receptively identify and label the items (i.e., tact).

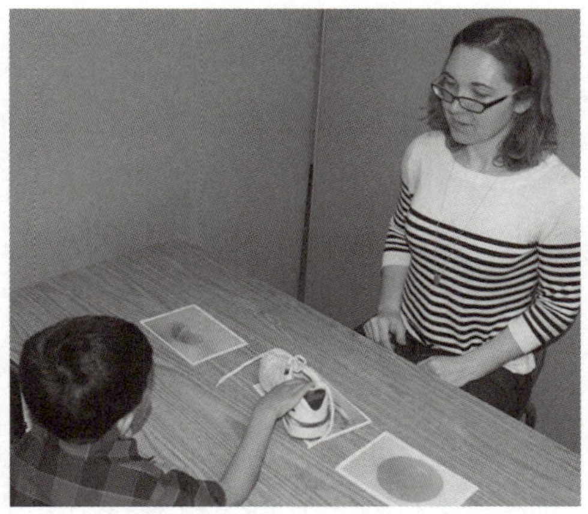
Child matching a shoe to a picture of a shoe.

Teaching Tip: Pair Names with Items

Some instructors will tell the child to "Match," or "Put with same." when presenting this task. However, those words do not pair the name of the object with the item. Many children often identify what they are supposed to do when handed an item when presented with an array of items. Sometimes the child may even repeat those words (i.e., "Match." "Put with same."). For a child with a limited vocabulary, it is better for him to have the name of the objects paired with the items rather than hearing words that really are not significant for the child's development of critical language skills.

Because the child has never been required to match objects, it is important to use prompts to get him to place the object in the proper location. Thus, an errorless teaching procedure can be utilized that includes having the adult point to the matching item in the array with one hand, and say "Put it here," while using the other hand to physically guide the child to place and release the object beside, or on top of, the matching object. The child should be reinforced for going along with the physically prompted matching response (i.e., the first "trial").

After the first matching response, the adult should then remove the item that was placed during the first trial, and repeat the process using a different object. The items in the display should remain the same. However, after the first two trials, it's important to change the positions of the items in the array. During the teaching of matching responses, the learner should be placing the objects based upon the similarity of the items. If the position of the items is not frequently changed, he may just learn to place them based upon their usual location. Additionally, the distance of the items from the child needs to be altered and the number of items in the array increased. The main issue is that the child should be developing his scanning ability so that he can find matching items no matter where they are located on the table: far to the left or right, directly in front of the child, etc. As the array gets larger, it's also important to ensure that the items are not always put in a line, but rather that they are placed in more random arrangements.

During a matching to sample session (i.e., a series of "trials" of matching objects), the items to be matched must vary within the session. Rather than working on a single item to be matched, the child should match two or more (preferably three or more) items within the session on a randomly alternating basis (See Figure 7-8). If he is only required to match a single item over and over again, he won't learn to scan and will disregard the non-matching items. The skill involves not only finding the matching item, but also the "ruling out" of the other items (Green, 2001).

Figure 7-8.

Example of Teaching MTS Using Objects

	Position of objects			***Object to match***
Trial #1	cup	shoe	spoon	shoe
Trial #2	cup	shoe	spoon	cup
Trial #3	cup	shoe	spoon	spoon
Trial #4	spoon	cup	shoe	spoon
Trial #5	spoon	cup	shoe	shoe
Trial #6	spoon	cup	shoe	cup
Trial #7	shoe	spoon	cup	cup
Trial #8	shoe	spoon	cup	shoe
Trial #9	shoe	spoon	cup	spoon
Trial #10	cup	shoe	spoon	shoe

Notice that, in this example, the positioning of objects in the array changes after several trials and the location of the matching object varies in position (left, center, right) from trial to trial.

As mentioned earlier, when teaching a child to match objects, a variety of prompts should be used during the first few trials. However, keep in mind that whenever prompts are used to teach a skill, they must be eliminated as quickly as possible. Thus, the full physical prompt of moving the child's hand and arm to place the object should be faded as soon as it's no longer needed. The prompt of pointing to the location of the matching object can be maintained while the full physical prompt is faded to a partial imitative prompt, and then eventually the physical prompts can be eliminated.

Before each trial begins, the instructor needs to ensure that the child has scanned the array (items should be frequently rearranged) and has looked at the item being handed to him. As the instructor observes that the child consistently scans both the item and those in the array, the prompt of pointing to the target item (i.e., correct object) should also be faded and eliminated.

Error Correction During Matching-to-Sample

During the teaching process, children often make mistakes. Some of these mistakes occur while the various prompts are being faded, and others occur after prompts are no longer being provided. In either case, it's important to implement a correction procedure following a child's incorrect response. The nature of the correction procedure will vary depending upon the child's response (See Figure 7-9).

One type of error that is frequently observed is due to the failure of the child to scan the array and the item prior to placing the object. If the instructor notices that the child isn't adequately attending to the objects, he should not be given the object (if it is still being held by the instructor) or allowed to just randomly place it. When the instructor is giving the item to the child, she should not release it until the child has looked at the array and the item. By doing so, the instructor increases the chance of the child making a correct response. However, if he did scan all the items and does not begin to place it within a few seconds, the adult should provide a prompt for him to respond (e.g., "match," gesture to item in the array). If he then correctly places the item, reinforcement should be provided for the correct matching response. If his pattern of responding during a matching to sample session is such that it requires numerous additional prompts after a trial has begun, it is necessary to ensure that he is properly motivated to respond correctly the first time the trial is presented. When he responds quickly and accurately, the amount or value of the reinforcer that is delivered should be greater than when a secondary prompt to respond is required. Thus, it is most beneficial for the child to respond quickly and accurately as each trial is presented.

In some situations, the child may start to play with the item after it is handed to him or will just appear to stop attending to the task. In such situations, it is usually best to remove the object from him and restart the trial. It is not beneficial to allow the child to "go off task" for a while before further prompting helps him to be successful and then he receives a reinforcer. If such a pattern develops, the child will not be reinforced for fully attending to and performing the task, but rather for not attending and responding at his own pace (not beneficial for his learning!).

Figure 7-9.

Correction Procedure for Errors When Matching-To-Sample

Instruction	→	Child's Response	→	Consequence
Give child a shoe and say "Shoe, put with shoe."	→	Child places the shoe with a shoe in the array.	→	• Reinforce with praise "Yes. Shoe." • Other reinforcer
	→	Child places the shoe with a different item (e.g., spoon).	→	• Remove shoe. • Repeat the instruction. • Provide gestural, partial or full physical prompt as necessary to get child to place shoe in correct location. • Move items to different locations in the array. • Repeat the instruction without prompts.
	→	Child does not respond.	→	• Remove shoe from child. • Repeat the instruction. • If still no response, use gestural, positional, partial or full physical prompt as necessary to get child to place the shoe with the shoe in the array. • Move items to different locations in the array. • Repeat instruction without prompts.

Extending Matching-to-Sample Skills

After the child has been successful in being able to consistently match any of at least 10 identical objects that are presented in an array of at least three objects, the matching skills should be further developed along several dimensions. One of the first extensions is to increase the number of objects in the array. The size of the array can be systematically increased so that there are at least six objects that are randomly placed in a nonlinear arrangement. Additionally, the objects can be rotated (e.g., 45o, 90 o, 180o) so that they have a slightly different appearance (See Figure 7-10).

Figure 7-10.

Large non-linear array of pictures.

Now that the child can match numerous items, he should be taught to fluently match items in succession (B 7). Rather than having him place one item, remove it, then place a second item, he should now be taught to place all three items in succession. Reinforcement should be provided for the completion of the matching of the three objects.

When handing the child successive items to match, care must be taken to ensure that he is given objects in an order that does not have a predictable pattern (e.g., all sequences of trials begin on left, then center, then right). For example, in the first sequence, the first item matches the middle item in the array, the second matches the one on the left and the third is placed on the right of the array. The next sequence begins with the first item being placed on the right, and the next sequence begins on the left, etc.

When the child is matching items in sequence, it is also important that that he learns to quickly complete the matches. He should learn to maintain focused attention and respond quickly (i.e., after he places one item, he immediately takes and places the next item). The ability to stay on task and complete multiple steps is critical for the development of many other skills that he will need to learn.

At this time, the child can start to learn how to match non-identical examples of those mastered items. The instructor may want to use an errorless learning procedure by using pointing prompts when each of the non-identical items is introduced. The first non-identical items should be fairly similar to the original objects. Over time, the objects should be increased along a variety of dimensions such as size, color, etc.

Figure 7-11.

Sample display for matching objects to pictures.

After the child is able to match both identical and non-identical objects, he can then be taught to match objects to a display of pictures and pictures to displays of objects (See Figure 7-11) **(B 4 & 5)**. He should also be taught to match pictures of objects to both identical and non-identical pictures. The teaching procedures and variances used in the matching of pictures and objects should be the same as those used to teach the matching of objects.

This basic matching-to-sample procedure really only requires the child to attend to the visual stimuli (i.e., the pictures or items) in order to be successful with the task. The words that are spoken to the child (i.e., "match" or "put with same") are not very important in the matching process in that the child learns to place the item in his hand with the appropriate item in front of him on the table. After a few successful trials with this type of procedure, the instructor doesn't need to say anything as she hands the item or picture to the child. The child has learned what he is supposed to do in this situation and merely matches the item to the one in the display.

Reverse Matching-to-Sample

Once the child is able to place objects with their matching items, there is another procedure that can be used that incorporates many of those same aspects to help teach the child to learn to receptively identify those items. In a "reverse matching-to-sample" procedure, the instructor can present an array of the same items that the child has matched in the "forward matching-to-sample" procedure. Note that in the forward matching procedure the instructor could be sitting either behind the child or across the table from him. However, in the "reverse" procedure, the instructor sits on the opposite side of the table across from the child, and rather than give him the item to be matched to the one in the array, the instructor holds up the item, says the name of the item, and instructs the child to give the matching item to her. For example, the instructor puts out a display of items (e.g., shoe, cup, plate, book), holds up an item that matches one of those items (e.g., shoe) and then says "Shoe, give me shoe."

Child correctly responding to a Reverse-Matching-to-Sample procedure.

Because the child has already learned to match a shoe to one in an array of items when instructed, "Shoe, put with shoe," this task is almost identical to the forward matching procedure. In this "reverse matching" procedure, the child must also attend to the individual item (held by the instructor rather than the child), scan the array of items, reach toward the matching item in the display, and finally place the two matching items together. However, in the reverse matching procedure, the child places the item in the hand of the instructor instead of matching the items on the table.

When the reverse matching procedure is being introduced, it is often helpful to use a visual prompt to help teach the child what is now being required of him. Specifically, when the adult says the name of the item and then shows him the example item, she can immediately hold her outreached palm in the direction of the matching item that the child should select. This prompt of gesturing toward the item to be selected can be quickly faded out as the child learns to look at the comparison item being held by the instructor if she begins to delay the gesture prompt after the first few trials are presented to the child.

The reverse matching-to-sample procedure is almost identical to a receptive discrimination training procedure in which the instructor places several items in front of the child, holds out her hand, and asks the child to give her the item she requested. For example, in a receptive discrimination procedure, several common items are placed on a table in front of the child (e.g., shoe, cup, plate, book), and then the instructor says, "Give me shoe." The child then scans the items, selects the shoe and hands it to the instructor. However, in the reverse matching-to-sample procedure, the child can also see the item that is being requested in the instructor's hand. Thus, it is not a true receptive discrimination in that the child doesn't need to only respond to the words spoken by the adult, but can also rely on the sight of the item to be selected and given to the instructor. With the inclusion of one additional step, the reverse matching-to-sample procedure can be changed to be a true receptive discrimination procedure.

Programming a Delay in the Prompt

Once the child is able to do the reverse matching-to-sample procedure, the next step is to teach him not to rely on the sight of the items to be able to respond to the instruction to give the named item. The goal is to have him hear the name of the item and then correctly select it. The method for accomplishing this skill of listening to the word involves the timing of when the child hears the word and when he is shown the item by the instructor. In the reverse matching-to-sample procedure, the item and the name of the item are presented together. In the next step, the word for the item is said to the child before he is shown the item to be selected from the array. At first, the instructor will say the name of the item (e.g., "shoe"), then immediately bring the example of the shoe into the child's line of sight (i.e., raise the shoe from a position below the table where it can't be seen by the child to a position above the table where it was previously held during the reverse matching-to-sample procedure). The instructor will then say, "Give me shoe" as she holds out her hand for the child to pass her the shoe. The critical element is that the child hears the word of the item before he sees the item. By carefully programming a slight delay between the time that the child hears the word for the item and sees the item, it is possible for him to respond by selecting the specified item only after hearing it named (Touchette, 1968). In this manner, he will demonstrate that he knows the name of the item that he is being asked to give to the instructor.

There are several critical components that must be attended to by the instructor as the delay is gradually increased during this procedure. As with any instructional task, the adult must remember to ensure that the child is sufficiently motivated to attend to the task stimuli (i.e., the words spoken by the instructor, the items on the table, and the actions of the adult). The instructions presented to the child need to occur only when the adult has him clearly focusing on the teaching activities. Additionally, the instructor needs to watch everything the child does as he is responding to the task.

For example, when the child is motivated and attending to the adult, the adult then says the name of the targeted item (e.g., "Shoe"), and then brings the item (i.e., the shoe) into the child's view. If the child wasn't attending to the spoken word "shoe," the instructor will want to regain his attention and re-present the word "shoe." If the child doesn't orient to the instructor when the word is spoken, there is no way to ensure that he is attending to the spoken word! If he was orienting toward the instructor as the word was spoken, as the adult raises the item into the child's view, it is important to watch to see where the child looks. Ideally, he will hear the word for the name of the item, and then either scan the array of items or the one being held by the adult, and then scan the array of items before he starts to reach for the named item. If he doesn't scan the held item or the items in the array, there is no need for the adult to continue with that trial. It is undesirable to just let the child make a random selection response. Even if he does select the correct item, we don't want to reward the poor attention to the task. Once again, stop the trial if the child isn't attending to the critical details of the task and require the child to scan the items. If he is listening to the word for the name of the object being requested, and is either scanning the held example or scanning the array of items from which he is to select, and is then selecting the appropriate (matching) item, the child's behavior of selecting the correct item needs to be reinforced.

Watching the Child's Responses

The next detail for the instructor to attend to is what the child does in between the time the word for the item is spoken and the matching item is shown to him. If the child "hears" the word and then scans the items and visually "locks-on" to the named item and begins to reach for it, the instructor may not need to show him the example that matches the named item. Under these circumstances, the instructor can merely wait for him to select and hand her the item. However, if the child doesn't scan but begins to reach for an incorrect item, the instructor can use her hand to block him from selecting the incorrect item as she shows him the example of the item being requested. It is often useful to place the objects on the side of the table closer to the adult, and to spread those items apart so that the instructor has more time to watch where the child is reaching and can better see which item he is attempting to select. There is no need to let the child make an error and then tell him that the item is not the one being requested. It is better to prevent the errors from occurring by being extremely careful with the use of prompts and the fading of those prompts during the teaching process.

Through the prompting and fading procedure just described, it is possible to teach the child that if he doesn't know the item that is being requested of him, he can merely wait for the adult to show him the item that he is being asked to select. However, once the child hears the name of the item and "knows" which one is being requested, his selection response will be reinforced faster if he doesn't need to wait for the instructor to show him the item. If the instructor is able to gradually increase the delay between the time when the word is spoken and the matching item is shown, the child will receive a greater amount of reinforcers during an instructional session if he is able to respond after only having heard the name of the item. Thus, this series of matching, reverse matching and delayed prompts for reverse matching can often lead to the development of some early receptive discrimination and labeling skills. The child who was also able to vocally imitate saying the names of the items involved in these tasks will often also learn to label some of those items.

Summary

One important set of skills involves a child being able to look closely at items, and especially those that he is asked to manipulate to complete a task. He needs to be able to identify his jacket and backpack among those that belong to others, and look closely to learn the difference between a dog and a cat. If a child is to learn common daily activities such as matching socks or putting away silverware, he must also be able to "match" or sort identical items. He must also pay attention to his actions if he is to learn how to use a zipper or to pour juice into a cup without spilling.

Thus, one of important set of skills a child needs to learn includes what professionals often refer to as "visual performance" tasks. These tasks require the child to carefully look at items as he performs actions involving them. They include such activities as completing puzzles, matching objects, sorting objects by categories, replicating block designs, and arranging items in order (e.g., smallest to largest).

Performing such activities actually involves several skills. The child must be able to scan displays of items, focus his attention on multiple items, and must attend to the similarities and differences among them. He must also be able to pay attention to his actions as he engages in the coordinated motor movements necessary to adjust the positioning of items. Furthermore, he must be able to identify when his actions have been successful in completing the desired outcome.

There are several types of tasks that are often used to teach some of these visual performance skills. These tasks include single-inset-piece puzzles, putting pieces into shape-sorter boxes, and matching identical and non-identical objects and pictures. A reverse matching-to-sample procedure along with a delayed prompting procedure can also be used to teach a child to receptively identify objects. The instructor must use and then fade a variety of prompts that help the child learn all the separate skills involved in performance of the tasks.

Potential Learning Objectives Related to the Development of Visual Performance Skills

The following objectives are provided to assist a parent or teacher in targeting specific skills that may be appropriate for a child's intervention plan. Please see the ABLLS-R® to assess the child's skills and to identify additional objectives for further skill development.

Each child is a unique individual and requires input from a variety of people who know him and are familiar with effective programming strategies. Therefore, these learning objectives are not being prescribed for any particular child, but rather are being provided as examples of objectives that are consistent with the skills described in this chapter.

B 1 When given five uniquely- shaped puzzle pieces from an inset puzzle presented as group; (Child's name) will place each of the pieces into their corresponding holes in a puzzle frame while looking and positioning each piece (i.e., not trial and error place ment).

B 2 When provided a form box or shape sorter and its pieces, Child's name) will be able to put four pieces into their corre sponding holes by looking at piece then visually locating the corresponding holes in the form box or shape sorter.

B 3 When given an object (Child's name) will match that object to an identical object presented in an array of three items.

(Cont'd on next page.)

B 4 When given a common object, (Child's name) will match at least ten objects to a picture of the object when presented with an array of three pictures of items.

B 5 When given a picture of an object, (Child's name) will be able to match at least ten pictures to an identical picture when presented with an array of at least three pictures.

C 5 Upon instruction, (Child's name) will readily touch a common item held in any position (up/down/left/right) within 3 seconds of the request (e.g., a pen held over head, off to side, etc.).

Appendix 1

- **First 220 Nouns List**
- **Receptive & Labeling Skills Generalization Data Sheet**

Appendix 1 – First 220 Nouns List

Group 1

WORD	CATEGORY	Receptive	Generalized Receptive	Tact	Generalized Tact
Cat	Animal				
Dog	Animal				
Cake	Food				
Candy	Food				
Chips	Food				
Cookies	Food				
Crackers	Food				
Ice Cream	Food				
Juice	Food				
Milk	Food				
Popcorn	Food				
Soda	Food				
Water	Food				
DVD/Movie	Miscellaneous				
Books	School Item				
Computer	School Item				
iPad/Tablet	School item				
Balls	Toy				
Bubbles	Toy				
Dolls	Toy				
Play dough	Toy				
Puzzles	Toy				
Swing (object)	Toy				
Airplane	Transportation				
Boat	Transportation				
Car	Transportation				
Train	Transportation				
Baby Bop	Character				
Barney	Character				
Big Bird	Character				
Cookie Monster	Character				
Diego	Character				
Donald Duck	Character				
Dora the Explorer	Character				
Elmo	Character				
Ernie	Character				
Grover	Character				
Handy Manny	Character				
Mickey Mouse	Character				
Minnie Mouse	Character				
Sponge Bob	Character				
Thomas the Train	Character				
Tigger	Character				
Winnie The Pooh	Character				

Data Collection Instructions

When completing this form for the first time, place a "+" in each collumn in which the student has acquired the skill. Leave the remaining cells blank. When updating the form, place the date in the column when the skill is known to be acquired (i.e., the date the form is updated).

Receptive = The student has demonstrated the ability to receptively identify at least one example of the item or action.

Generalized Receptive = The student can receptively identify at least five examples of the item or action that have specifically been taught, or can identify at least one example that had not previously been taught.

Tact = The student has demonstrated the ability to tact (i.e., label) at least one example of the item or action.

GeneralizedTact = The student can tact (i.e., label) at least five examples of the item or action that have specifically been taught, or can tact at least one example that had not previously been taught.

Appendix 1 – First 220 Nouns List (Cont'd)

Group 2

WORD	CATEGORY	Receptive	Generalized Receptive	Tact	Generalized Tact
Bird	Animal				
Fish	Animal				
Coat / Jacket	Clothing				
Hat	Clothing				
Shirt	Clothing				
Shoes	Clothing				
Socks	Clothing				
Swimsuit	Clothing				
Apples	Food				
Bananas	Food				
Fries	Food				
Hamburger	Food				
Hot Dog	Food				
Oranges	Food				
Sandwich	Food				
Bed	Household				
Bowl	Household				
Chair	Household				
Cup	Household				
Door	Household				
Fork	Household				
Garbage Can	Household				
Phone	Household				
Pillow	Household				
Plate-Dish	Household				
Refrigerator	Household				
Sink	Household				
Sofa-Couch	Household				
Spoon	Household				
Table	Household				
Toilet/Potty	Household				
TV	Household				
Window	Household				
Flower	Outside				
House	Outside				
Tree	Outside				
Backpack	Personal Item				
Brush-Hairbrush	Personal Item				
Comb	Personal Item				
Keys	Personal Item				
Paper	School Item				
Pencil	School Item				
Scissors	School Item				
Balloons	Toy				
Bike	Toy				
Slide	Toy				
Bus/School bus	Transportation				
Truck	Transportation				

Appendix 1 – First 220 Nouns List (Cont'd)

Group 3

WORD	CATEGORY	Receptive	Generalized Receptive	Tact	Generalized Tact
Bear	Animal				
Cow	Animal				
Duck	Animal				
Horse	Animal				
Turtle	Animal				
Eyes	Body Part				
Feet	Body Part				
Mouth	Body Part				
Nose	Body Part				
Button	Clothing				
Pants	Clothing				
Pocket	Clothing				
Bagels	Food				
Bread	Food				
Cereal	Food				
Grapes	Food				
Pizza	Food				
Pudding	Food				
Raisins	Food				
Soup	Food				
Spaghetti/Noodles/Pasta	Food				
Yogurt	Food				
Bathtub-Tub	Household				
Blanket	Household				
Dresser	Household				
Lamp-Light	Household				
Soap	Household				
Stove	Household				
Toothbrush	Household				
Toothpaste	Household				
Towels	Household				
Bell	Miscellaneous				
Candle	Miscellaneous				
Clown	Miscellaneous				
Fire	Miscellaneous				
Wheel	Miscellaneous				
Moon	Outside				
Rain	Outside				
Stars	Outside				
Sun	Outside				
Barn	Outside				
Glasses-Eyeglasses	Personal Item				
Umbrella	Personal Item				
Crayons	School Item				
Broom	Tool				
Drum	Toy				
Wagon	Toy				
Fire truck	Transportation				

Appendix 1 – First 220 Nouns List (Cont'd)

Group 4

WORD	CATEGORY	Receptive	Generalized Receptive	Tact	Generalized Tact
Chicken	Animal				
Elephant	Animal				
Frog	Animal				
Giraffe	Animal				
Lion	Animal				
Monkey	Animal				
Pig	Animal				
Rabbit	Animal				
Sheep	Animal				
Snake	Animal				
Squirrel	Animal				
Tiger	Animal				
Whale	Animal				
Zebra	Animal				
Ankle	Body Part				
Arm	Body Part				
Ear	Body Part				
Elbow	Body Part				
Fingers	Body Part				
Hair	Body Part				
Hands	Body Part				
Head	Body Part				
Hips	Body Part				
Knee	Body Part				
Leg	Body Part				
Shoulders	Body Part				
Teeth	Body Part				
Toes	Body Part				
Tummy	Body Part				
Belt	Clothing				
Blue Jeans	Clothing				
Boots	Clothing				
Diaper	Clothing				
Dress	Clothing				
Pajamas	Clothing				
Panties/Underpants	Clothing				
Shorts	Clothing				
Sweater	Clothing				
Carrots	Food				
Cheese	Food				
Corn	Food				
Eggs	Food				
Goldfish (Crackers)	Food				
Meat- Steak-Beef	Food				
Peas	Food				
Potatoes	Food				
Strawberries	Food				
Tomatoes	Food				

APPENDIX 1 – FIRST 220 NOUNS LIST (CONT'D)

Group 4 (Continued)

WORD	CATEGORY	Receptive	Generalized Receptive	Tact	Generalized Tact
Closet	Household				
Mirror	Household				
Knife	Household				
Microwave	Household				
Napkin	Household				
Paper Towels	Household				
Pot-Pan	Household				
Toaster	Household				
Toilet Paper	Household				
Washcloth	Household				
Box	Miscellaneous				
Clock	Miscellaneous				
Drum	Miscellaneous				
Guitar	Miscellaneous				
Piano	Miscellaneous				
Radio-Music	Miscellaneous				
Stereo-Record Player	Miscellaneous				
Bridge	Outside				
Fence	Outside				
Flag	Outside				
Gate	Outside				
Grass	Outside				
Leaf	Outside				
Swimming Pool					
Watch	Personal Item				
Paints	School Item				
Hammer	Tool				
Ladder	Tool				
Blocks	Toy				
Coloring Book	Toy				
Teddy Bear	Toy				
Helicopter	Transportation				

Appendix 1 – First 220 Nouns List (Cont'd)

Special Words for the Individual Learner

WORD	CATEGORY	Receptive	Generalized Receptive	Tact	Generalized Tact

Appendix 1 – Receptive & Labeling Skills Generalization Data Sheet

		Receptive						Tact					
	WORD	Object	Pict 1	Pict 2	Pict 3	Black & White	Different Person	Object	Pict 1	Pict 2	Pict 3	Black & White	Different Person
1													
2													
3													
4													
5													
6													
7													
8													
9													
10													
11													
12													
13													
14													
15													
16													
17													
18													
19													
20													
21													
22													
23													
24													
25													
26													
27													
28													
29													
30													
31													
32													
33													
34													
35													
36													
37													
38													
39													
40													
41													
42													
43													
44													
45													
46													
47													
48													
49													
50													

Appendix 2 – PISA

The Partington Imitation Skills Assessment

The following assessment was developed to provide a comprehensive review of imitation skills. It has been administered to typically developing preschool age children who were able to do most of the skills at slightly more than three years of age, and all of the skills before reaching four and a half to five years of age (Partington, Doud & Partington, 2011). Therefore, it can be used to identify responses to teach a child who is in need of developing his ability to focus on a model and then imitate a wide range of actions.

This list includes many different types of actions. Some of them require the child to imitate actions that remain present (P) while the child is imitating the response. For example, the instructor is still clapping while the child claps. Other actions are presented and then the model stops before the child is to respond (i.e., the model is gone–G). For example, the instructor taps a drum three times and then gives the child the drumstick to tap the same number of times. The list includes actions requiring the use of numerous body parts, manipulation of objects, and movement of the body to perform sequences of actions. It also assesses the child's ability to imitate a specific number of responses, and to imitate actions with a specific speed or intensity.

To use this assessment, ask the child to imitate each of the actions. The child should be scored a "+" if he accurately imitates the response. A "-" should be scored if he was unable to accurately imitate the response, and a "/" should be scored if he was able to make a fairly good approximation of the modeled response. In addition, it is often helpful to note why the response was scored as being an approximation.

Partington Imitation Skills Assessment

Date of Assessment: ___ Yr ___ Mo ___ Day
DOB: ___ Yr ___ Mo ___ Day
CA: ___ Yr ___ Mo

Child: ______________
Assessor: ______________

Simple Imitation with Objects

#	Item		Model P/G	1st				2nd			
1	tap drum with stick		P	+	--	NR	Aprox	+	--	NR	Aprox
2		Tap slow/fast	P	+	--	NR	Aprox	+	--	NR	Aprox
3		Tap hard/soft	P	+	--	NR	Aprox	+	--	NR	Aprox
4		Tap 3x vs 1x	G	+	--	NR	Aprox	+	--	NR	Aprox
5	rub stick on top of drum		P	+	--	NR	Aprox	+	--	NR	Aprox
6	wave stick up and down		P	+	--	NR	Aprox	+	--	NR	Aprox
7	wave stick side-to-side		G	+	--	NR	Aprox	+	--	NR	Aprox
8	stack a block on another block	array of 3	G	+	--	NR	Aprox	+	--	NR	Aprox
9	put block in a can	array of 3	G	+	--	NR	Aprox	+	--	NR	Aprox
10	place block on a book	array of 3	G	+	--	NR	Aprox	+	--	NR	Aprox
11	tap block on a table		P	+	--	NR	Aprox	+	--	NR	Aprox
12	push block with a finger		P	+	--	NR	Aprox	+	--	NR	Aprox

Arm & Hand Gross Motor Movements

#	Item		Model P/G	1st				2nd			
13	clap hands		P	+	--	NR	Aprox	+	--	NR	Aprox
14		Clap slow/fast	P	+	--	NR	Aprox	+	--	NR	Aprox
15		Clap hard/soft	P	+	--	NR	Aprox	+	--	NR	Aprox
16		Clap 3x vs 1x	G	+	--	NR	Aprox	+	--	NR	Aprox
17	arms up (over head)	1 arm	P	+	--	NR	Aprox	+	--	NR	Aprox
18		both arms	P	+	--	NR	Aprox	+	--	NR	Aprox
19	arms out to sides		P	+	--	NR	Aprox	+	--	NR	Aprox
20	hands to cheeks (model gone)		G	+	--	NR	Aprox	+	--	NR	Aprox
21	hand cover mouth (model gone)	1 hand	G	+	--	NR	Aprox	+	--	NR	Aprox
22		2 hands	G	+	--	NR	Aprox	+	--	NR	Aprox
23	hands together over head		P	+	--	NR	Aprox	+	--	NR	Aprox
24	wave with hand, up & down		P	+	--	NR	Aprox	+	--	NR	Aprox
25	wave with hand, side to side		P	+	--	NR	Aprox	+	--	NR	Aprox
26	arms out in front (like to catch a big ball)		P	+	--	NR	Aprox	+	--	NR	Aprox
27	arms out to side		P	+	--	NR	Aprox	+	--	NR	Aprox
28	arms out to side & move up and down		P	+	--	NR	Aprox	+	--	NR	Aprox
29	hands on head (model gone)		G	+	--	NR	Aprox	+	--	NR	Aprox

Date of Assessment: ___ Yr ___ Mo ___ Day
DOB: ___ Yr ___ Mo ___ Day
CA: ___ Yr ___ Mo

Partington Imitation Skills Assessment

Child: ____________
Assessor: ____________

		Model P/G								
30	hands on shoulders (model gone)	G	+	--	NR	Aprox	+	--	NR	Aprox
31	hand on stomach - one hand (model gone)	G	+	--	NR	Aprox	+	--	NR	Aprox
32	hand on knees - one hand(model gone)	G	+	--	NR	Aprox	+	--	NR	Aprox
33	touch toes with one hand (model gone)	G	+	--	NR	Aprox	+	--	NR	Aprox
34	rub hands (palms together)	P	+	--	NR	Aprox	+	--	NR	Aprox
35	tap table with palms	P	+	--	NR	Aprox	+	--	NR	Aprox
36	turn palms up & down	P	+	--	NR	Aprox	+	--	NR	Aprox
37	arms out in front & palms down	P	+	--	NR	Aprox	+	--	NR	Aprox
38	arms out in front & palms up	P	+	--	NR	Aprox	+	--	NR	Aprox
39	arms out in front & palms sideways	P	+	--	NR	Aprox	+	--	NR	Aprox
40	arms out in front & spread fingers	P	+	--	NR	Aprox	+	--	NR	Aprox
41	arms out in front & spread fingers, then to fist, etc	P	+	--	NR	Aprox	+	--	NR	Aprox

Date of Assessment: ___ Yr ___ Mo ___ Day
DOB: ___ Yr ___ Mo ___ Day
CA: ___ Yr ___ Mo

Partington Imitation Skills Assessment

Child: ______________
Assessor: ______________

Static Vs. Kinetic Motor Movements

#	Item	Model P/G	1st				2nd			
42	hold palms together vs. clapping	P	+	--	NR	Aprox	+	--	NR	Aprox
43	hold palms together vs. rubbing palms together	P	+	--	NR	Aprox	+	--	NR	Aprox
44	rest palm on table vs. tapping table with palm	P	+	--	NR	Aprox	+	--	NR	Aprox
45	rest palm on table vs. rubbing palm on table	P	+	--	NR	Aprox	+	--	NR	Aprox

Gross Motor with Legs

#	Item	Model P/G	1st				2nd			
46	lift & hold one leg (bent at knee)	P	+	--	NR	Aprox	+	--	NR	Aprox
47	lift foot & point toes up & down	P	+	--	NR	Aprox	+	--	NR	Aprox
48	lift foot & point toes side to side (shake foot)	P	+	--	NR	Aprox	+	--	NR	Aprox
49	spread feet apart (about 12-15 inches)	P	+	--	NR	Aprox	+	--	NR	Aprox
50	place foot forward	P	+	--	NR	Aprox	+	--	NR	Aprox
51	place foot forward and draw it back next to othe foot	G	+	--	NR	Aprox	+	--	NR	Aprox
52	hop with two feet	G	+	--	NR	Aprox	+	--	NR	Aprox
53	stomp one foot	G	+	--	NR	Aprox	+	--	NR	Aprox
54	kick a ball	G	+	--	NR	Aprox	+	--	NR	Aprox

Hand Fine Motor Movements

#	Item	Model P/G	1st				2nd			
55	open and close fist	P	+	--	NR	Aprox	+	--	NR	Aprox
56	thumb up position	P	+	--	NR	Aprox	+	--	NR	Aprox
57	thumb up and down (repetitive)	P	+	--	NR	Aprox	+	--	NR	Aprox
58	hold up pointer finger	P	+	--	NR	Aprox	+	--	NR	Aprox
59	make fist to pointer finger (repetitive)	P	+	--	NR	Aprox	+	--	NR	Aprox
60	touch index fingers together	P	+	--	NR	Aprox	+	--	NR	Aprox
61	touch index fingers together & bounce	P	+	--	NR	Aprox	+	--	NR	Aprox
62	index finger held closed on thumb (pincer grip)	P	+	--	NR	Aprox	+	--	NR	Aprox
63	index finger bounce on thumb (pincer grip)	P	+	--	NR	Aprox	+	--	NR	Aprox
64	fist on table knuckles down	P	+	--	NR	Aprox	+	--	NR	Aprox
65	fist on table side of hand on table	P	+	--	NR	Aprox	+	--	NR	Aprox
66	fold hands (fingers interwoven)	P	+	--	NR	Aprox	+	--	NR	Aprox

Date of Assessment: ___ Yr ___ Mo ___ Day
DOB: ___ Yr ___ Mo ___ Day
CA: ___ Yr ___ Mo

Partington Imitation Skills Assessment

Child: ______________
Assessor: ______________

Model P/G

#	Head and Mouth Movements	Model P/G	1st				2nd			
67	shake head "Yes"	P	+	--	NR	Aprox	+	--	NR	Aprox
68	shake head "No"	P	+	--	NR	Aprox	+	--	NR	Aprox
69	Move head side to side (toward shoulders)	P	+	--	NR	Aprox	+	--	NR	Aprox
70	tongue out	G	+	--	NR	Aprox	+	--	NR	Aprox
71	tongue out & side to side	P	+	--	NR	Aprox	+	--	NR	Aprox
72	tongue licking motion	P	+	--	NR	Aprox	+	--	NR	Aprox
73	purse lips together ("mmm")	P	+	--	NR	Aprox	+	--	NR	Aprox
74	open mouth	P	+	--	NR	Aprox	+	--	NR	Aprox
75	open and close mouth twice	P	+	--	NR	Aprox	+	--	NR	Aprox
76	blows	P	+	--	NR	Aprox	+	--	NR	Aprox
77	blow slow/fast	P	+	--	NR	Aprox	+	--	NR	Aprox
78	blow hard/soft	P	+	--	NR	Aprox	+	--	NR	Aprox

Date of Assessment: ___ Yr ___ Mo ___ Day
DOB: ___ Yr ___ Mo ___ Day
CA: ___ Yr ___ Mo

Partington Imitation Skills Assessment

Child: ______________
Assessor: ______________

Sequences of Actions

#	Item	Model P/G	1st				2nd			
79	Array of 4 objects touch in sequence w/ model	P	+	--	NR	Aprox	+	--	NR	Aprox
80	Array of 4 objects touch in sequence w/ model after demo	G	+	--	NR	Aprox	+	--	NR	Aprox
81	Sequence of actions switch with model	P	+	--	NR	Aprox	+	--	NR	Aprox
82	Sequence of actions after model	G	+	--	NR	Aprox	+	--	NR	Aprox
83	block into dumptruck, turn truck & roll backwards into garage	G	+	--	NR	Aprox	+	--	NR	Aprox

Facial expressions

#	Item	Model P/G	1st				2nd			
84	blink eyes	P	+	--	NR	Aprox	+	--	NR	Aprox
85	surprised face	P	+	--	NR	Aprox	+	--	NR	Aprox
86	sour puss face	P	+	--	NR	Aprox	+	--	NR	Aprox
87	kiss action	P	+	--	NR	Aprox	+	--	NR	Aprox

Actions with vocals

#	Item	Model P/G	1st				2nd			
88	Pretend to cry with vocal	P	+	--	NR	Aprox	+	--	NR	Aprox
89	"Sh" with finger to lips	G	+	--	NR	Aprox	+	--	NR	Aprox
90	"Yeah/Yipee" with fist to air	G	+	--	NR	Aprox	+	--	NR	Aprox
91	Open mouth & say "ah"	P	+	--	NR	Aprox	+	--	NR	Aprox

Imitations with body movement

#	Item	Model P/G	1st				2nd			
92	Stand, go ring a bell, return & sit	G	+	--	NR	Aprox	+	--	NR	Aprox
93	Stand, go walk around a chair, return & sit	G	+	--	NR	Aprox	+	--	NR	Aprox
94	Stand, go touch an item, return & sit	G	+	--	NR	Aprox	+	--	NR	Aprox

Mirror

#	Item	Model P/G	1st				2nd			
95	tap head	P	+	--	NR	Aprox	+	--	NR	Aprox
96	Arms over head	P	+	--	NR	Aprox	+	--	NR	Aprox
97	surprise face	P	+	--	NR	Aprox	+	--	NR	Aprox

Date of Assessment: ___ Yr ___ Mo ___ Day
DOB: ___ Yr ___ Mo ___ Day
CA: ___ Yr ___ Mo

Partington Imitation Skills Assessment

Child: ______________
Assessor: ______________

		Model P/G								
98	Open mouth	P	+	--	NR	Aprox	+	--	NR	Aprox
99	tongue out	P	+	--	NR	Aprox	+	--	NR	Aprox
100	touch nose with index finger	P	+	--	NR	Aprox	+	--	NR	Aprox

	Imitation at a distance		1st				2nd			
101	Clap hands (13)	P	+	--	NR	Aprox	+	--	NR	Aprox
102	Arms ober head (17)	P	+	--	NR	Aprox	+	--	NR	Aprox
103	Arms out to side (19)	P	+	--	NR	Aprox	+	--	NR	Aprox
104	Stomp one foot (53)	G	+	--	NR	Aprox	+	--	NR	Aprox
105	Shake head "Yes" (67)	P	+	--	NR	Aprox	+	--	NR	Aprox
106	Shake head "No" (68)	P	+	--	NR	Aprox	+	--	NR	Aprox
107	Mouth open and closed (75)	P	+	--	NR	Aprox	+	--	NR	Aprox
108	Sequence of actions switching with model (81)	P	+	--	NR	Aprox	+	--	NR	Aprox

Appendix 3 – Echoic Assessment

The following Vocal Imitation/Echoic Assessment is being provided for a simple method of determining a child's ability to say a variety of sounds and words. It should be noted that there are a variety of assessments that are available to help determine a child's articulation skills. Speech and language pathologists have more sophisticated assessments that can determine the ability of a child to say specific sounds (phonemes) and sound combinations. These evaluations assess a child's ability to produce sounds in the beginning, middle and end of words, and use normative data to compare the articulation skills of a child to those of his same-age peers.

This current assessment was developed with input from speech and language pathologists who have considerable experience working with children on the autism spectrum. It is not a replacement for those more sophisticated assessments. However, it provides parents and teachers a simple way to identify a child's vocal imitation skills and to select specific sounds and combinations to teach him. By completing this assessment, it is possible to identify a wide variety of specific sounds or words that a child can be taught and to track the development of his vocal imitation skills.

The column on the left specifies a specific sound, letter, number, word or phrase to be assessed. Some of the sounds are actually variations of a particular sound. For example saying a short "mm" sound Vs. an extended version of that sound "mmmmmmm." Other items assess the child's ability to not only make the sounds, but also to listen and repeat a sequence of two separate sounds (e.g., "ma"-"ma" vs. "ma"-"me"). For many of the sounds, the next column provides an example of a word that would include the specific sound to help the evaluator determine the specific sound being reviewed (e.g., "duh" as in the word 'dug'). The third column allows the assessor to write what she hears the child say when he can only make an approximation to the sound or word. The remaining columns are for the assessor to indicate at various points in time whether the child was able to accurately say the sound (+), or was unable to make the sound (-). The child should only be given credit for being able to make the sound if he is consistently able to make the sound upon request.

Echoic Evaluation

Dates of Assessment

Sounds	As in the word	Sounds like				
Aa	ape					
aah	hot					
a	hat					
aw	awful					
ah - ah						
ah - ee						
Bb	bee					
bih	big					
bah	Bah humbug					
buh	bubble					
boe	bow tie					
boo	booth					
boo - boo						
bah - bah						
br	bread					
cuh	cup					
ca	cat					
coe	copilot					
da	dash					
duh	dug					
daw	dog					
dih	dip					
dee	deep					
doe	dough					
due	dew					

Echoic Evaluation

Dates of Assessment

Sounds	As in the word	Sounds like				
dah - dah						
dee - dee						
duh - duh						
doe - doe						
due - due						
doe - dee						
dee - dah						
dah - dee						
Ee						
eh	egg					
ee - oh						
ee - ee						
ee - ah						
el	Elmo					
er	Ernie					
Ff (unvoiced)	fish					
fah	father					
feh	fetch					
fih	fish					
foe	foam					
guh	girl					
grr	green					
Hh (unvoiced)	hat					
ha	happy					
heh	help					
hi	high					

Echoic Evaluation

Dates of Assessment

Sounds	As in the word	Sounds like				
hih	hip					
hah	hop					
ha - ha	(laugh)					
hee	heed					
hee - hee						
Ii	eye					
ih	fish					
ip	sip					
Kk	kick					
lah	(musical note)					
lee						
low						
lah - lah						
loe - loe						
mee	me					
mm	men					
mmmm	(extended mm)					
mah	Mama					
may	maybe					
moe	mow lawn					
moo	cow sound					
my	myself					
ma - ma						
ma - mee						
ma - moe						
mm - oo						

Echoic Evaluation

Dates of Assessment

Sounds	**As in the word**	**Sounds like**				
Nn	nickle					
Oo	open					
oo	move					
oo - ee						
oy	boy					
peh	pen					
pah	potty					
pa	pat					
puh	push					
pih	pin					
ip	lip					
pee	peep					
poe	potato					
pah - pah						
pee - pee						
Rr	red					
ruff	(barking)					
Ss (unvoiced)	sip					
sssss	(snake sound)					
sh	ship					
shuh	shut					
tih	tip					
toe	tomato					
tae	table					
tah	Tom					
ta	tab					

Echoic Evaluation

Dates of Assessment

Sounds	As in the word	Sounds like				
tuh	tub					
Uu	you					
vee	(letter)					
vih	victory					
whih	which					
wah	water					
way	(word)					
wee	we					
woe	woeful					
wih	with					
woo	(word)					
wah - wah						
yah	Yahoo					
yeh	yes					
yell	yellow					
yay	yeah					
Zz	zip					

Echoic Evaluation

Letter Names	Sounds like		Dates of Assessment			
A						
B						
C						
D						
E						
F						
G						
H						
I						
J						
K						
L						
M						
N						
O						
P						
Q						
R						
S						
T						
U						
V						
W						
X						
Y						
Z						

Echoic Evaluation

Dates of Assessment

Sounds of Numbers		Sounds Like				
1						
2						
3						
4						
5						
6						
7						
8						
9						
10						
11						
12						
13						
14						
15						
16						
17						
18						
19						
20						
21						
22						
23						
24						
25						

Echoic Evaluation

Dates of Assessment

Words	Sounds like					
aim						
am						
and						
bald						
ball						
banana						
bat						
bed						
blow						
blue						
bolt						
book						
boot						
boy						
brake						
breakfast						
broken						
brush						
bubble						
bus						
bush						
bye-bye						
calm						
car						
caught						
chip						
chop						
city						

Echoic Evaluation

Words	Sounds like					
cloudy						
cost						
cup						
curl						
dew						
dime						
dinner						
doe						
doll						
eat						
elbow						
Elmo						
eye						
face						
fancy						
fault						
few						
finger						
fit						
ghost						
girl						
gold						
halt						
hat						
head						
high						
house						
how						
jump						

Echoic Evaluation

Dates of Assessment

Words	Sounds like					
just						
key						
kind						
kite						
lunch						
Mama						
man						
men						
mirror						
movie						
mop						
oil						
oat						
open						
out						
own						
peek						
pen						
people						
pill						
pillow						
pin						
quack						
quit						
rabbit						
rainy						
ray						

Echoic Evaluation

Dates of Assessment

Words	Sounds like					
roll						
say						
sheep						
ship						
shoe						
sign						
ski						
sky						
snack						
squash						
sun						
sunshine						
talk						
tent						
they						
tie						
train						
truck						
tummy						
you						
yours						
want						
water						
wax						
win						
window						
yellow						

Echoic Evaluation

Phrases	Sounds like		Dates of Assessment			
stand up						
help me						
open door						
open the door						
big cat						
give me hug						
eat pizza						

Glossary

Antecedent Any condition, stimulus, or event that is present or occurs prior to a behavior.

Behavior Any observable or measureable act of an individual (also called a response).

Behavioral objective A statement that indicates a proposed change in behavior. An objective must include the expected behavior, the conditions under which the behavior is expected to be performed, and the criteria to evaluate the behavior.

Conditioned reinforcer A type of reinforcer that has acquired its reinforcing function (i.e., it increases the behavior that preceded its delivery) through the pairing of a previously neutral stimulus (now the conditioned reinforcer) with an unconditioned or other conditioned reinforcer. (See the definition of a reinforcer.)

Consequence Any stimulus or event that immediately follows a particular behavior.

Dependent variable The behavior to be changed as a result of an intervention.

Deprivation A condition in which a person has minimal or no access to a desired reinforcer for a period of time.

Differential reinforcement Reinforcement is provided only under certain conditions. Typically the reinforcement is provided when a behavior meets a specific criterion for accuracy, or is performed at a certain rate.

Discrimination The ability to differentiate among stimuli or environmental events.

Discriminative stimulus (SD) A stimulus that indicates the current availability of a reinforcer contingent upon the occurrence of a specific behavior.

Echoic A type of verbal response that matches a vocal verbal stimulus. It is often referred to a vocal imitation.

Emit To make or produce a response or action.

Errorless learning An instructional procedure that arranges instructions and prompts to only result in correct responses.

* Note that these definitions are not the technical descriptions of these terms as they are written for parents and teachers to be able to understand the concepts presented in this book.

Glossary (Cont'd)

Extinction The withholding of reinforcement for a previously reinforced behavior or response. The procedure is used to decrease the occurrence of the behavior.

Generalization The expansion of the child's skills so that they will occur under conditions that differ from the conditions under which the original behavior was acquired.

Generalized conditioned reinforcer A reinforcer that is associated with a variety of other learned and unlearned reinforcers.

Independent variable Any factor that is manipulated so as to have an effect upon a behavior (the dependent variable).

Intermittent reinforcement Patterns of the delivery of reinforcement in which some, but not all, responses are followed by a reinforcer.

Intraverbal A type of verbal behavior that is controlled by a verbal stimulus and the response doesn't match that verbal stimulus. It is often referred to in relation to answering questions and talking about things that are not present.

Maintenance The ability for the child to perform the response over an extended period of time, even though there may not have been the opportunity to engage in that behavior.

Mand A type of verbal behavior that is controlled by a motivational operation and is reinforced with specific reinforcement. It is often referred to as "requesting" or "asking."

Modeling The demonstration of a behavior in order to prompt an imitative response.

Motivational operation A change in the environment that results in a change in the reinforcing value of a stimulus, object or event, and alters the current frequency of the behavior that has previously been reinforced by that stimulus, object or event.

Operant conditioning The arrangement of environmental variables to establish a functional relationship between a voluntary behavior and its consequences.

Pairing The simultaneous presentation of stimuli. It is a procedure that is used to develop conditioned reinforcers by presenting neutral stimuli immediately prior to, or at the same time as, presenting an existing reinforcer. It is often used to increase the reinforcing value of an individual who delivers reinforcers following desired behavior performed by a child.

Primary reinforcer A stimulus that has reinforcing value without the need for previous learning (e.g., food, water, warmth). These types of reinforcers are also referred to as unlearned reinforcers.

Prompt A stimulus that is added to increase the probability that a certain response will occur. There are a variety of types of prompts that are often used in teaching skills to children, including: imitative, gestural, verbal, positional, and physical.

Punisher A consequence that results in a decrease in the future rate or probability of a certain behavior.

Rate The frequency of a behavior over a specified period of time.

Reinforcer The presentation of a stimulus or event following a behavior (a consequence) that results in the increased probability (rate) of that behavior occurring under similar circumstances in the future.

Response Any observable or measureable act of an individual (also referred to as behavior).

Satiation A condition that occurs when there is no longer a state of deprivation.

Schedules of reinforcement The pattern in which reinforcers are provided based on the number of responses or the timing of responses. For example, every instance of a response may result in a reinforcer, or the reinforcer may be delivered after a certain number of responses.

Secondary reinforcers Stimuli or events that obtained their reinforcement value due to their pairing with other primary or conditioned reinforcers. These reinforcers are often referred to as learned reinfrocers.

Selection-based response Behavior that involves a single type of physical motor movement (e.g., point or pick up) to select one of several possible options of items or pictures

Glossary (Cont'd)

Shaping A method for developing new behaviors by systematically reinforcing responses that are closer to the desired performance of a behavior. Often referred to as the differential reinforcement of successive approximations to a desired behavior.

Social reinforcers A type of secondary or conditioned reinforcer that includes statements of acknowledgement, praise, and facial expressions.

Stimulus Anything that is able to be detected by one of a person's senses (i.e., visual, hearing, smell, taste, felt).

Stimulus control The relationship between an environmental event or stimulus that serves as a cue for a behavior to occur or not occur.

Tact A type of verbal behavior in which the response is controlled by a nonverbal stimulus (item). It is often referred to as "labeling" or "naming" an item that is seen, heard, smelled, tasted or touched by an individual.

Task analysis A technique of breaking down sequences of responses necessary to perform an activity into each of the stimuli and behaviors involved in the task. It is the identification of each of the specific responses involved in a more complex activity.

Topography A description of the physical movement of a motor action.

Topography-based response Behavior that involves unique physical motor movements for each response (e.g., making the ASL sign for 'shoe' vs. the sign for 'eat").

Trial A discrete opportunity for a response to occur. It is defined by the antecedent stimuli, the behavior, and the consequence that follows the behavior.

Verbal behavior Behavior which is reinforced through the mediation of another individual. It is generally thought of as speaking, but can also include nonvocal behavior such as using sign language and typing or writing.

Verbal stimulus A stimulus that is a result of sombody's verbal behavior (e.g., a spoken or written word, an ASL sign).

References

Alberto, P. A. & Troutman, A. C. (1999). *Applied behavior analysis for teachers.* Upper Saddle River, NJ: Merril Publishing Company.

American Psychiatric Association. (2013). *Diagnostic and Statistical Manual of Mental Disorders (5th Ed.)*. Washington, DC: Author.

Baer, D., Peterson, R., & Sherman, J. (1967). The development of imitation by reinforcing behavioral similarity to a model. *Journal of Experimental Analysis of Behavior, 10*, 405-416.

Beaulieu, L., Hanley, G. P., & Roberson, A. A. (2013). Effects of responding to a name and group call on preschoolers' compliance. *Journal of Applied Behavior Analysis, 45*, 685–707.

Becker, W. C., Engelmann, S., & Thomas, D. R. (1975). *Teaching 2: Cognitive learning and instruction*. Chicago, IL: Science Research Associates.

Bijou, S. W., & Baer, D. M. (1965). *Child development II: Universal stage of infancy*. Englewood Cliffs, NJ: Prentice-Hall.

Bloom, L. (1974). Developmental relationship between receptive and expressive language. In R. L. Schiefelbusch and L. L. Lloyd (Eds.). *Language perspectives, acquisition, retardation, and intervention*. (285-311). Baltimore: University Park Press.

Carr, E. G. & Durand, V. M. (1985). Reducing behavior problems through functional communication training. *Journal of Applied Behavior Analysis, 18*(2), 111-126.

Catania, A. C. (1998). Learning, 4th edition. Englewood Cliffs, NJ: Prentice-Hall.

Charlop M. H., & Trasowech, J. E. (1991). Increasing autistic children's daily spontaneous speech. *Journal of Applied Behavior Analysis. 24*, 747–761.

Dube, W. V., Ahearn, W. H., Lionello-Denolf, K., McIlvane, W. J. (2009). Behavioral momentum: Translational research in intellectual and developmental disabilities. *The Behavior Analyst Today. 10*(2): 238-253.

Foxx, R. M. (1982). *Decreasing behaviors of severely retarded and autistic persons.* Champaign, IL: Research Press.

Foxx, R. M. (1982). *Increasing behaviors of severely retarded and autistic persons.* Champaign, IL: Research Press.

Frost, L. A., & Bondy, A. S. (1994). *The picture exchange communication system training manual.* Cherry Hill, NJ: Pyramid Educational Consultants, Inc.

Grandin, T. (2012). Personal communication, 7 September.

Green, G. (2001). Behavior analytic instruction for learners with autism: Advances in stimulus control technology. *Focus on Autism and Other Developmental Disabilities, 16*, 72-85.

References (Cont'd)

Greer, R. D., & Ross, D. E. (2008). *Verbal behavior analysis: Inducing and expanding new verbal capabilities in children with language delays.* Boston, MA: Pearson Education, Inc.

Grow, L. L., Carr, J. E., Kodak, T. M., Jostad, C. M., & Kisamore, A. N. (2011). A comparison of methods for teaching receptive labeling to children with autism spectrum disorders. *Journal of Applied Behavior Analysis, 44*(3): 475–498.

Halle, J. W., Baer, D. M., & Spradlin, J. E. (1981). Teachers' generalized use of delay as a stimulus control procedure to increase language use in handicapped children. *Journal of Applied Behavior Analysis, 14*, 389-409.

Hart, B., & Risley T. R. (1975). Incidental teaching of language in the preschool. *Journal of Applied Behavior Analysis, 8*, 411-420.

Howard, J. S., Sparkman, C. R., Cohen, H. G., Green, G., & Stanislaw, H. (2005). A comparison of intensive behavior analytic and eclectic treatments for young children with autism. *Research in Developmental Disabilities, 26*, 359–383.

Jones, W. & Klin, A., (2013). *Attention to eyes is present but in decline in 2–6-month-old infants later diagnosed with autism.* Nature doi:10.1038/nature12715

Kent, L. (1974). *Language acquisition program for the retarded or multiply impaired.* Champaign, IL: Research Press.

Laraway, S., Snycerski, S., Michael, J., & Poling, A. (2003). Motivating operations and terms to describe them: some further refinements. *Journal of Applied Behavior Analysis, 36*(3): 407-14.

Lerman, D. C., Parten, M., Addison, L. R., Vorndran, C. M., Volkert, V. M., & Kodak, T. (2005). A methodology for assessing the functions of emerging speech in children with developmental disabilities. *Journal of Applied Behavior Analysis, 38*, 303-316.

Lovaas, O. I. (1987). Behavioral treatment and normal educational and intellectual functioning in young autistic children. *Journal of Consulting and Clinical Psychology, 55*, 3–9.

Lovaas, I., Freitas, L., Nelson, K., & Whalen, K. (1967). The establishment of imitation and its use for the development of complex behavior in schizophrenic children. *Behavioral Research and Therapy, 5*, 171-181.

Martin, G. & Pear, J. (2002). *Behavior modification: What it is and how to do it (7th Ed.)*. Englewood Cliffs, NJ: Prentice-Hall, Inc.

Michael, J. (1993). Establishing operations. *The Behavior Analyst, 16*, 191-206.

Michael, J. (1988). Establishing operations and the mand. *The Analysis of Verbal Behavior, 6*, 3-9.

Mowrer, O. H. (1950). *Learning theory and personality dynamics.* New York: The Ronald Press Company.

Nadel, J., & Peze, A. (1993). What makes imitation communicative in toddlers and autistic children. In J Nadel, L Camaioni (Eds.), *New Perspectives in Early Communication Development* (pp. 139-56). London: Routledge.

National Research Council (2002). Educating children with autism. Committee on educational interventions for children with autism. Catherine Lord and James P. McGee, Eds. *Division of Behavioral and Social Sciences and Education.* Washington, DC: National Academy Press.

Novak, G. (1996). *Developmental psychology: Dynamical systems and behavior analysis.* Reno, NV: Context Press.

O'Neill, R. E., Horner, R. H. Albin, R. W., Sprague, J. R., Storey, K., & Newton, J. S. (1997). *Functional assessment and program development for problem behaviors.* Pacific Grove: Brooks/Cole.

Osgood, C. E. (1953). *Method and theory in experimental psychology.* New York: Oxford University Press.

Partington, J. W. (2010). *Assessment of Basic Language and Learning Skills-Revised: An assessment, curriculum guide and skills tracking system for children with autism or other developmental disabilities.* Pleasant Hill, CA: Behavior Analysts, Inc.

Partington, J. W. (2008). *Capturing the Motivation of Children with Autism or Other Developmental Delays.* Pleasant Hill, CA: Behavior Analysts, Inc.

Partington, J. W., Bailey, A., Pritchard, J. K., Nosik, M. & Doerr, M. (2010, January). *An update of the data on the developmental patterns of specific language and learning skills of typically developing children as measured by the ABLLS-R.* Presentation at the Association for Behavior Analysis International 2010 Autism Conference, Chicago, IL.

Partington, J. W., & Bailey, J. S. (1993). Teaching intraverbal behavior to preschool children. *The Analysis of Verbal Behavior, 11*, 9-18.

Partington, J. W., Doud, M. & Partington, S. W. (2011). *Measuring the Imitation Skills of Typically Developing Children to Assist in the Development of Imitative Skills in Children with Autism.* Presentation at the Association for Behavior Analysis International Conference. Granada, Spain.

Partington, J. W., & Mueller, M. M. (2012). *The Assessment of Functional Living Skills: Essential Skills for Independence at Home, School, and in the Community.* Pleasant Hill, CA: Behavior Analysts, Inc.

References (Cont'd)

Payne, S., Radicchi, J., Rosellini, L., Deutchman, L., & Darch, C. (1983). *Structuring classrooms for academic success*. Eugene, OR: Association for Direct Instruction.

Pelaez, M., Virues-Ortega, J., & Gewirtz, J. L. (2011). Reinforcement of vocalizations through contingent vocal imitation. *Journal of Applied Behavior Analysis, 44*(1), 33-40.

Risley, T. R. (1968). The effects and side effects of punishing the autistic behaviors of a deviant child. *Journal of Applied Behavior Analysis, 1*(1), 21-34.

Ross, D. E., & Greer, R. D. (2003). Generalized imitation and the mand: Inducing first instances of speech in young children with autism. *Research in Developmental Disabilities, 24*, 58-74.

Rogers, S., & Vismara, L. (2008) Evidence-based comprehensive treatments for early autism. *Journal of Clinical and Child and Adolescent Psychology, 37*(1), 8-38.

Sallows, G., & Graupner, T. (2005). Intensive behavioral treatment for children with autism: Four-year outcome and predictors. *American Journal on Mental Retardation, 110*(6), 417-438.

Schreibman, L. (2005). *Are there Core Deficits in Autism?. In: The science and fiction of autism*. Cambridge, Massachusetts: Harvard University Press.

Siegel, B., (2003). *Helping Children with Autism Learn*. New York: Oxford University Press, Inc.

Skinner, B. F. (1957). *Verbal behavior*. New York: Appleton-Century-Crofts.

Slaughter, V. & McConnell, D. (2001). Emergence of joint attention: relationships between gaze following, social referencing, imitation, and naming in infancy. *Journal of Genetic Psychology, 164*(1), 54-71.

Sloane, H. N., & MacAuley, B. D. (Eds.) (1968). *Operant procedures in remedial speech and language training*. Boston: Houghton Mifflin.

Spradlin, J. E. (1974). Development of receptive language. In R. L. Schiefelbusch & L. L. LLoyd (Eds.). *Language perspectives, acquisition, retardation, and intervention*. (285-311) Baltimore: University Park Press.

Spradlin, J. E. (1963). Assessment of speech and language of retarded children: The Parsons language sample. *Journal of Speech and Hearing Disorders Monograph, 10*, 8-31.

Sundberg, C. T., & Sundberg, M. L. (1990). Comparing topography-based verbal behavior with stimulus selection-based verbal behavior. *The Analysis of Verbal Behavior, 8*, 31-41.

Sundberg, M. L., Michael, J., Partington, J. W., & Sundberg, C. A. (1996). The role of automatic reinforcement in early language acquisition. *The Analysis of Verbal Behavior, 13*, 21-37.

Sundberg, M. L., & Partington, J. W. (2013). *Teaching language to Children with Autism or Other Developmental Disabilities*. Pleasant Hill, CA: Behavior Analysts, Inc.

Terrace, H. (1963). Discrimination learning with and without "errors." *Journal of the Experimental Analysis of Behavior, 6*, 1-27.

Tomasello, M. (2001). Perceiving intentions and learning words in the second year of life. In M Tomasello, E Bates (Eds.), *Language Development: The Essential Readings* (pp. 11-128). Oxford, UK: Blackwell.

Thompson, T. (2011). *Individualized Autism Intervention for Young Children*. Baltimore, MD: Paul H. Brookes Publishing Co.

Thompson, T. (2007). *Making Sense of Autism*. Baltimore, MD: Paul H. Brookes Publishing Co.

Touchette, P. E. (1971). Transferring of stimulus control: Measuring the moment of transfer. *Journal of the Experimental Analysis of Behavior, 15*, 347-354.

Touchette, P. E. (1968). The effects of graduated stimulus change on the acquisition of a simple discrimination in severely retarded boys. *Journal of the Experimental Analysis of Behavior, 11*, 39-48.

Touchette, P. E. & Howard, J. S. (1984). Errorless Learning: Reinforcement Contingencies and Stimulus Control Transfer in Delayed Prompting. *Journal of Applied Behavior Analysis, 17*, 175-188.

Van Riper, C. (1978). *Speech correction principles and methods (6th ed.)*. New York: Prentice-Hall.

Vaughan, M. E., & Michael, J. L. (1982). Automatic reinforcement: An important but ignored concept. *Behaviorism, 10*, 217-227.

Volkert, V. M., Lerman, D. C., Trosclair, N., Addison, L., & Kodak, T. (2008). An exploratory analysis of task-interspersal procedures while teaching object labels to children with autism. *Journal of Applied Behavior Analysis, 41*(3), 335–350.

Weiss, M. J. (1999). Differential rates of skill acquisition and outcomes of early intensive behavioral intervention for autism. *Behavioral Interventions, 14*(1), 3-22.

Whaley, D., & Malott, R. W. (1968). *Elementary Principles of Behavior*. Kalamazoo, MI: Behaviordelia.

References (Cont'd)

Wing, L. (2003). *The autistic spectrum: A guide for parents and professionals*. London: Constable and Robinson, Ltd.

Winterling, V., Dunlap, G., & O'Neill, R.E. (1987). The influence of task variation on the abberant behaviors of autistic students. *Education and Treatment of Children, 10*, 105

Wolfberg, P. (2003). *Peer play and the autism spectrum: The art of guiding children's socialization and imagination*. Shawnee Mission, KS: Autism Asperger Publishing Company.

Wolff, P. H. (1969). The natural history of crying and other vocalization in early infancy. In B. M. Foss (Ed.), *Determinants of infant behavior (Vol. 4)*. London: Methuen.

Wraikat, R., Sundberg, C. T., & Michael, J. (1991). Topography-based and selection-based verbal behavior: A further comparison. *The Analysis of Verbal Behavior, 9*, 1-17.

Wynn, J. W., & Smith, T. (2003). Generalization between receptive and expressive language in young children with autism. *Behavioral Interventions, 18*, 245-266.